ADVANCE PRAISE FOR
CERULEAN BLUES

FROM THE GENTLE APPALACHIAN RIDGES of West Virginia to the rebel-haunted cloud forests of Colombia, Katie Fallon immerses herself in the world of the cerulean warbler—a tiny, lovely songbird few Americans have heard of, but which is emblematic of the increasingly desperate plight of migratory birds in general. In *Cerulean Blues*, Fallon tracks not just the bird's globe-hurtling journeys, but the passion and determination of the people in two hemispheres who are trying to save it. — *Scott Weidensaul, Pulitzer Prize finalist and author of more than twenty books*

KATIE FALLON INHABITS THE WORLD of cerulean warblers with directness, humor, and real joy. In prose as clean and clear as water, she invites us into the world of both birds and birders. It's a fascinating world, a world that bristles with life, and a world that expands far beyond the merely human. This book is a pleasure to read, and will open the eyes of many to the life of a small creature fighting an enormous fight. —*David Gessner, author of* Return of the Osprey *and* Soaring with Fidel

BIRDS HAVE THE POWER TO captivate, even change lives. Told here is the story of a woman who could and a small, blue, bellwether bird that increasingly cannot maintain itself in this world of our making. *Cerulean Blues* is part journey, part documentary, and wholly engaging; a tribute to a bird that bridges continents with its wings and to a rising star among contemporary nature writers. —*Pete Dunne, author of* Hawks in Flight *and director of the Cape May Bird Observatory*

OUR READERS KNOW THE CERULEAN Warbler as one of the more difficult warblers to find on a spring bird walk. Katie Fallon knows it as much more: a sky-blue third-of-an-ounce link between the way we grow coffee in the tropics, mine coal in Appalachia, and teach children the value of preserving wildlife. Her timely, important book introduces us to the bird, the challenges it faces, and the people who are working to protect it. —*Matt Mender¹ ¹¹* ——*——— ——-*** BirdWatching Magazine

Cerulean Blues

Cerulean Blues

A PERSONAL SEARCH
FOR A VANISHING SONGBIRD

Katie Fallon

Ruka Press®
Washington, DC

For Rachael

First edition published 2011 by Ruka Press®, PO Box 1409, Washington, DC 20013.
www.rukapress.com

Photography by the author, except pp. 112, 137, and 190 by T. J. Boves.

Map of the cerulean warbler's range based on data provided by NatureServe in collaboration with Robert Ridgely, James Zook, The Nature Conservancy–Migratory Bird Program, Conservation International–CABS, World Wildlife Fund–US, and Environment Canada–WILDSPACE. Available online at http://www.natureserve.org.

Other map data is from OpenStreetMap and copyright OpenStreetMap contributors, under the Creative Commons Attribution-ShareAlike 2.0 license.
See: http://www.openstreetmap.com and http://creativecommons.org/licenses/by-sa/2.0.

Lyrics from "Green Rolling Hills of West Virginia" by Bruce D. "Utah" Phillips ©1973. Used by permission of the estate.

"Interpreters of Cerulean" © 2011 by Tom Will. Used by permission.

Portions of Chapter Nine appeared in a different form in the anthology *Appalachia's Last Stand* (Wind Publications, 2009).

Library of Congress Control Number: 2011926412

ISBN 978-0-9830111-1-8

10 9 8 7 6 5 4 3 2 1

Printed in the United States of America

Design by Sensical Design & Communication

CONTENTS

Fall

Cerulean Blues

INTERPRETERS OF CERULEAN

WE COME TO THE TABLE
wearing our agencies, committed
to bring back a warbler,
Dendroica cerulea,
from the presumed spiral of its demise…

to conjure significant landscape—
the arching hardwood canopy
of sunlight, shadow, and space
that gifts this bird its green canyons
from which to plummet unannounced
like a fragment of heaven
into a waif body barely weaned
left homeless on the forest floor.

When you cradle this lost creature in your arms,
when you look into the receding blue of its eyes,
you understand
that there is not much time left,
that every act of wonder and caring
must count.

Perhaps only three hundred thousand pairs of wings
are left
to carry the sky across continents
and inspire gestures of benevolence
on their behalf.

We prune the forest just so,
adjust a net or balance an equation,
arrange a meeting in another language,
search the dense foliage
or listen for the ascending song
that promises
that these birds will remain *our* guardians
as we adjust *our* course
from the edge of helplessness
toward the center of faithful action.

—Tom Will

*Tom Will is a wildlife biologist and founding member of the Cerulean Warbler
Technical Group.*

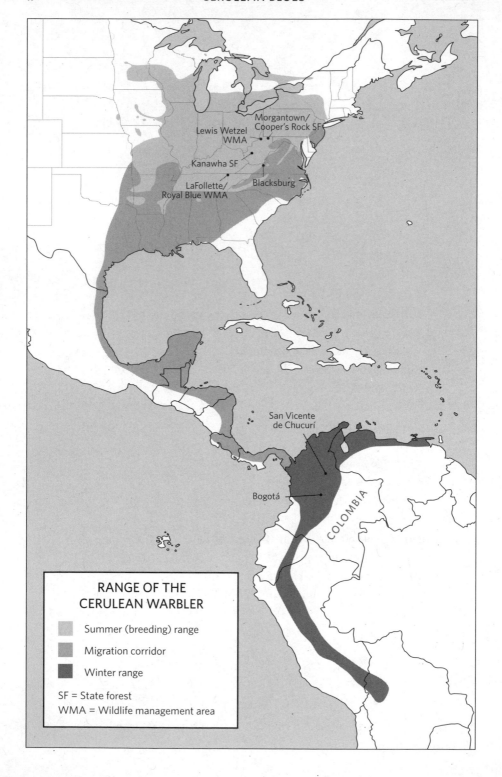

RANGE OF THE
CERULEAN WARBLER

Summer (breeding) range

Migration corridor

Winter range

SF = State forest
WMA = Wildlife management area

INTRODUCTION

I STEPPED ONTO THE TARMAC in Bucaramanga, a city of more than five hundred thousand people in northeastern Colombia, and blinked in the fierce October sun. Black vultures lazily circled in the clear blue sky overhead, and swallows chittered to each other as they cut and dove above the Avianca jets idling on the runway. I wasn't the only one to notice the birds; the two dozen or so ornithologists who'd deplaned with me dropped their suitcases and frantically rummaged through their backpacks for binoculars. Mine were buried too deep—below souvenirs from my stay in Bogotá, balled-up dirty laundry, and the hefty six-hundred-page *Birds of Northern South America* identification guide—and besides, I knew I could rely on the experts for positive identifications. I tilted my head and squinted at the vultures, drifting on the updrafts from the Andes Mountains that surrounded us. The Colombian air traffic controllers and baggage handlers raised their eyebrows as the *gringos locos* called out the names of the birds: "White-winged swallow!" "Martin—gray-breasted?" "Is that a blue and white swallow?"

Earlier this morning, all of us—members of the Cerulean Warbler Technical Group, the Golden-winged Warbler Working Group, and me, the invading writer—had boarded an airport shuttle at our hotel in downtown Bogotá. We'd spent the previous three days sitting in the posh auditoriums of the *Federación Nacional de Cafeteros de Colombia* headquarters, listening to presentations about research and monitoring, education and publicity, and habitat management of cerulean and golden-winged warblers. The conference, which was the combined Third Annual Cerulean Warbler Summit and Second Annual Golden-winged Warbler Summit, brought together about eighty experts from North, South, and Central America.

These warbler species are two of the fastest-declining Neotropical migratory songbirds in the Western Hemisphere. While the plight of the golden-winged warbler interested me, too, it was my fascination (perhaps "my obsession" is more accurate) with the cerulean warbler that prompted me to travel to one of the world's most dangerous countries.

I'm not alone in my affection for the cerulean warbler; a favorite challenge for birders, this four-and-a-half inch, nine-gram bird is notoriously difficult to spot as it forages high in the forest canopy, flicking its wings as it gleans aphids, treehoppers, caterpillars, and other small insects from the undersides of leaves. From below—the only view most humans get of a cerulean—its belly appears whitish, its throat ringed with a necklace of dark feathers. But the cerulean's back and wings are a brilliant blue unlike any other bird's—bluer than an Eastern bluebird and a shade lighter than an indigo bunting—like the blue of the clear Colombian sky. Two parallel white bars adorn each of the cerulean's shoulders, and flecks of black mimic shadows on its wings. Because of its quick movements, small size, and penchant for the forest's canopy, most birders identify the cerulean warbler not by sight, but by the male's buzzy, ascending song.

Data from the United States Geological Survey's annual Breeding Bird Survey shows that since 1966 cerulean warbler numbers have dropped by about 3 percent a year, which meant that in 2006 the size of their total population was almost 80 percent smaller than it had been forty years earlier. These grim statistics compelled the avian conservation organization Partners in Flight to list the species as a top priority for conservation action. In 2001, a coalition of biologists, birders, foresters, and wildlife managers (known collectively as the Cerulean Warbler Technical Group, many of whom stood in my company on the tarmac), alarmed by the bird's steep and steady decline, launched several collaborative research projects and conservation initiatives. But even after several years of intense study, the reasons for the cerulean's plummeting numbers remained somewhat murky; researchers had a difficult time pinpointing a single, smoking-gun culprit. Instead, it quickly became clear that the cerulean warbler faced significant threats throughout its entire range: in its breeding, migratory, and wintering habitats.

I first heard of the cerulean warbler in 2002, when my husband, Jesse, and I lived in West Virginia. Wildlife biologist Dr. Petra Bohall Wood gave a presentation at a meeting of the local Mountaineer Chapter of the National Audubon Society that described the cerulean's decline and explained some of her research investigating possible reasons for the bird's falling population numbers. Afterward,

I read a few articles and learned that on October 30, 2000, the Southern Environmental Law Center and twenty-seven other organizations filed a petition with the
US Fish and Wildlife Service to list the cerulean warbler as "threatened" under the
Endangered Species Act. For several months, I casually followed the news about
the cerulean, and I even started a file folder of articles. But then other issues in my
life took center stage. Jesse and I married and finished graduate school. We left
West Virginia and moved further south to Blacksburg, Virginia, for Jesse to attend
veterinary school and for me to teach creative writing in Virginia Tech's English
Department. The world changed, too, from the September 11, 2001, attacks and
the subsequent wars in Afghanistan and Iraq, to the Asian tsunami, to Hurricane
Katrina. My "Cerulean Warbler" folder sat idle in our filing cabinet between "Car
Insurance" and "Credit-Card Statements.".

Several years later, I began thinking about the cerulean warbler again, and I
looked up the status of the Southern Environmental Law Center petition. To my
surprise, I discovered that the Fish and Wildlife Service still hadn't released their
"twelve-month finding," even though more than five years had passed since the original petition had been filed. I became interested, then suspicious, then intrigued, and
finally *obsessed* with the cerulean warbler. It firmly lodged itself in my imagination;
its buzzy call echoed in my daydreams. The cerulean warbler was a neighbor, a kin-
dred spirit trying to forge a life in the old Appalachian hills. It became my symbol for
a changing hemisphere, a sentinel singing a warning of dark days to come if we refused to pay attention. With my new obsession as my guide, I compulsively read every cerulean-focused scientific and legal document I could find. And while it seemed
like a lot of information at first, I soon realized that quite a bit about this bird and its
natural history remained uncertain or entirely unknown.

I learned that cerulean warblers mate, nest, and raise their young in large tracts
of contiguous deciduous forests throughout much of the eastern United States and
Canada, from Ontario in the northeast to northern Georgia in the south; however, about 80 percent of the total cerulean warbler population breeds in the central
Appalachian Mountains. This core breeding area, which lies within Partners in
Flight's Appalachian Bird Conservation Region, stretches from southwest Pennsylvania through all of West Virginia and south to eastern Kentucky and Tennessee. This part of the country may not always have been the heart of the cerulean's
breeding range; historically, they could be found nesting in great numbers in the
old-growth riparian forests of the Mississippi and Ohio River Valleys. Sadly, most
of those bottomland hardwood forests were heavily logged in the nineteenth and
early twentieth centuries, displacing wildlife and forcing the animals to attempt to
adapt to other habitats. For the cerulean warbler, this meant shifting their breeding
range to the north and east, into the mixed mesophytic and oak forests of Central

Appalachia. While tracts of mature hardwoods still exist in these ancient mountains, preserving this important breeding habitat could prove a daunting task.

In addition to the usual suspects—urban sprawl, development, forest fragmentation—a startling landscape change is transforming our Central Appalachians; a
relatively new method of extracting the region's plentiful bituminous coal, known
as mountaintop removal mining, not only eliminates the trees (along with all the
other plants and animals), but flattens entire ridges and fills in the surrounding
valleys and hollows with dirt, rock, and other material from the former mountaintop. Coal companies are required by the Surface Mining Control and Reclamation
Act of 1977 to restore surface-mined land to "approximate original contour"; however, if returning the mountain to its former height and shape is too costly or not
possible, coal companies can apply for a variance. Variances—waivers or exemp-
tions from parts of the law—can be granted if the company renders the mined land
"suitable for an industrial, commercial, residential, or public use." Unfortunately,
rendering the land "suitable" for these uses often means leaving behind flat, grass-
covered plateaus where forested mountains once stood.

While mountaintop removal coal mining is deplorable for a wide variety of
reasons—economic and social as well as environmental and emotional—it may
permanently destroy the preferred breeding habitat of the cerulean warbler. According to the US Fish and Wildlife Service, "In the core of the [cerulean warbler's] range, Kentucky and West Virginia, ...mountaintop coal mining and valley
fill operations through 2012 are expected to remove 567,000 hectares (1.4 million
acres)"—an area roughly the size of Delaware—"of suitable forest habitat.... The
total cumulative forest loss from these activities will likely eliminate breeding
habitat for 10 to 20 percent of the total cerulean warbler population currently occurring within that core area." In addition to literally removing cerulean breeding sites, mountaintop removal further fragments the region's contiguous forests,
creating large-scale "edges" that could make surviving ceruleans (and their nests)
more susceptible to predation. While reforestation efforts are under way on some
abandoned and "reclaimed" mine lands in Appalachia, it could take more than
a hundred years for those forests to mature enough to harbor breeding cerulean
warblers.

The news didn't get much better for ceruleans in their migratory and wintering habitats. They begin leaving North America in late summer—as early as the
end of July—for their long migration south. Many ceruleans follow the Mississippi
River to the Gulf of Mexico. Then, amazingly, they take off across the open water on their tiny two-and-a-half inch wings; their exact route is unknown, though
they may stop briefly when they reach Mexico's Yucatán Peninsula. Or, instead
of Mexico, they might recuperate in Belize or Honduras before making another

over-water flight above the western Caribbean Sea before finally reaching their wintering grounds on the South American continent. Ceruleans then continue to disperse southward to the Andes Mountains of Colombia, Venezuela, Ecuador, Peru, and perhaps Bolivia, where they spend the winter months in middle elevations of forested slopes. Unfortunately, biologists in Colombia estimate that no more than 40 percent and perhaps *less than 10 percent* of the cerulean's preferred wintering habitat remains. Much of the original mountain forest has been cleared for agriculture or to meet the United States' demand for coffee. Cerulean warblers can and do live in the canopy trees of traditional shade-grown coffee farms; unfortunately, many of these farms have been converted to higher-yield full-sun plantations. Like mountaintop removal coal mining in Appalachia, Andean deforestation could have negative social and economic impacts in addition to obvious environmental drawbacks.

At the height of my cerulean obsession—November of 2006, more than six years since the Southern Environmental Law Center's petition had been filed and more than four years late—the Fish and Wildlife Service finally reached a decision about listing the cerulean warbler. They concluded that granting the cerulean additional legal protections as a threatened species under the Endangered Species Act was "unwarranted," even though they acknowledged that the cerulean's population numbers would probably continue to drop at a rate of more than 3 percent a year.

I puzzled over this; how could so many birds disappear and the species not be "threatened"? I studied the report the service published in the Federal Register, and learned that according to the Endangered Species Act, a species had to be literally "in danger of extinction" before it could be recognized as "endangered," and "likely to become endangered" in order to qualify as threatened. Apparently, even though their numbers continued to plummet, there were still too many cerulean warblers—estimated at about four hundred thousand individuals in 2006, according to the service to be in danger of extinction. This number seemed adequately high until I did some math: if four hundred thousand individuals existed in 2006, and that represented an annual decline of 3 percent since 1966, then in 1966 about 1.3 million cerulean warblers existed in the world. If this trend continued and did not accelerate, by 2050 the population will have dropped to fewer than a hundred thousand birds. Federally recognized or not, this bird species was obviously in jeopardy.

So, in late 2006 I decided to take my relationship with the cerulean warbler to a more serious level; I indulged my obsession and began investigating the bird for myself. I wanted to know the mysterious, elusive cerulean warbler as intimately as I possibly could. This journey to South America marked the culmination of my personal search for this vanishing bird, which took me from the hills and hollows

of West Virginia and Tennessee to the high plains and Andean slopes of Colombia. During the previous two years, I'd accompanied wildlife biologists on field
research projects, interviewed cerulean experts, hiked in areas known to harbor
breeding ceruleans, and tried to learn everything I could about the bird. Before
beginning my cerulean investigation, I had a strong suspicion that this little blue
bird could show us not only how our actions are to blame for its decline, but also
how its decline mirrors a decline in the quality of life of its human neighbors in
Appalachia, the Andes, and indeed the rest of the world. What follows is an account of my discoveries, experiences, and frustrations with this charismatic sprite
of the treetops.

PART ONE

Spring

Audubon's cerulean warbler, painted in 1822.

ONE

★

PIONEERS

*H*ANGING A FRAMED John James Audubon print on a prominent wall is almost a requirement for a bird-lover's home. My Audubon print—"Cerulean Warbler," of course—hangs in our living room, above a twenty-gallon fish tank. The caption along the bottom claims it was painted in 1822 with watercolor and graphite on paper. The bird, a bright blue male, is poised to snatch a small black spider from a bearberry leaf. The bird's wings are slightly drooped, his head cocked toward his prey. One tiny foot clings to a thin branch, and the other trails behind, as if the bird is frozen in mid-hop. The tail is my favorite part; its twelve feathers are fanned, showing off their white splotches and black tips. Parallel white shoulder bars stand out against the blue and black of the wings. It seems, however, that Audubon left out the cerulean's blue-black "necklace" of feathers—but I give him the benefit of the doubt and blame the angle.

While John James Audubon is the most famous early naturalist to paint and chronicle North American birds, he wasn't the first. Scottish-born artist, naturalist, and poet Alexander Wilson, known as "the father of American ornithology," was the first to "officially" describe the cerulean warbler and dozens of other North American bird species. Wilson arrived in America in 1794 when he was twenty-eight years old. According to *Of a Feather: A Brief History of American Birding*, in 1803 Wilson launched the idea of creating "a book documenting all of his adopted land's birds." For years he traveled the United States "collecting" (i.e. shooting)

individuals to paint and describe for his project. The first volume of Wilson's
American Ornithology appeared a few years later, in 1808, and the fourth (and final)
volume appeared in 1814, a year after his untimely death at age forty-seven. The
volumes included hand-painted engraved copperplates of every North American
bird species known to Wilson, along with a narrative description of each species'
habitats and natural history, followed by a detailed physical description.

The cerulean warbler appears in Volume II of *American Ornithology*, completed in 1810. Wilson bestowed upon the bird the scientific name *Sylvia cerulea*. This
made sense at the time, since many Old World warblers were categorized in the
Sylvia genus. (The cerulean would later be reclassified as *Dendroica cerulea*, and in
July 2011, as this book was preparing to go to press, the American Ornithologists
Union changed the designation again, to *Setophaga cerulea*.) In the beginning of
his description Wilson announces, "This delicate little species is now, for the first
time, introduced to public notice. Except my friend, Mr. Peale, I know of no other
naturalist who seems to have hitherto known of its existence." After that somewhat
dramatic opening, the tenor of the entry changes: "At what time it arrives from the
south I cannot positively say, as I have never met with it in spring, but have several
times found it during summer. On the borders of streams and marshes, among the
branches of the poplar, it is sometimes to be found. It has many of the habits of
the Flycatcher; though…from the formation of its bill, [I] must arrange it with the
Warblers. It is one of our scarce birds in Pennsylvania, and its nest has hitherto
eluded my search. I have never observed it after the 20th of August, and therefore
suppose it retires early to the south." Wilson was correct on most counts; ceruleans are not a bird of early spring or fall, and their tiny nests are almost impossible
to find. Wilson's poetic side surfaces in his physical description of the cerulean:
"This bird is four inches and a half long, and seven and a half broad; the front and
upper part of the head is of a fine verditer blue; the hind end and back, of the same
color, but not quite so brilliant; a few lateral streaks of black mark the upper part of
the back; wings and tail, black, edged with sky blue…"

Wilson's painted etching of the cerulean warbler shares Plate 8 with the "American Siskin," "Rosebreasted Grosbeak," "Green black throated Warbler," "Yellow
rump Warbler," and "Solitary Flycatcher." The birds seem to be painted in scale to
each other; the largest bird of the plate, the grosbeak, takes center stage. It is portrayed as if standing upright; the bird's head is tilted back, and its wings are gently
spread. The grosbeak's underside and breast face the reader; its posture and position on the page make the bird appear almost like Christ on the cross. Surrounding the grosbeak, clockwise from the upper right side, are the "American Siskin"
(known today as the pine siskin), then the yellow-rumped warbler, and then the
solitary flycatcher (a.k.a. the blue-headed vireo) in the lower right-hand corner of

the page. The cerulean is in the lower left, and the black-throated green warbler in the upper left.

Wilson's cerulean is extraordinarily unlifelike. It looks as if it's about to fall off the bottom of the page; the bird is facing downward, its wings open but pulled back slightly to denote a dive or swoop. Its bill is slightly parted, and its black eye looks dull. I realize that using watercolor paints to tint copperplate etchings must be extremely difficult, and I feel guilty about being critical, but it looks like a painting of a dead cerulean warbler (which, of course, it is). The plumage looks too gray, and this bird, too, seems to be missing its blue-black necklace. The tail would also benefit from additional detail and refinement. The black-throated green warbler in the upper corner looks much better; this bird is portrayed hanging from a branch, head cocked in a curious manner, as if looking for a meal. The siskin looks alright, too, and is even pictured with a pine cone, suggesting the habitat where the species is most likely to be found. Actually, every bird on the plate looks better than the cerulean, even the Christ-like grosbeak. I think, at least in the contest of depicting cerulean warblers, John James Audubon must be declared superior.

Like Alexander Wilson, Audubon immigrated to the United States as a young man. Born in Haiti in 1785, he was reportedly the illegitimate son of a French sea captain and his mistress. Audubon grew up in France with his stepmother, and according to the National Audubon Society, fled to America in 1803 to avoid conscription into Napoleon's army. Unsuccessful at virtually everything except for painting birds, he was jailed in 1819 for bankruptcy. Shortly thereafter, he set off on a journey down the Mississippi and Missouri rivers, with a goal similar to Wilson's: to paint and describe all of North America's birds.

On Sunday, August 12, 1821, Audubon wrote about cerulean warblers in his Mississippi River journal [all *sic*]:

We left this Morning after an early breakfast to go and explore a Famous Lake about 5½ Miles from this where we were to find (as told) great many Very fine Birds.... I was fortunate in Shooting a Male of the Green blue Warbler [cerulean warbler]—One Week ago I had shot one but Never could find it...these birds sing sweetly, and No doubt breed here; Look much like the blue Yellow Backs Warblers [Northern parula] and hang downwards by the feet like these and the Titmouse. Saw only the one I shot to day and having as much as I Know I could Well draw before they would be Spoiled by the heat of the Wheather returned to the House. This Male Measured 5 Inches in Length and 7¼ in breadth...every Tail feathers having White on their inner Vane except the Two Middle ones—so fat was this bird and of so solid a Nature was that fat that it Cut like Mutton fat; its

gizzard Was filled entirely with some Small brown Shelly Insects and the remains
of the same Kind that are extremely plenty on the Cipresses of these Swamps...

I wondered if the fat cerulean warbler (no doubt stocking up for his long migration) that Audubon so vividly described dissecting was the model for the print
hanging on my wall.

By the mid-1820s Audubon was promoting his legendary book, *Birds of America*, in Europe. The paintings therein were all life-sized, and therefore the volumes
themselves were huge—each page measured 39½ inches long by 28½ inches wide.
The print on my wall differed slightly from the one that appeared in the 1840 version of *Birds of America*; in that book, the plate is entitled "The Coerulean Wood-
Warbler," and while the male cerulean is obviously the same one featured in my
print, lower on the branch a female joins him. The branch, too, seems to have
sprouted more berries and leaves, and its position on the page is turned slightly to
allow room for the female bird.

Unfortunately, some of Audubon's accompanying description is inaccu-
rate, and his discussion of the nesting site is almost completely wrong. Audubon
claims that "the nest is placed in the forks of a low tree or bush, more frequently
on a dog-wood tree." Today, biologists have discovered that ceruleans usually construct their nests on horizontal branches more than thirty feet from the ground.
Audubon also errs when he discusses the range of the cerulean warbler: "The
whole breadth of our country, from the Atlantic shores to those of the Pacific, is
visited by this bird, which was found along the Columbia River at Fort Vancou-
ver by Mr. TOWNSEND." The cerulean warbler typically occurs in the eastern
United States; Audubon's colleague Mr. Townsend (of Townsend's solitaire and
Townsend's warbler fame) is probably incorrect in this instance.

In addition to Wilson and Audubon, another important contributor to the
body of knowledge about North American birds was Massachusetts amateur ornithologist Arthur Cleveland Bent. Born in 1866, Bent achieved success in the busi-
ness world as a young man, but he never lost his childhood love for birds. When he
was forty-four, he, too, began compiling the life histories of all of America's bird
species. While chief researcher and organizer of the project, he relied upon the
help of more than eight hundred collaborators from across the continent. He prepared and compiled twenty-one volumes of work; nineteen were published in his
lifetime, and the final two appeared in the years after his death in 1954. Each volume consisted of between three hundred and six hundred pages; according to *Of a
Feather*, the twenty-one volumes totaled 9,500 pages of text.

Bent's *Life Histories of North American Wood Warblers* (in two volumes) appeared in 1953. His section on the cerulean warbler compiles observations from

Wilson and Audubon as well as other ornithologists up to the year 1924. In the introduction to the cerulean's section, Bent writes, "This warbler, a bird of treetops in heavy deciduous woods, where its colors make it difficult to distinguish among the lights and shadows of the lofty foliage and against the blue sky, is well named cerulean!" He describes the bird's habits, including its migration route and nesting information. Unlike Audubon, much of Bent's information has since been validated. He quotes a letter from "Burutch" to "Dr. Chapman" (presumably Frank M. Chapman of the American Museum of Natural History) that claims the cerulean's nest "is usually placed on a horizontal branch or drooping branch of an elm, ranging from twenty-five to sixty feet from the ground, and from four, to fifteen, or eighteen feet from the body of the tree *over an opening*" [emphasis his]. Another contributor, W. E. Saunders of southern Ontario, reported on eight nests: "two of these were in oaks...two in maples, and four in basswoods." These claims are all accurate; ceruleans nest in deciduous hardwoods, and in addition to oaks, maples, and basswoods, they also nest in elms, sycamores, and hickories.

Bent's discussion also includes information about young, plumages, food, behavior, voice, enemies, field marks, range, and arrival and departure dates. My favorite of Bent's inclusions comes from S. Harmsted Chubb: "A bird more difficult to observe I have rarely if ever met with. His life seemed to be confined almost entirely to the tops of the tallest deciduous trees, where he would generally feed, with apparent design, on the side most remote from the would-be observer, exhibiting a wariness not expected on the part of a warbler, and finally leaving the tree, the first intimation of his departure being a more distant song." I, too, have had this frustrating experience while searching for ceruleans in a forest canopy. Chubb continues, "Had it not been for the almost incessant singing, being heard almost constantly from daybreak until nearly dark, the task of identification would have seemed hopeless." Another humorous portion of Bent's account is the summary of the different ways observers have described the cerulean's song: "*wee wee wee wee bzzz*," "*trill, trill, trill, bzz*," and "*Just a little sneeze*." Fifty years later, Bent's work still shows up in the citation sections of scientific papers.

IT WOULD BE THE 1980s before scientists began taking a closer look at ceruleans. Paul B. Hamel—sort of the godfather of cerulean warblers—was one of the first researchers to specifically study them. He's authored and coauthored dozens of papers on management, silviculture, conservation, and habitat, and he continues to be the world's preeminent authority on all things cerulean.

Although Hamel began studying ceruleans in the 1980s, birds had been a part of his life since at least the fourth grade. In school that year, he'd been assigned a

book report; like many students, he procrastinated. On the Saturday before the
report was due, young Paul went to the library and selected the skinniest book
he could find: the *Golden Field Guide to the Birds of North America*. He wrote the
report, and a few months later, after the Michigan snow had melted and signs of
spring had begun to appear, Paul was walking home from school when he noticed
bird activity in multi-flora rose bushes. Much to his surprise, he recognized the
species. "They were cedar waxwings," he told me. "It was like the sentence was
given that day. I wrote it down—it was the first day I ever wrote down a bird I
knew—March 23rd, 1959."

After the cedar waxwings, Paul Hamel's fate was sealed; he went on to study
zoology at Michigan State University and eventually earned his doctorate from
Clemson. Upon graduation, he accepted a job with the Tennessee Department of
Environment and Conservation and relocated to Nashville. Though he'd studied
other bird species, he'd never officially investigated cerulean warblers; there were
few—if any—ceruleans in South Carolina, so when Hamel noticed the small blue
birds in the trees of the Warner Parks near his Nashville apartment, he found them
"interesting." "That was my first contact with the birds," he said. "I realized I really
didn't know very much about them, so I did a little research on the side to kind of
compare ceruleans with the other warblers that I knew about."

Hamel began talking with his colleagues; one of them, Chandler S. Robbins,
had US Geological Survey Breeding Bird Survey data that suggested cerulean
population numbers were dropping. Another colleague, John W. Fitzpatrick, had
preliminary data from observing ceruleans on their Peruvian wintering grounds.
Robbins's and Fitzpatrick's data, combined with Hamel's new information about
cerulean breeding habitat in Tennessee, provided the basis for the paper "A Warbler in Trouble: *Dendroica cerulea*," presented at a symposium in 1989; afterwards,
it was published in the volume *Ecology and Conservation of Neotropical Landbirds*.
In the article, the authors report that "from 1966 to 1987 the Cerulean Warbler
showed the most precipitous decline of any North American warbler (3.4% per
year). Unless steps are taken to protect large tracts of habitat of this ecologically
specialized species, both on the breeding grounds and in the Andean foothills, we
believe the future of this warbler is in serious jeopardy." In 1992, Hamel's "Cerulean Warbler: *Dendroica cerulea*" appeared in *Migratory Nongame Birds of Management Concern in the Northeast*, published by the US Fish and Wildlife Service. He
echoed many of his concerns about ceruleans and, like Bent, summarized current
and historical research on the species.

In 1993, Paul Hamel had the opportunity to move from Tennessee to Mississippi to work for the US Forest Service on a long-term cerulean study. Since early
research on the bird seemed to suggest that it favored mature, "high dollar" trees,

the Forest Service took notice. Hamel began studying ceruleans in some of the large remaining forest patches in the Mississippi Alluvial Valley. Soon thereafter, the US Fish and Wildlife Service asked him to work on a status assessment of the species. Interest among members of the scientific community began to increase as well, and by the late 1990s several groups of biologists were studying ceruleans; in addition to Hamel's work in the Deep South, researchers in Appalachia and Ontario studied the birds in their respective regions. At that time, according to Hamel, the groups "were interacting sort of loosely, but there wasn't a coordinated interaction among us. The mindset of each group was different, but in our interactions with each other we were always cordial."

The groups became a more formal collective after a meeting in Knoxville, Tennessee, in the summer of 2001 to ensure that all of their research was "moving in the same way and not counteracting each other's efforts." From that meeting of approximately thirty biologists, foresters, land managers, federal and state employees, representatives from nongovernmental organizations, and academics, the Cerulean Warbler Technical Group was formed. According to the article Hamel co-authored with Deanna K. Dawson and Patrick D. Keyser, "How We Can Learn More About the Cerulean Warbler (*Dendroica cerulea*)," the group sought to "focus on identifying meaningful conservation solutions through sound science, clear communication, and trust." They hoped that the group could "serve as an example for concentrating and coordinating research, monitoring populations, and implementing conservation of forest bird species," with an "underlying philosophy of...drawing circles to include and leaving agendas at the door." In the winter of 2002, the CWTG met again to develop a more comprehensive and broad-based strategy for conserving ceruleans. This workshop involved more than sixty people, and during the meeting they divided themselves into several sub-committees, including a Breeding Season Research Group and a Non-Breeding Season Group (known as El Grupo Cerúleo). Collectively, the CWTG identified gaps in cerulean knowledge and priorities for future research, both on the breeding and wintering grounds.

In addition to helping coordinate the CWTG, Dr. Hamel wrote the bird's species account in *The Birds of North America*, which according to its introduction is "a joint 10 year project of the American Ornithologists' Union, the Cornell Lab of Ornithology, and the Academy of Natural Sciences." *The Birds of North America* is "only the fourth comprehensive reference covering the life histories of North American birds. Following in the footsteps of Wilson, Audubon, and Bent, *BNA* makes a quantum leap in information beyond what these historic figures were able to provide." Hamel's account summarizes the cerulean's natural history, including details about its diet (which consists primarily of insects from the orders

Homoptera and *Lepidoptera*, such as cicadas, aphids, treehoppers, leaf hoppers, spittlebugs, mealybugs, and caterpillars), habitat, nesting, and migration. The reference was completed in 2002, and it is now available in its entirety online, where it serves as an invaluable resource for any would-be ornithologist or bird-obsessed writer. Virtually every scientific and popular article on cerulean warblers cites Paul Hamel's species account.

I SPENT MANY LATE-MARCH HOURS staring at the Audubon print on my wall, waiting for ceruleans to arrive back in North America after their long journeys. While I hadn't dedicated my life to researching, painting, or "collecting" birds, I understood what being consumed by them felt like. I faulted Wilson and Audubon for shooting so many birds, but their fascination, their love, must have come from the same place that mine did, and perhaps from the same place as Paul Hamel's curiosity about the tiny blue warblers in the park near his apartment. I admired the dedication and determination of pioneering researchers, artists, and naturalists, and I harbored an ambitious secret desire to stand among them.

As March faded to April, I grew more and more restless with anticipation. I wanted to abandon my job and flee to the forested mountains, leaving a stack of un-graded freshman composition papers in my wake. In addition to learning more about this tiny, vanishing songbird, I needed to actually see one in the wild; as embarrassing as it was to admit, the cerulean warbler had heretofore eluded my best birding efforts. I'd been on birding hikes when others in the group claimed to hear ceruleans, but I'd never been able to get one in the sights of my binoculars. They stayed too high in the canopy, were too small, and blended in too well with the leaves and sky. The cerulean seemed more like a ghost or a shadow than a breathing, flesh-and-blood creature. I had to see one.

In the coming months, I planned to make several forays into the world of cerulean warbler research. In early May, I would head to Morgantown, West Virginia, to meet with cerulean biologist Petra Bohall Wood. One of my friends who also lived in Morgantown, expert birder Hillar Klandorf, had promised to take me birding and find a cerulean for me. Then I would join doctoral student Greg George and his crew of field technicians at their study site near Jacksonburg, West Virginia; the field crew would be attempting to capture and band ceruleans as they jockeyed for mates and territories. I stared up at Audubon's cerulean and sighed; May could not come soon enough.

TWO

★

UNDER THE OPEN SKY

O N MOST DAYS, SOUTHWEST VIRGINIA is the very picture of peace and tranquility. On one side of highway 460—to my left as I drove west out of town—were the Allegheny Mountains and West Virginia. To my right were the rounded peaks of the Blue Ridge. Pasture-covered hills rolled on both sides of the road, and an old farmhouse stood in the center of a field filled with Black Angus cattle. The pasture on the other side of the road held horses—paints, bays, roans. The town of Blacksburg is creeping slowly in this direction, and I fear it won't be long before the remaining farmland is converted to subdivisions.

The New River snakes through this valley as it flows north and west into West Virginia, where it eventually meets the Gauley to form the Kanawha. The Kanawha then continues to flow west until it merges with the mighty Ohio. Blacksburg sits on the Eastern Continental Divide; on the west side of town, water flows into the New, which is part of the Mississippi River watershed. On the east side of town, water flows to the Atlantic Ocean via the Chesapeake Bay. Soon, this road would leave Montgomery County and begin to follow the New River through Giles County and into West Virginia.

Two days earlier—May 4—I had submitted my final grades for the semester; I was finally embarking on the first of what I hoped would be many cerulean warbler adventures. As I drove out of Blacksburg, however, my heart was heavier than it had ever been; the last three weeks had been marred by unimaginable violence. I shouldered a heavy sadness that I feared would never completely leave me.

Mid-April in our southern mountains is a gentle time; blooming forsythia lights up yards like bursts of yellow fireworks, magnolia trees sport gaudy white and pink blossoms, and median strips swell with lilacs and tulips. The daffodils on Virginia Tech's campus were nearly finished already, their yellow-and-white flowers brown around the edges and drooping. This spring, the weather had been so unseasonably hot that even the small dogwood next to our house had tentatively begun to open its buds. Iridescent tree swallows lined the power lines behind our house, and two Eastern bluebirds moved into the box that Jesse had built and hung on one of our fence posts. It appeared that spring had sprung; certainly summer was just around the corner. And mid-April marked the return to Appalachia of the first cerulean warblers after their three-thousand-mile journey from the mountain forests of the Andes.

I had trouble believing the weather reports that warned of a vicious nor'easter heading for the United States. But on April 15, a cold wind whipped up overnight and the skies darkened. My parents called from Pennsylvania to say they'd had six inches of snow, and it was still coming down. Blizzard conditions were reported throughout New England. A cold rain began to pelt southwest Virginia, but I assumed the worst of the erratic storm would miss us. Still, I worried about the birds.

On the morning of Monday, April 16, Jesse got up early; he was showered and out the door before 7:00 a.m. to do some last minute studying before his exam at eight. I fed the dog, filled the bird feeders, toasted a whole-wheat bagel, poured coffee into my travel mug, and headed to campus. My freshmen composition students' research papers were due the following day, and that Monday I'd scheduled office hours from 8:00 a.m. until 1:00 p.m. I planned to stop at the local bird store after my office hours to buy more sunflower seed.

Around 7:45, I pulled into the faculty parking lot. The biting wind whipped snow flurries through the gray dawn. I hoped that none of the cerulean warblers had made it back here yet; would this storm disrupt their migration patterns? How could tiny, fragile birds fly in this relentless wind? My hair was still wet from my shower, so I scurried across the lot, cut through a dining hall, and crossed in front of a dorm to the English Department building. Soon I was sitting in front of my computer in my warm office, checking news sites for information about the violent weather. When I didn't learn anything new, I puttered around the building— I checked my mailbox in the main office, joked with the secretary, dropped off a grading rubric that I needed copies of. I finished my coffee, rinsed out my mug, and filled it with water, which I then heated in my office microwave for tea. I propped my door open so my students would feel welcome and wouldn't have to knock.

Around 9:15 or so, Kara, the colleague with whom I shared the office, came in. She had just been downtown at the post office, mailing her taxes at the last minute.

We asked about each other's weekends and complained about the stupid weather. I was beginning to tell Kara how worried I was about the returning cerulean warblers when her cell phone rang. It was her mother calling from Pennsylvania, asking if we knew anything about a shooting on Virginia Tech's campus. We didn't. I went online, and sure enough, there was an email telling the university community to be alert because of a "shooting incident" in a dormitory.

"I'm sure it's nothing," I shrugged. "They're probably overreacting." I went back to surfing news sites, and Kara unpacked her school bags.

But then, a few minutes later, another email came, this one warning of a gunman loose on campus. It instructed us to lock ourselves in our offices and stay away from windows. Kara switched off the lights, lowered the blinds, and kicked out the doorstop.

"I'm sure it's nothing..." I said again, as our office door clicked shut. I glanced around, and my head filled with ridiculous thoughts. My tea was almost gone; we couldn't lock ourselves in here yet, I needed to get more water first. I had to use the bathroom. How long would we have to stay here? I had things to do. I needed more birdseed. I needed to obsess about the storm and its effect on exhausted ceruleans. I could get to the parking lot without getting hurt. Why would anyone shoot me? Why would anyone shoot anyone? It was probably an isolated incident, a domestic dispute of some kind. I said as much, but Kara grew more and more nervous with each passing moment and wouldn't let me leave our office.

I called Jesse's cell phone. He was safe, and the veterinary school was locked down, too.

At around ten o'clock, a student emailed to tell me that he was locked in a classroom and was watching police outside, with guns drawn, running past the windows. Then I heard ambulance sirens. I peeked out the large window (much to Kara's dismay) and glimpsed police cars speeding up and down the street near our building, lights spinning. What was going on? From somewhere outside, I heard an amplified click, then a voice through a loudspeaker—I'm not sure if it was a recording or a real person—repeating, "This is an emergency. Stay away from doors and windows," over and over.

I called my parents. "Hi, Kate!" my mother said cheerfully. "What did you think of those snow pictures I emailed you?"

I told her I hadn't seen them yet because something was happening on our campus. She turned on her television. "They're saying one person is dead and seven are wounded," she gasped. "Oh, Kathleen, please be careful." I told her I would, that I was locked in my office, and not to worry. She told me they were reporting that emergency medical helicopters couldn't fly in the high winds, so Virginia Tech had requested ambulances from nearby communities. *Helicopters?*

For the next two hours, Kara and I crouched on the floor with our backs against the wall, listening to wailing ambulance sirens and the loudspeaker's persistent warnings. Our cell phones rang and rang. My friend Lisa called from her nearby apartment; she could hear the sirens and the loudspeaker, too—did I know what was going on? I called my friend Julie, locked in her office across campus. She had a police scanner, but the news coming across it was cryptic. Through the slats in the window blinds, I could see blowing snow outside. I *really* had to go to the bathroom, but Kara still wouldn't let me leave. In a moment of glowing professionalism, I threatened to urinate in the corner, which under other circumstances might have been funny.

I felt helpless and isolated, and like I should be doing something—writing or grading papers or researching ceruleans or going outside to see what the hell was going on. Maybe they needed help out there. Maybe my students had been hurt. *I needed to leave.* My bones ached from sitting on the thin carpet. The pinched nerve between my spine and right shoulder blade twinged. I tapped the back of my head against the wall and stared at the ceiling tiles. The sirens kept screaming, and the loudspeaker's "This is an emergency" mantra reverberated between the stately brick and limestone buildings—classrooms, laboratories, offices, dining halls, lives.

Finally, around noon, we were told by email to go home. I hurried to the bathroom and then out onto the cold walkways of campus. Faculty, staff, and students trickled from nearby buildings. No one seemed to know what was going on or what had happened, but the sirens and the loudspeaker were finally quiet. The parking lot felt still and cold. Wind whipped my hair into my eyes as I glanced over my shoulder. My colleagues' faces looked confused, or worried, or blank. *Should I still go and get birdseed?* I thought, and then hated myself.

I pulled out of the parking lot, and my cell phone rang again: "I just want to let you know," my father said, slowly, "that the news has made a mistake. You know how they always get things wrong. They're saying twenty-two people are dead. I'm sure they meant 'two.' It's a mistake."

By one o'clock, I was sitting safely on my couch at home with my husband, my dog, and my friends Julie and Steve, both of whom were English instructors, too. We watched the news in horrified shock as the number of murdered students and faculty rose from twenty-two to thirty-three. Thirty-three people killed on our campus, they reported, most of them in Norris Hall; as many as twenty more were injured. *Forty people* had been shot just a few hundred feet from where I'd been all morning. While I checked my email, sipped tea, and read weather reports, my colleagues and our students were dying violent deaths. On the days I taught class, I walked past Norris Hall twice, along its looming, Gothic walls, lined with mature tulip trees and beds of yellow and white daffodils. Was this really happening?

It seemed every person I'd ever met in my life emailed or called that afternoon—high school classmates I hadn't talked to in ten years, people I'd met at academic conferences, distant cousins, former professors, even former students. Our phones rang nonstop. That evening I was scheduled to teach a short course entitled "Birding for Beginners" at the local YMCA; the director called and asked if I still wanted to hold class. "I don't know," I stammered. The media had dubbed the morning's tragedy a "massacre" and claimed it was "the worse mass shooting in United States history." Would anyone, now, want to learn about ways to identify a northern waterthrush or a black-throated green warbler? "No," I replied, "let's cancel. Or, let's reschedule. Whatever. I don't know." As I hung up the phone, I think common sense, reason, and perhaps my sanity began to unravel. The world took on a bizarre, surreal quality; I felt like I was watching a tragic drama unfold all around me. Images flashed across my television and I felt exposed, struck dumb by the absolute improbability of what had apparently occurred. At some point all of our phones quit working—cell towers were jammed and my mother emailed to say she'd gotten a busy signal when she tried to call our landline. Without ringing phones to distract us, we focused, for better or for worse, on the television.

The next morning, Tuesday, April 17, when the world heard that the shooter was an English major, I felt sure that they must have meant "engineering." It's a common mistake—we abbreviate English ENGL instead of ENG to avoid such confusion. Everyone at Virginia Tech majors in engineering. But then I learned that it wasn't a mistake. He was one of our own. I felt that I had to go to campus, had to see my friends and colleagues and students, even if only to look briefly into their eyes.

Jesse and I drove to campus, unsure of what we'd find. When we neared Virginia Tech's Inn and Conference Center, we pulled over and gawked. Its parking lots and lawns were filled with satellite trucks—hundreds of them. From all across Virginia, but also New Jersey, North Carolina, Pennsylvania, Georgia, and everywhere else. CNN. Fox. NBC. ABC. CBS. Lots of cords and wires and men in dark jackets and women in heels, all pacing around on the pavement, holding cell phones to their ears or talking into cameras. Bright morning sunshine glinted off hundreds of windshields.

We weren't sure if we'd be allowed in the lot near the English Department building, so Jesse parked across campus and we walked. People from the media were everywhere—toting cameras, clutching notebooks and microphones, wandering around looking for any sign of tears or anger. As we passed a dorm, a side door opened and a rumpled student stepped out. The media were waiting. They surrounded him, pointed their cameras and fired questions: *Were any of your friends killed? Did you know the shooter?* The student stammered, shoved his hands in his jeans pockets, and looked around for an escape. *How do you think the administration is handling this?* A woman with a notebook noticed Jesse and me watching and began to advance. Jesse took me by the arm and pulled me down the sidewalk. I focused on the ground. If I didn't make eye contact with them, maybe they'd leave me alone. I felt naked. We didn't stay long on campus.

On Tuesday evening, I sat on the couch at Julie and Steve's house with a laptop open on the coffee table in front of me. I kept hitting the refresh icon, because every few minutes *The New York Times* added names to the casualty list on its website. The television showed images of bloody students being carried out of Norris Hall, of police sprinting through the snow flurries, of huddled students standing around looking shocked. I saw my colleagues, my friends, being interviewed, being asked painful and often ignorant questions about the shooter and the university. One of my freshman students appeared on *Larry King Live*. Another wept on CBS. Dan Rather, Geraldo Rivera, Anderson Cooper, and all the heavy hitters were here, on our beautiful, usually quiet, usually peaceful campus tucked away in the mountains.

I hit the refresh icon again and noticed that the casualty list had been updated. I recognized one of the just-added names, but second-guessed myself. Same last name, same first name. But that can't be *my* Rachael, I thought. Not the Rachael with the brilliant smile whom I'd taught in a freshman English class the previous semester. Not the intelligent young woman who sometimes lamented the traffic problems around her hometown, who wrote about her love of quiet, pre-dawn mornings. I forced myself to focus. The website also listed an age: eighteen. And a hometown, which I recognized.

The room dissolved. I could suddenly see her sitting cross-legged on the floor of the hallway outside our classroom in McBryde Hall, her back against the wall, waiting for the students in the class before ours to clear out. She'd be wearing jeans and a Virginia Tech sweatshirt. Her shoulder-length brown hair, the color of chestnuts, would be tucked behind her ears. Her elbows would rest on her knees, and her head would be bent over the novel she'd be reading. She'd look up, smile at me and say hello, and then resume reading. When we'd finally get into the classroom, I'd drop my bags on the front desk, she would set her backpack on the floor, and the two of us would arrange the desks in a circle before the other students arrived.

Rachael took notes. She paid attention. She never rolled her eyes, she came to office hours, she volunteered to read aloud when no one else would. She had perfect attendance for the semester. Even during the most tedious of lectures on MLA citation or logical fallacies, I could look across the circle at her, and she would be listening, textbook open on her desk. She wasn't afraid to make eye contact. She had a quiet confidence and a level of maturity rare among college freshmen. She was poised, focused, respectful, and kind. Her beautiful smile could brighten a boring class. And she smiled often.

"Oh no," I said. I started to shake. Jesse was next to me on the couch. My mouth twisted. I stammered a few times and tried to say something about Rachael, about her smile, about her intelligence, but instead, I think I said, "She was probably sitting in the front row." My mind rushed to a horrible place and filled with images of chaos and overturned desks and arms, legs, blood. "Oh no," I said again, and then sobbed.

I'm not sure about the order of the rest of the week's events. I know I cried a lot and slept little. We watched news reports, went to vigils, wept at convocations; it felt like everything good had been drained from the world. At times, my mind felt like a vacuum—totally empty of everything, hollow and useless. At other times, questions rushed in. Between the murders at the dormitory and at Norris Hall, the shooter went downtown to the Blacksburg Post Office to mail his manifesto to NBC; why, after mailing the package, didn't he stop in the English Department? Had Kara been behind him in line as she waited to mail her taxes? I must have passed him many times in the hallways of the department over the last three years. Why didn't he go to the building that held his professors' offices? Who would he have found at nine o'clock on that Monday morning, shuffling around her office, checking email, heating water for tea in the microwave?

The university decided that classes would meet during the last two weeks of the semester. Our department invited counselors to a faculty meeting to help us know what to say to our students. At the meeting, we were told that we could request counselors to come with us to our classes, and counselors would automatically be sent to classes where there would be empty desks. *Empty desks.* I didn't hear much of anything else he said until the question and answer session at the end of the meeting. One of my colleagues asked if we were allowed to hug our students. The counselor told us that if we weren't sure, we should "err on the side of the hug." While it was the best advice I'd heard in a long time, it only added to the surreality; what kind of bizarre world did we live in? It might not be appropriate for a professor to hug a grieving adult student, but apparently it *was* appropriate—and legal—for someone with a history of mental illness and extreme antisocial behavior to purchase semiautomatic handguns.

The following Tuesday I was afraid to go to class. I considered canceling my classes and giving all my students automatic A's. What if someone wanted to further terrorize us by repeating the events of the previous week? One of the classrooms that I taught in didn't have windows or a lock—should I push the instructor's desk in front of the door? I'd never been afraid to go to work before. What would I say to my traumatized, beautiful students? They'd be looking to me for some sort of guidance, wouldn't they? What if I said the wrong things? What if none of them showed up?

When I walked into my first classroom, I was surprised to see all but one or two of my students. They seemed eager to see each other, to see me, and to have a chance to talk. I gave them handouts about counseling services on campus and about the symptoms of Post Traumatic Stress Disorder. I told them about Rachael. I cried. I admitted that I hadn't been sleeping, that my stomach hurt, and that I had to turn off an episode of *CSI*. I gave them each a copy of Wendell Berry's soothing poem "The Peace of Wild Things," and as my classes ended, I erred on the side of the hug and embraced every one of my students, except for a young man who said he'd cry if he hugged me, and he didn't want to cry in front of people.

I dreaded walking past Norris Hall, but I had to in order to get to my second class. My feet felt heavy as I approached its looming countenance. I had an hour-long break between classes, during which I forced myself to sit on a bench near the building's backside. A new chain-link fence covered in green mesh encased the entire structure, so no one could really see in. Students rushed by en route to class. Most avoided looking at Norris. Two young women, walking together, laughed and talked. It was an odd sound. The landscaped daffodils were all dead. Their green stalks remained, but the flowers had dropped some days before.

Yellow police tape was stretched around the outside of the fence and wrapped around the thick trunks of tulip trees. CRIME SCENE DO NOT CROSS CRIME SCENE DO NOT CROSS... From inside the fence, I heard a bird singing. At first, the twangy song sounded like a mockingbird, but then I realized it was a gray catbird, the first I'd heard that season. He had probably recently arrived from points south. What did he think of all this yellow tape? I imagined him wooing a mate, building a nest, and raising young birds, all inside the police boundary. The possibility of new, fragile life—so close to where so many lives had brutally ended—seemed impossible.

I stared at the towering tulip trees and imagined a forest full of them. An old-growth, hardwood forest, thick with oaks and maples, hickories and buckeyes. For the first time in more than a week, I thought about cerulean warblers. In light of everything that had happened, it felt petty to have been so worried about them during the storm, so consumed by their fate. Surely most survived the nor'easter—but perhaps not the ones most determined to arrive here first, perhaps not the strongest and the brightest.

My eyes followed the tulip tree trunks up toward their crowns. I noticed they were taller than Norris. The building stopped, but the trees kept going, reaching sunward, stretching into the sky. I ran my gaze back down their trunks to where they met the earth; their roots had caused the sidewalk to crack. I visualized them plunging deep into the ground, below Norris's foundation. Compared to the trees, the building suddenly seemed small and impermanent. I felt the sun's warmth in the metal bench under me.

I forced my eyes to the building's second floor windows. I wanted to make some personal vow, to reach a revelation, but I kept coming back to the trees. The trees, the catbird, the dead flowers. Students hurrying past. A state police officer standing guard near an opening in the chain-link fence. I knew I'd find a way to go on, but I also knew that everything would be different—for Virginia Tech, for our students and faculty, for me.

IN THE HECTIC WEEKS THAT followed, I did my best to focus on cerulean warblers, on the work I wanted to do, and on the future. On several occasions, I tried to read a poem that usually comforted me, William Cullen Bryant's "Thanatopsis":

> ...When thoughts
> Of the last bitter hour come like a blight
> Over thy spirit,...
> Go forth, under the open sky, and list
> To Nature's teachings...

Even though the poem didn't work this time (I couldn't even get all the way through it without breaking down), I was trying to take Bryant's advice; I would "go forth under the open sky" and "list to Nature's teachings." I did my best to bury my feelings of sorrow, despair, and the choking anxiety that gripped me late at night, and I tried to concentrate on the purpose of this trip: to search for and investigate my little blue friends, the cerulean warblers.

I had been looking forward to this trip to West Virginia for several months; after recent events, though, I'd considered canceling it. Jesse insisted that I go. He reminded me, at times not so gently, that I must keep living, that I couldn't let this ruin my life. So, after finishing my grades, I loaded up my old, red Jeep Cherokee and headed west. As Blacksburg's green river valley faded behind me and the mountains loomed closer, I felt an almost magnetic pull backward. In spite of it, I kept driving.

The woods on both sides of the road thickened as I passed the sign letting me know that I was entering the Jefferson National Forest. A brown-and-gold Montgomery County police cruiser was parked in the grassy median near the turn for the Pandapas Pond day-use area of the forest. I breezed by it and crossed into Giles County, which bordered West Virginia. The steepening highway gently twisted into the hills. *Montani semper liberi*, I remembered: mountaineers are always free. I slid in a Hillbilly Gypsies CD and headed for the horizon.

THREE

★

CERULEAN BLUES

I PULLED INTO A PARKING SPOT in front of Percival Hall, the oddly shaped building that housed West Virginia University's Division of Forestry and Natural Resources. I'd arranged to meet Dr. Petra Wood at two o'clock, but because of my paranoia about being late, I arrived almost half an hour early. The sun shone high and bright in a cloudless sky, and a gentle breeze swept down the hill from WVU's greenhouses, lifting my hair away from my face.

I pushed through Percival Hall's glass doors and my arms goose-bumped in the cool of the air-conditioned lobby. I'd only been in this building a few times before, but it was exactly how I'd remembered it. Wooden display cases with glass panes lined one of the wood-paneled walls, which were hung with framed portraits of official-looking men. A flat plasma screen hung from the ceiling, and every few seconds the message on it changed from "WVU Forestry Ranks Top 10 in Research Citations" to information about the upcoming graduation ceremony to pictures of smiling students. I sat down on a chair beneath the screen and watched a woman across the lobby spread navy blue cloths over rectangular tables. Every few minutes a student, backpack slung over one shoulder, would amble through the lobby and exit to the beautiful spring afternoon.

I glanced at the clock on the wall and chewed on my bottom lip; I still had fifteen minutes to wait before my meeting with Dr. Wood. For the tenth time that day, I mentally ran through each of my previous interactions with her. The one that stood out, of course, was the time I saw her deliver the presentation on cerulean

26

warblers at the Audubon Society meeting several years before. I opened my folder and flipped though highlighted copies of scientific articles. I'd recently reread and partially memorized Dr. Wood's published research projects, most of which focused on cerulean warbler habitat in southern West Virginia. Her titles included: "Cerulean Warbler (*Dendroica cerulea*) Microhabitat and Landscape-Level Habitat Characteristics in Southern West Virginia"; "Cerulean Warbler Abundance and Occurrence Relative to Large-Scale Edge and Habitat Characteristics"; "Cerulean Warbler Use of Regenerated Clearcut and Two-age Harvests"; and my favorite, a report submitted to the USGS Biological Resources Division Species-At-Risk Program, "Cerulean Warbler (*Dendroica cerulea*) Microhabitat and Landscape-level Habitat Characteristics in Southern West Virginia in Relation to Mountaintop Mining/Valley Fills." I hoped I knew enough about the birds and her research to not embarrass myself.

As I shuffled through the papers, Dr. Wood suddenly emerged from a nearby hallway, clutching a coffee mug and a notebook. She did a double take when she saw me, then smiled. I'd forgotten how tall and thin she was; when I stood to greet her I felt short and a bit stumpy.

We decided to go outside and enjoy the warm spring weather, and we sat down across from each other at a table near the entrance to Percival. Suddenly this project became more real to me; while I loved and obsessed over charismatic, elusive cerulean warblers, here was someone who'd devoted years of her life to researching them. Because of my overactive nerves, I babbled incoherently at Dr. Wood for almost twenty minutes about friends we had in common, my husband Jesse, veterinary school, the weather. She listened politely and smiled often; eventually, nervous energy expended, I took a deep breath and asked how she'd first become involved with cerulean warbler research.

"I actually kind of just fell into it, in a way," she said, smiling and pushing her brown hair out of her eyes. "When we first started out doing mountaintop mining research, our project was to look at wildlife populations and how they changed in reclaimed areas versus forested areas." In addition to cerulean warblers, Dr. Wood's research included projects on bald eagles, American woodcocks, wood thrush, wood rats, and other species. (I thought it curious that she shared a name with so many of the species she studied, but I kept that to myself.) She continued, "Around that same time, people started talking about cerulean warblers, so one of the things we looked at was how many cerulean warblers there were; we noticed that in the intact forest we had a lot more birds than in the fragmented patches of forest that were left on the mines. And it kind of kept building from there."

Dr. Wood's research has shown that in this part of the United States—Central Appalachia—cerulean warblers preferred to nest within large tracts of mature forest on ridgetops. One of the most significant threats to cerulean habitat in this core breeding area is, obviously, mountaintop removal coal mining, the focus of several of Dr. Wood's projects. Begun in the late 1970s, this surface mining practice "removes" layers of the mountain to reach the coal within. Once a company secures the necessary state and federal permits and determines that coal lies within a mountain, it clears away all the trees and other vegetation. Sometimes the trees are sold for timber, but other times they are simply pushed into a huge pile and burned. Then the coal company drills holes on the mountain's surface, into which high-powered explosives are dropped; the resulting blasts destroy the top of the mountain to expose thin coal seams. Usually, the former mountaintop (now reduced to dirt and rocks called "spoil") is pushed into surrounding valleys and hollows. These valley-fills often bury headwater streams and cause problems for nearby communities with increased erosion and run-off; local residents complain of structural damage to their homes from the blasting, contamination of their drinking water because of the landscape changes, and an increase in flooding. Once the top layers of the mountain have been removed, heavy equipment scrapes coal from the now-exposed seam. The coal is then trucked to a processing plant, where it's cleaned up and ground down to burnable size before being shipped off to power plants, where it (along with coal recovered from deep-mining and other methods) is converted into 50 percent of our nation's electricity.

When an entire Appalachian ridge (and its mature hardwood forest) is removed, so is critical cerulean warbler breeding habitat. Some of Dr. Wood's research in southern West Virginia focused specifically on how ceruleans reacted to deforested "reclaimed" mine sites; the results revealed that the density of their breeding territories increased with distance from the mine's edge. In other words, not only do mountaintop removal mines destroy cerulean habitat outright, but they also make nearby remaining habitat less hospitable.

Despite the obvious problems caused by mountaintop removal coal mining, Dr. Wood pointed out that it probably wasn't solely the loss of habitat in Appalachia that was affecting ceruleans. "A lot of bird species need forested habitat," she said, again brushing her hair out of her eyes, "the cerulean is just one of them. But there's something going on with this bird. A lot of species are declining, but this one's really declining more quickly, and we don't know if it's the habitat here, or if it's wintering habitat, or migratory habitat. It very well could be all three. But," she continued, slowing down for emphasis, "the *only* place where you can produce *more* birds is in the breeding season in the breeding habitat. If we keep letting the habitat degrade here, then we're going to add to the decline. Our job is to keep the breeding habitat and help out more birds to offset the ones that"—she paused, opening her hand and making a sweeping gesture—"you know."

"Right," I nodded. "The ones that don't make it back here."

While all the factors that could be affecting cerulean warblers in their winter-ing and migratory habitats are not completely understood (and perhaps not yet identified), most biologists agree that the loss of primary forest is a major contrib-utor. Ceruleans spend the winter months on the forested slopes of the northern Andes Mountains, where they devote much of their time to foraging for insects in the canopy of broadleaf evergreen trees. Biologists in Colombia estimate that 60 percent of this ideal forested habitat has been converted to other uses; however, they admit that their model might be too generous, and as little as 10 percent of pre-ferred cerulean habitat may actually remain in the northern Andes.

Many primary Andean forests have been razed to make way for agriculture, es-pecially coffee plantations. In South America, coffee was traditionally grown in the shade of canopy trees. In recent years, however, many shade-grown coffee opera-tions have been converted to full-sun. Coffee shrubs do grow more quickly in the full sun (meeting the coffee demands of the United States and other countries), but they also require additional pesticides and fertilizers because nature's pesticides the insectivorous songbirds that live in the shade trees—don't frequent the tree-less plantations. While primary Andean forests are probably ideal for wintering ceru-lean warblers, the birds have also been known to thrive in the canopies of trees that provide shade for coffee plants. Shade-grown coffee farms not only provide a winter home for ceruleans, but they reduce the need for potentially dangerous chemicals, making them safer for the farmers and nearby human residents, too.

The breeze picked up a bit and threatened to whisk my papers off the table. A blue jay called Thief! Thief! from a nearby tree. I tied my unruly hair in a knot in an attempt to keep it out of my eyes.

I asked Dr. Wood if she thought any non-habitat factors could be contribut-ing to the cerulean's decline. "Well," she began, "climate change could be affect-ing things. Climate change could affect the cerulean's food resources. Or changing weather patterns. This year we had that really weird late snow and cold weather, and the birds came back a lot later. Since their nesting was delayed this year, how is that going to affect their nesting success? Just the act of migration, too—try-ing to fly in these changing weather patterns—could affect their population num-bers." Dr. Wood sipped her coffee and continued. "Contaminants are also an issue for some species, but I guess we don't really know about that with ceruleans." She thought for a moment, and then nodded. "I think as far as their decline, most peo-ple think it has something to do with habitat, because habitat affects both survival and reproductive success."

The "most people" Dr. Wood referred to were her fellow members of the Ceru-lean Warbler Technical Group, which, she explained, "is an ad hoc group of people interested in cerulean warbler conservation. Some state people, some federal people, university people, and industry people. Pat Keyser, a biologist who used to work for a timber company, was one of the main people who got the group going."

The wind kicked a stapled stack of pages across the table. I squealed and jumped, trying to slap my hands down on the sheets before they blew away. Dr. Wood laughed, and once I'd collected everything, she continued. "The thought was, no one's going to stop timber harvesting. Everybody uses trees and timber products."

"Yeah," I said, restacking the sheets, "look at all this paper."

She nodded and laughed again. "And it's not going to go away. But the timber companies want to be responsible, too. They don't want a spotted owl situation, where it's the timber company against everybody else. So we thought, maybe there would be a way to start proactively doing conservation for this bird and have everybody work together instead of having everybody fighting each other."

This of course sounded like a good idea to me, even though I remained skeptical.

"One of our ideas," Dr. Wood continued, "was that since the timber industry is not going to go away, can we make it less damaging to the birds? Ceruleans seem to require some kind of structure in the forest canopy—gaps, for instance—but once a forest starts maturing, you get a closed canopy. Until the forest reaches old-growth conditions, you don't get that canopy structure back. And getting to the old-growth stage takes a really long time. So, we thought, instead of viewing timber harvesters as the bad guys, is there a way to design timber harvests to benefit ceruleans and possibly other forest birds? Can you actively manage for the kind of canopy gaps that would exist in an old-growth forest?"

I nodded slowly, still silently skeptical. But the Cerulean Warbler Technical Group probably did have it right—certainly folks in the timber industry didn't hate trees and wildlife, and people working together instead of at odds with each other stood a better chance of being successful. I wondered, however, where the coal mining industry fit in with the group's vision. I understood and respected the efforts of the timber industry in this situation; several of my friends worked as foresters, and for the most part they were genuine outdoorsy types who enjoyed hiking in the woods more than they enjoyed cutting them down. But I couldn't find many redeeming qualities of mountaintop removal coal mining, and I doubted a mining company would willingly abandon a potential site because of some breeding warblers. Still, I admired the congenial and cooperative spirit of the group; I hoped they'd be able to help the birds.

"At the first cerulean meeting," Dr. Wood continued, "we sat down and identified research needs and information gaps and tried to figure ways to address them. There had been a lot of anecdotal information that ceruleans seemed to like canopy gaps—they seemed to like a heterogeneous canopy structure—but there hadn't been specific studies looking at that. So we set up the same study in seven different areas."

In one of these seven areas, the Lewis Wetzel Wildlife Management Area, Dr. Wood's doctoral student Greg George and a team of field technicians were currently at work. I'd be visiting them the following afternoon. Another one of the seven study areas was located in the Royal Blue Wildlife Management Area in eastern Tennessee; I had plans to travel there later in the summer.

"In each of our study areas," Dr. Wood explained, "we have four different forest plots with three different intensities of timber harvest and one unharvested control plot. What we wanted to do was to say, 'OK, if you go in and do a really light harvest, and just take out a few trees here and there, and make a few canopy gaps, how do the birds respond to that?' That's not a timbering method that's used much, though. But there's another method, called 'shelterwoods,' where you end up with about 40 percent of the canopy left, and that's used a lot in Appalachia. And then there's a clear-cut plot, where they take most of the canopy, since that's used a lot in timber harvesting, too. We also have uncut buffer plots on either side to determine when we start seeing edge-effects."

I nodded again, and Dr. Wood smiled. "So that's the basic study design. We'll look at the different harvesting intensities and see if there's an optimum range where the timber companies can make money without screwing up the forest for the birds. We had two years of data collected before the harvests went in this winter. All the harvests were completed, so now the research teams are monitoring the post-harvest forests. They're doing point counts, looking for the presence or absence of birds, spot-mapping, looking for nests, and doing some banding. They'll also try to look at return rates in future years to kind of get at the survival question."

"That all sounds great," I agreed. I re-wound my hair into its knot and watched two blue jays hopping after each other on the lawn in front of Percival Hall. Something I'd read in the article "History of the Cerulean Warbler Technical Group" stuck in my mind: "The basic premise of the group was to develop a broad-based, technically sound approach to conservation of the Cerulean Warbler, preempting the contentious and unproductive approach that could otherwise result if the species is listed.... Too often in the past, endangered species conservation issues and listing actions have been characterized by controversy, misinformation, mistrust, and gridlock."

The first time I'd read this, I thought, *of course* there's controversy and mistrust. And there always will be when the public learns about the ways industries abuse our natural resources. Was the article implying that if the cerulean warbler were listed for protection under the Endangered Species Act, the industry people would stop cooperating? Or was the article suggesting that the group was formed in anticipation of the cerulean's listing, to get the recovery process underway early? It sounded to me like the group generally opposed listing the cerulean warbler as "threatened," and they hoped to work to conserve the species without the additional protections of the Endangered Species Act.

I was probably naïve, but I had confidence in federal legislation designed to protect wildlife. I'd grown up hearing about Endangered Species Act success stories like the bald eagle, the peregrine falcon, the California condor, the humpback whale, and the grizzly bear. In addition to the legal protections required by the ESA, listed animals often become media darlings; what elementary school science class doesn't talk about the decline and subsequent recovery of the bald eagle? The ESA and resulting attention even made the California condor—an enormous carrion-eating vulture with a naked, bulbous head—somehow loveable.

The story of the petition to list the cerulean warbler as "threatened" is an interesting one. On October 30, 2000, in response to the cerulean's steady decline, the Southern Environmental Law Center and twenty-seven other organizations, including the National Audubon Society, Defenders of Wildlife, The Sierra Club, and The Wilderness Society, filed a petition under the Endangered Species Act to list the bird as a federally threatened species. Combined, these twenty-seven organizations boast more than two million members. In addition to a discussion of the natural history of the species, the fifty-page petition summarizes scientific research on the birds' decline and provides justifications for listing it as threatened.

The US Fish and Wildlife Service defines an endangered species as "one that is in danger of extinction throughout all or a significant portion of its range"; they define a threatened species as "one that is likely to become endangered in the foreseeable future." The SELC petition argues that the cerulean fits this definition: "Long term Breeding Bird Survey (BBS) trends, many recent studies, peer-reviewed scientific papers, and state and federal agency reports indicate that the decline of the Cerulean Warbler continues and that the threats to its habitats and existence are severe, pervasive, and ongoing." Not only would listing the bird as a threatened species help conserve the remaining population, but it would require the service to designate habitat critical to its survival and recovery. The petition continues: "This listing and designation would prohibit federal land managers from engaging in clear-cutting or other fragmenting activities which might jeopardize the species or adversely impact its critical habitat. Moreover, all federal agencies would be charged with affirmatively promoting and restoring the forests so as to promote the recovery of these warblers, which in turn would benefit the many other birds and other species which depend on intact forests for survival." That sounded splendid to me; it sounded like it would be a significant hurdle for mountaintop removal operations.

According to the Endangered Species Act, the Fish and Wildlife Service had ninety days to review the petition before making a preliminary decision about whether or not there was substantial information to warrant moving to the next stage, which included gathering information and a more thorough review. After receiving the cerulean petition, the service took almost two years—until September 2002—to announce their "ninety-day finding," which it published in Volume 67, Number 205 of the Federal Register. It found "that the petition presented substantial information indicating that listing this species may be warranted." The service asked the public to submit comments on the petition by January 21, 2003. According to the Federal Register, "After considering the comments and information submitted to us during the status review comment period following this 90-day finding, we will issue an additional finding (i.e., the 12-month finding) determining whether listing is in fact warranted."

Twelve months passed, then another twelve months, and then another twelve months, but no "12-month finding" was issued. In February 2006, more than *three years* after the service was required to make a decision, the Southern Environmental Law Center submitted a Complaint for Declaratory and Injunctive Relief to the United States District Court for the District of Columbia. The Complaint "challenge[d] Defendant's failure to issue a finding on Plaintiff's petition to list the Cerulean Warbler as a threatened species." It contended that the Secretary of the Interior's and the Fish and Wildlife Service's "failure to process [the] petition... frustrate[d] efforts to protect the Cerulean Warbler and its habitat..." They asked that the court compel the defendants to issue a finding. On August 7, 2006, a stipulated settlement agreement was reached; the service agreed to submit a twelve-month finding by November 30, 2006. On November 28, 2006—more than six years since the original petition and more than four years late—the service decided to deny the cerulean warbler protection under the Endangered Species Act. It cited budget shortfalls as the reason for the delay.

The service published its decision in the Federal Register, Volume 71, Number 234. While it agreed that the cerulean warbler had declined at an average annual rate of 3.2 percent over the last forty years, and it "anticipate[d] continued, gradual decline of this species," it "[did] not believe this species [was] likely to become endangered within the foreseeable future." The service "also conclude[d]...that abundance will remain high enough that the species effectively is in no danger of extinction in the near term...." Essentially, it argued that even though ceruleans are expected to continue to decline at a rate of about 3 percent a year, there were still too many of them to warrant a listing as "threatened." The service reasoned that if there were about four hundred thousand ceruleans left in the world, in one hundred years there would still be twenty thousand. Since the likelihood of extinction in the "foreseeable future" seemed low, the service did not believe that cerulean warblers qualified for additional federal protection under the Endangered Species Act.

Interestingly, the service acknowledged in the Federal Register that "large-scale habitat loss is occurring in the core of the species' range, Kentucky and West Virginia, where mountaintop coal mining and valley fill operations through 2012 are expected to remove 567,000 ha (1.4 million acres) of suitable forest habitat." It continued, "The total cumulative forest loss from these activities will likely eliminate breeding habitat for 10 to 20 percent of the total cerulean warbler population currently occurring within that core area. The loss of breeding opportunities for birds in this area may have a disproportionate effect on the species' total population size." These statistics do not seem to consider the areas of forest already altered by mountaintop removal mining; by many accounts, more than four hundred Appalachian peaks have been blasted away since the late 1970s.

As the service explained, "Reclamation at mountaintop mine sites has focused on erosion prevention and backfill stability and not on reclamation with trees. The compacted backfill material that is normally used for reclamation hinders tree establishment and growth. ... As a result, natural succession by trees and woody plants on reclaimed mine land...is slowed." Instead of listing the species, the service suggested another route: "The conservation of the cerulean warbler could be improved by additional focus by the regulatory programs under SMCRA [Surface Mining Control and Reclamation Act] and section 404 of the CWA [Clean Water Act] on the additional protection and improved reclamation of the species' habitat." But where will this "additional focus" come from? The Office of Surface Mining refuses to comment on whether or not the benefits of mountaintop removal coal mining are worth the environmental costs. Its website states that while this question "is certainly valid...for debate, it doesn't fall within [its] ability to address"; however, in 2004 the Office of Surface Mining partnered with scientists, industry representatives, citizens' groups, and all seven Appalachian coal states to launch the ambitious Appalachian Regional Reforestation Initiative (ARRI).

ARRI's mission is to restore hardwood forests on mined lands in the eastern United States. Unlike the currently popular reclamation methods, ARRI advocates a methodology known as the Forestry Reclamation Approach (FRA). This approach encourages reclamation with forests instead of grass-covered plateaus. Dr. Patrick Angel, a forester and soil scientist with the Office of Surface Mining, explained the FRA to me this way: "Basically, first of all, select the very best growth medium, whether that's topsoil or sandstone, and secondly, don't compact it. Keep it loose. Maybe just do one pass with a light dozer instead of twenty. Scientists have figured that compaction of surface mines is the most limiting factor for reforestation." Currently, as the Fish and Wildlife Service stated in the cerulean ruling, most mine reclamation involves densely packing and terracing the soil to prevent landslides. ARRI's solution is to use trees to prevent erosion instead.

Dr. Angel continued, "The third concept in our methodology is to be very careful in what kinds of grasses and legumes we put down, because some of those are pretty aggressive—fescue, sericea lespedeza—they can smother out little tree seedlings. There are many grasses and legumes that are compatible with small trees, like birdsfoot trefoil." Reclaiming mines with fast growing, invasive grass species makes the sites appear green; unfortunately, the grass species currently popular with mine companies do not allow much else to grow on the sites. "The fourth step," Dr. Angel told me, "is to plant two types of trees. The first category is early successional species—dogwood, redbud, black locust, Virginia pine—for wildlife purposes and soil development. And the other category is native hardwood high-value species, like white oak and red oak, yellow poplar, and black walnut, too. We never were able to talk about black walnut and strip mine reclamation in the same breath until the scientists we've partnered with showed us how to do it. And the fifth step—the last step—is to plant the trees right, by hand, the old-fashioned way."

Dr. Angel, who in 1972 began working as a state mine inspector in Lecher County, Kentucky (where the mountains are "as steep as a mule's face"), before securing a job with the federal Office of Surface Mining in 1978, wholeheartedly believes in ARRI's potential for reforesting old strip mines. In addition to the possibility of oaks, maples, and walnut trees, ARRI has been working with the American Chestnut Foundation to restore the near-extinct trees to Appalachia. Almost all of the United States' American chestnuts had disappeared by the 1940s, victims of an accidentally introduced Asian blight. Since American chestnuts can no longer thrive in their native range, the American Chestnut Foundation has worked hard to develop back-cross trees that are fifteen-sixteenths American chestnut and one-sixteenth Chinese chestnut; ARRI hopes to plant these trees, which will look and "act" like American chestnuts but will be blight-resistant because of the Chinese portion, on reclaimed mine sites. While the foundation has not yet produced mass quantities of these trees, Dr. Angel claimed that this program had the potential to be "the biggest ecological restoration ever," because "we're talking about restoring an entire ecosystem that was dependent on one species."

Restoring American chestnut trees—and native Appalachian hardwood forests in general—to old surface mine sites sounds like responsible, appropriate reclamation; ARRI's ambitious plans will certainly help future cerulean warblers repopulate formerly unusable portions of their range. I hope ARRI's reclamation approach will become the norm; in the meantime, however, huge swaths of forested mountains were still being leveled for "cheap" electricity.

I wondered: Without the additional protections of the Endangered Species Act, would the cerulean warbler be doomed to a fate of gradual, steady decline? Or could their decline be turned around by the Cerulean Warbler Technical Group's collaborative research projects without added federal protection? Would industries such as lumber and coal mining *really* cooperate to help save such a tiny creature? I felt in my deepest heart of hearts that protecting wildlife species—no matter how small or delicate or seemingly insignificant—was vital to the health of our planet and to our own health. But it didn't seem that the coal industry even cared about *humans* who resided near their mines. The situation made me feel a bit desperate.

The breeze gusted down the hill again toward Percival Hall. I leaned back on the wooden bench and asked Dr. Wood if she had any wisdom about the "so what" factor.

"You mean, 'So what if we lose all the ceruleans?'" she asked.

I nodded.

"Well," she smiled, pushing her hair out of her eyes again, "to me, they're not 'the canary in the mine' or anything, but they're a part of the system. If we start losing pieces of things, where will we stop?"

I smiled back at Dr. Wood. I couldn't agree more. Although the cerulean's situation was complex—not only because of its steep and steady decline, but also because of the polite disagreements about how to best help the species—it seemed that everyone involved had the same goal: to conserve cerulean warblers, and to make sure they didn't disappear from our forests and mountains.

As I walked back up the sidewalk to my Jeep (after expressing my deep and eternal gratitude to Petra Wood), I felt that I had a much clearer understanding of the big cerulean picture. I was ready to take the next step; it was long past time for me to *see* an actual cerulean, in the flesh.

FOUR

★

SANCTUARY

T 5:45 A.M., THE ALARM buzzed in my ear. The soft motel pillow tried to convince me to stay in bed, but I resisted—I had a cerulean warbler hike planned, and I wouldn't let mere lack of sleep spoil it. I kicked off the covers and rubbed my eyes. After talking with Dr. Wood yesterday, I couldn't stop thinking about seeing a cerulean warbler. I'd contacted my friend Hillar Klandorf, who had accepted the challenge to find one of the elusive blue birds for me.

I had plans to pick up Hillar at his house near campus at seven, and I knew I'd have to hurry if I wanted to grab a quick bagel and cup of coffee first.

Hillar had been Jesse's graduate school mentor, director of his Master's thesis, and was, in large part, responsible for where we had ended up in life. After we got our bachelor's degrees, Jesse and I moved to West Virginia for me to attend graduate school. Jesse took a full-time staff position with the university's library; when he learned that staff members were allowed to take up to six course credits per semester for free, he decided to enroll in an animal behavior class as a non-degree-seeking student. The class was taught by Dr. Hillar Klandorf. Hillar, impressed with Jesse's enthusiasm and work ethic, encouraged him to become a full-time graduate student in the Animal Science Department. Jesse accepted his offer, and his graduate research project resulted in two published papers as well as several conference posters and presentations. When Jesse decided to pursue veterinary medicine, his master's degree and Hillar's recommendation helped him get accepted.

In addition to Hillar's academic achievements as a poultry physiologist—he'd co-authored at least one textbook on the subject—he was a skilled and energetic birder, known for leaping from moving vehicles to find an illusive kinglet or warbler. Hillar had taken Jesse on his first Christmas Bird Count and introduced us to the Morgantown area's birding hot spots. I considered him a "serious" birder. Also a serious practical joker, Hillar had a wry sense of humor; he was notorious around the Animal Science Department for his electronic "fart machine," which he sounded at highly inappropriate times, such as during a colleague's promotion and tenure presentation. He also enjoyed having a good time with his friends and students. At the end of Jesse's graduate program, he and Hillar went to a conference in Arizona together, and after a long, exhausting day of birding in the desert, they decided to hang out in a bar and recite Robert Service poetry instead of attending the conference's poster session.

Now that we lived four hours apart, we missed Hillar, and I was excited to see him, even though I felt guilty that Jesse couldn't join us. We planned to go birding in nearby Cooper's Rock State Forest, where he would attempt to find a cerulean warbler for me. Cooper's Rock's Raven Rock Trail was along Hillar's North American Breeding Bird Survey (BBS) route. According to its website, the mission of the BBS, a cooperative program of the US Geological Survey, the Canadian Wildlife Service, and Mexico's National Commission for the Knowledge and Use of Biodiversity, is to "provide scientifically credible measures of the status and trends of North American bird populations at continental and regional scales to inform biologically sound conservation and management actions." The BBS relies on skilled volunteers who annually survey non-game landbirds along predetermined 24.5-mile routes. The volunteers stop every half-mile (fifty stops total) and record every bird seen or heard during three-minute point counts. Since its official launch in 1966, data from the BBS has been used in more than three hundred scientific articles. BBS data is extremely important to bird conservation—analysis of data collected on cerulean warbler abundance during point counts alerted scientists to the cerulean's steady population decline.

According to Hillar, he almost always saw a cerulean near the Raven Rock Trail. Jesse and I had birded that trail many times when we lived in West Virginia, but we'd never definitively identified a cerulean. Hillar, though, was a much better birder than Jesse and I, and if anyone could find a bird, he could.

I quickly showered, dressed, and stomped down the stairs to the motel's lobby, where I was surprised to find a line of guests waiting to check out. I shifted my weight nervously from foot to foot as I stood in line, my room keys and credit card in hand. The man ahead of me had keys for six different rooms, and he insisted on paying for each one individually and obtaining separate receipts. The desk clerk worked slowly and deliberately. I checked my watch—6:50 a.m. I would never make it across town to Hillar's house in ten minutes. Finally, the man handed over the last of his keys and carefully folded the stack of receipts. He made some final flirtatious comment to the plodding checkout clerk before shuffling out of the way. I paid, signed, and rushed out to my Jeep as fast as my flip-flop-wearing feet could carry me. I tried to pull on my boots as I swerved recklessly out of the parking lot.

I arrived at Hillar's house about ten minutes late, and he came out to greet me before I'd even parked. Hillar, thin and athletic with light blonde hair and mischievous blue eyes, was followed by a younger man wearing a Pittsburgh Pirates baseball cap and a "Spend a Semester at Sea" T-shirt. Hillar introduced him as Andy, a graduate student who hoped to become a high school English teacher. Andy was new to birding, so Hillar thought this outing would be a good learning experience for him. The two had been drinking a bit the night before and claimed to be groggy, but in my sleep-deprived state, they seemed chipper and alert. The two of them tried to explain a sort of jogging race they participated in every Tuesday night—apparently, one group of runners were "hares" and the other group, "chasers." The hares started the run first, and left chalk directions on sidewalks and roads for the chasers to follow. Alcohol was somehow involved, too.

Hillar sat in the passenger seat next to me and Andy climbed in the back. We caught up on the details of each other's lives, and soon the conversation headed in the inevitable direction of politics. After cursing the antics of certain elected officials and lamenting the depletion of the earth's natural resources, I offered my grim opinion that a pandemic would strike before we used everything up. "It's coming," I said, "we're due for another deadly influenza outbreak."

"She seems like a nice girl, doesn't she?" Hillar said over his shoulder to Andy, "And then she starts talking about pandemics and such."

Andy and I laughed, and I began to perk up a bit as we headed northeast out of town.

Five miles later, we pulled off Interstate 68 after a steep drive up the mountain, turned right, and entered the 12,698-acre Cooper's Rock, the largest state forest in West Virginia. As I drove deeper into the forest on the winding, two-lane road, I was reminded of how much I missed this place. Cooper's Rock State Forest gets its name from a fugitive. According to legend, the escaped criminal—a "cooper," or barrel-maker, by trade—hid in the forested mountains and evaded capture for many years. I, too, had often escaped to Cooper's Rock. This forest had been a quiet place of refuge for me during troubled times. I remembered coming here with my dog, Mr. Bones, on September 12, 2001; we sat together on a rocky outcrop and I took comfort in the permanency and strength of the mountains and the Cheat River far below. Cooper's Rock was a place of inspiration, as well; the forest appeared in several chapters of my thesis, and one of my graduate creative writing classes had met here occasionally to read and discuss poetry.

Besides being a place for quiet reflection and refuge, Cooper's Rock was a popular ecotourism destination. In addition to the magnificent Cheat Canyon—through which the Cheat River flows 2,150 feet below the forest's rocky overlooks—Cooper's Rock offered many miles of hiking, mountain biking, and cross-country ski trails. Adventurers could rock-climb around the mountains' summits or kayak the Cheat's rapids, and anglers could cast their lines into the stocked trout pond. There were pavilions available for rent, a family campground, picnic areas with tables and grills, and even a gift shop that sold lumps of coal, Appalachian cookbooks, and pepperoni rolls (a West Virginia specialty). While the more accessible areas of the forest could be crowded during the fall leaf-peeping season, a lone hiker could usually find a deserted trail for meandering. Cooper's Rock didn't disappoint history buffs, either. Early in the 19th century, the area was mined for iron ore and limestone; one of the forest's many trails led to an iron furnace from this era.

The road through the forest was deserted at this early morning hour. No cars passed us, and the small gravel parking area across from the trailhead had been empty when we pulled into it. The 1.8-mile Raven Rock Trail, popular with hikers and birders, gradually descended into a hollow. Piles of gray boulders surrounded by rhododendron occasionally lined the trail, which eventually climbed back up out of the hollow and ended at Raven Rock, an overlook that provided a spectacular view of the Cheat River far below and the wooded mountain on its opposite bank. Unfortunately, power lines had been cemented to Raven Rock's natural boulders, and a cleared power-line cut ran down the mountain to the river. While this thin strip of edge broke up the contiguity of the forest, it provided great birding opportunities.

We all got out of the Jeep and gathered our binoculars, field guides, and snacks. Hillar pulled a light windbreaker over his faded "Life is Good" T-shirt. The morning was bright and sunny, but the mountain air at this altitude was always several degrees cooler than in nearby Morgantown. Most of Cooper's Rock—except for the cross-country ski trail near the entrance—was closed from December 1 to April 1 because of potentially dangerous snow and ice conditions. I took Hillar's hint and decided I should wear something heavier over my T-shirt, too. I opened the back tailgate door of the Jeep, revealing the embarrassing mess inside. Clothes, camping gear, random shoes, books, and granola bars threatened to spill out onto the gravel parking area. I giggled nervously and rummaged through the disarray, looking for my fleece jacket. I finally found it, freed it from beneath a cooler, and slipped it over my head.

As soon as I slammed the door shut, we began to hear and see birds. A Northern parula—a small, bluish-yellow warbler—buzzed from a tree across the road and a wood thrush called from the deep forest beyond the Jeep. In my opinion, the wood thrush has the most beautiful and musical voice of any bird. Of the wood thrush's song, Henry David Thoreau wrote, "Whenever a man hears it he is young, and Nature is in her spring; whenever he hears it, it is a new world and a free country, and the gates of heaven are not shut against him." I completely agree—it's difficult to feel despair and hopelessness when a wood thrush is singing. I took a deep breath and smiled.

"Hear that, Andy?" Hillar pointed, then paused. "There—that liquidy call? That's the wood thrush. They're able to make two sounds at the same time."

Andy nodded. Since he was new to birding, and Hillar and I were both teachers who loved birds, we found it nearly impossible to pass up opportunities to educate Andy.

"And did you hear that?" I interjected. "From over there, near the trailhead? *Zee, zee, zoo zoo zee*? That's a black-throated green warbler."

A tree branch bobbed above us, and we tilted our heads. "Chipping sparrow," said Hillar. "We haven't even started down the trail yet, and we have quite a few birds right here."

From behind us, we heard a scratchy, robin-like song. "Scarlet tanager," said Hillar, turning over his shoulder to scan the trees. "A robin with a sore throat. And the rose-breasted grosbeak, who we might get later, sounds like a robin with voice lessons." Andy laughed. I took this opportunity to tell him about the scarlet tanager's other common call, the *chip-burr*. Hillar nodded happily in agreement.

The three of us crossed the road and walked towards the brown gate and sign that marked the trailhead. Raven Rock Trail began here as a wide, grassy road. Just as we reached the gate, a small bird flew down onto the grassy trail about twenty feet in front of us. Three pairs of binoculars were swiftly raised, and we all saw the yellow head and dark neck of a black-throated green warbler. He hopped around on the old road's grass for a few seconds before fluttering up into a sugar maple and disappearing behind its green leaves.

We lowered our binoculars and stepped lightly along the trail, eyes and ears adjusting to the thick, cool forest, which shaded us from the morning sun. Birds seemed to call from every shadowy branch, and unseen chipmunks scurried in the dry undergrowth. The trail veered away from the old road and led us down the side of the mountain, soon becoming narrower and rocky. Trees towered on both sides, almost closing the canopy above us. I apparently hadn't paid attention during the dendrology lessons in my high school biology class, because I had trouble identifying common trees—especially ones with oval or teardrop-shaped leaves.

Fortunately, I'd read Cornell University's Cerulean Warbler Atlas Project before coming here, and I knew that they characterized the forested habitat of Cooper's Rock as both "mesic slope" and "dry ridgetop." Mesic forests, which grow from "moderately moist" soil, typically consist of hardwoods such as sugar maple, white ash, hickory, and basswood. Along this trail, most of the trees looked like oaks and maples, though another corner of Cooper's Rock sheltered a virgin hemlock grove.

As we slowly descended, Andy's education continued. "That, Andy, that questioning call—'*Where are you? Can you hear?*'—that's a red-eyed vireo, one of the most common birds in the forest right now," Hillar explained, smiling.

A thin *weesa-weesa-weesa* from the right side of the trail made us pause and listen. "Is that a black-and-white warbler?" I ventured softly.

"No," said Hillar, "Black-and-white is more like a squeaky wheel. That's a redstart, I believe." He raised his binoculars. "Ah, yes. Redstart. Do you have him yet, Andy? See those two trees? He's on the tree just behind and in between them, on a branch about halfway up..."

As Andy and I both searched for a flash of the bird's orange and black body, I silently (but good-naturedly) swore at the American redstart. His song confused me every time I heard it. For some reason I just could not commit it to memory; I usually misidentified it as the song of a black-and-white warbler (which, to be fair, was virtually the same, only higher-pitched) or a Blackburnian warbler (whose variable call could also sound similar). To make things even more confusing, the American redstart and Blackburnian both sported patterns of orange, black, and white feathers. The Blackburnian was streakier, while the redstart's head and back were a more solid black. That darn redstart often embarrassed me in front of more experienced birders.

We hadn't been on the trail for more than fifteen minutes when Hillar, who had been walking just a few steps ahead of me, froze. He cocked his head. A quick, buzzy call floated down to us from somewhere off the trail to the right and high above us. With a sudden burst of catlike agility, Hillar bounded up the steep bank next to the trail, into the woods. Andy and I scrambled through the ankle-deep fallen leaves after him, but by the time the bank leveled out a bit, Hillar was far ahead of us. He'd stop after every few steps to listen, would hear the buzzy call, then move off quickly again, adjusting his direction slightly each time. Greenbrier snagged my jeans, and I got several face-fulls of spider webs as I attempted to gracefully jog through the woods after him.

Andy and I finally caught up with Hillar when he stopped running. Binoculars glued to his eyes and head tilted all the way back, he stood between two towering trees. One was a sugar maple and the other had jaggy oval leaves, exactly the kind I couldn't identify. "He's up there," Hillar said to us in a hushed voice, "in the canopy."

I tried to catch my breath as I lifted my binoculars and searched the highest branches for whatever bird Hillar had found. I thought I saw movement, perhaps a flick of quick wings, a vibrating branch. It could have been just shadows on leaves…but then I saw it! A tiny, tiny bird, hopping from leaf to leaf near the very top of the tree, toward the ends of its branches. I couldn't tell what color the bird was, but its breast seemed whitish. It fluttered, and suddenly I had a good view. "I see his necklace!" I squealed, my heart pounding. "His necklace—look!"

"Yes," said Hillar, "that confirms it, then. Cerulean warbler for sure. Do you have him, Andy?"

While Hillar gave Andy directions, I kept my binoculars on the cerulean and watched him hop and flit around the leaves. He'd stop after every few hops to sing *zhrzhrzhrZEEEEE,* and then he'd hop some more. I watched him pull his head back and open his dark bill to sing. The way he hopped and paused, then hopped and paused again, reminded me of Hillar running through the woods to get to this spot.

The three of us stood silently and watched the cerulean through our binoculars until he suddenly flew deeper into the woods, out of sight. Then we celebrated, patting each other on the back. "Great job, Hillar!" I laughed.

"I was a bit worried we wouldn't find one," he admitted.

"I think you ran faster to see that bird than you did last night in the race," Andy chuckled.

The three of us were so excited that we strutted off though the woods on a thin deer path instead of Raven Rock Trail. As we approached a tangle of thick brush and a few fallen trees, our happy chatter was cut short by a bird calling close by. "This bird sounds like he's—oh. He's right there," I whispered.

"That's the redstart again," Hillar said, raising his binoculars.

"He flew—" I said, pointing at the damned confusing redstart.

"He's still over—" Hillar began.

"Oh, I see him," I said softly.

"He's really orange," Andy remarked.

"He really is," agreed Hillar, lowering his binoculars. "I think this is almost a spiritual thing, being birding. It's a celebration of what they are, the awareness of nature, the color, the song…"

"The contrast," Andy offered. "A dot of color amid all this green."

We walked a few more steps, our footfalls crunching last fall's dry leaves, discussing the spirituality of nature, when we were again distracted by a bird. "Ooh!" I pointed, raising my binoculars. "Who's that? He's yellow…has a little black behind his eyes, olive wings, he just flew down to the ground. Can you see that fallen—?"

"Yeah," said Hillar, "I had him for a second."

"He's in front of that fallen log back there," I whispered.

"Oh yeah. Got him," Hillar said. "He's little."

"He's got a yellow body and olive wings and black behind his—"

"I think it's a hooded," said Hillar quickly.

"Oh! There's a towhee," I said.

There was a flutter in the tangled underbrush that surrounded the fallen trees. "The towhee scared him off," said Hillar disappointedly.

I lowered my binoculars. Activity in a nearby sapling caught my attention, and I quickly raised them again. "There," I said, "he's in the green—"

"It's the hooded!" Hillar whispered again, more confidently this time. "There he is. He went in the brush back there."

Andy, finally finding the bird we'd been looking at, said, "There he is, sitting right there."

As we all tried to keep focused on the hooded warbler, another bird flew through my binoculars' sights. "Oh, there's your wood thrush," I told Hillar. "No wait, that's not a wood thrush. That's, um, a waterthrush? Did you see that guy fly through?" I stuttered. "He's got pink legs. Oh, there he goes. Ovenbird?"

I searched, but couldn't relocate the mysterious pink-legged bird, which neither Hillar nor Andy had seen. After the excitement died down a bit, Hillar got out his field guide to show Andy the hooded warbler. "Yes," said Hillar, as he pointed to the bird in the guide, "That's what it was, yes. And that's the one we're hearing now, that *weety weety weetyo*. I know them by song because I so rarely see them here. You actually saw that, Andy?"

"Yeah, mm hm," Andy nodded.

"Oh, lucky. You've seen ceruleans and hoods on the same day."

We began to slowly walk again when we discovered that we weren't on the trail to Raven Rock anymore. We backtracked a bit, then left the narrow path to search for the wide, rocky trail. "That's all we need, is to just get lost," said Hillar. "We'll be fighting over Andy's bottle of water in a minute." I laughed and realized that it had been gradually getting hotter outside. I took off my fleece jacket and tied it around my waist.

We found the trail after only a few moments and continued down it towards Raven Rock. We heard and saw many other birds, including a black-throated blue warbler whose song fooled us for a moment; we had ceruleans on the brain, and the black-throated blue's call is somewhat similar to a cerulean's, only deeper and slower—*zurrr zurrrr zurrrr ZEE*—sometimes described as *I am la-ZYY!* Their blue feathers are also similar to a cerulean's, but Hillar pointed out a small white dot on the edge of the bird's long primary flight feathers. This white dot stood out starkly on the blue and black bird.

Near the bottom of the hollow, Raven Rock Trail cut steeply uphill. This climb, though short, always used to wind me, and this day was no different. We finally reached the top and trudged the short distance to the sunny outcropping of boulders that overlooked the Cheat River far below. A densely forested mountain rose sharply from the other side of the river. I recently learned that a wood-products company had purchased land across from Cooper's Rock. The state had tried to buy the land, too, in the hopes of adding it to the state forest, but they were outbid. I think it would be anti-climactic and disheartening to reach Raven Rock after a brisk, two-mile hike only to see a deforested mountain across from the overlook. In addition to marring the spectacular view, logging the opposite mountain could destroy important habitat for the cerulean warbler and other imperiled species. Several species of conservation concern made their homes in Cooper's Rock State Forest, including the Allegheny woodrat, the federally threatened flat-spired three-toothed land snail, and the federally threatened Cheat Mountain salamander, a creature endemic to West Virginia.

Hillar, Andy, and I fanned out and across the rocky outcrop. I sat cross-legged on the boulders just above the cleared power-line cut. The grassy strip, probably about twenty feet wide, ran all the way down the steep mountain to the river. I noticed bird commotion in the crowns of some of the trees below me. Pointing my binoculars in the direction of the sounds, I spotted a blue-gray gnatcatcher foraging towards the end of a tree branch that overhung the clearing. After every few hops, the small bird stopped and sounded his *spew! spew!* call while flicking his long tail. I watched him for a while, but then movement on the other side of the clearing caught my eye. A dark, streaky-backed warbler fluttered in another tree. I gasped. "Cerulean! Cerulean!" I yelled, pointing. I trained my binoculars on the bird, then felt embarrassed again. "Never mind," I called to Hillar and Andy, who were both searching the treetops. "It's a black-and-white, not a cerulean." After watching the black-and-white warbler for a few minutes, I stood, brushed myself off, mopped the sweat from my forehead, and walked across the outcrop to where Hillar and Andy sat.

"Sorry about that," I said, shaking my head. "I'm still excited about the cerulean we saw earlier."

I plopped down next to Hillar, and the three of us gazed out over forest, river, and mountains. A few houses perched on the tops of very distant ridges, but other than that, this part of north-central West Virginia looked like pristine, unbroken wilderness. The May sunshine warmed my face—and without warning, I was suddenly filled with happiness. The fact that places like this still existed in the world comforted me. All the critters—birds, bears, snails, salamanders, deer, bobcats, people—breathing air made pure by the trees, drinking water made clear by the river rocks far below. We all fit somewhere in the intricate web of life, interconnected whether we liked it or not. But if one part of this came loose, the whole thing could unravel, sort of like a knit sweater. I didn't want Cooper's Rock to ever come unraveled. It was my sanctuary, much like it was the barrel-maker's. I could escape here and remember what's real and necessary and at the core of all life. I took a deep breath and let it out slowly.

"Yes," said Hillar, nodding and smiling at me. "It's too bad Jesse couldn't be here."

"I know," I sighed. "He's probably spaying something right now."

"Moment of silence for Jesse, then," said Hillar, "trapped in the clinic."

After the moment passed, I said, "I heard a pewee."

Hillar said, "I still hear a scarlet tanager."

The three of us laughed, and we talked about all the birds we'd seen that morning. I pulled out my notepad and made sure I had taken an accurate species list. When we finally stood up, stretched, and began to make our way back down the trail and into the forest, I checked my watch and was surprised to see that it was almost eleven. It had taken us more than three hours to walk two miles—time flies (no pun intended) when birding with Hillar.

When we arrived back at the gravel parking area, we decided we weren't ready to go back to civilization just yet. After sharing a few granola bars, we hopped in the Jeep and crossed the highway to the other side of the state forest. I pulled off the road near the start of the Virgin Hemlock Trail, took a huge swig of water, and gathered my binoculars.

"Have you ever seen a Baltimore oriole, Andy?" Hillar asked, getting out of the Jeep and closing the passenger door.

Andy shouldered his backpack and shook his head.

"Well, you'll see one here," said Hillar.

I smiled, shoved my notepad into the back pocket of my jeans, and followed Hillar and Andy into the forest.

BIRD LIST, MAY 9
Cooper's Rock State Forest, Raven Rock and Virgin Hemlock Trails

Mourning Dove

Yellow-billed Cuckoo

Red-bellied Woodpecker
Downy Woodpecker

Eastern Wood-pewee
Acadian Flycatcher
Eastern Phoebe

Yellow-throated Vireo
Blue-headed Vireo
Red-eyed Vireo

Blue Jay
American Crow

Black-capped Chickadee
Tufted Titmouse

White-breasted Nuthatch

Blue-gray Gnatcatcher

Wood Thrush
American Robin

Gray Catbird

Ovenbird
Black-and-white Warbler
Nashville Warbler
Hooded Warbler
American Redstart
Cerulean Warbler
Northern Parula
Blackburnian Warbler
Chestnut-sided Warbler
Black-throated Blue Warbler
Yellow-throated Warbler
Black-throated Green Warbler

Eastern Towhee
Chipping Sparrow
Song Sparrow
Dark-eyed Junco

Scarlet Tanager
Northern Cardinal
Rose-breasted Grosbeak
Indigo Bunting

Brown-headed Cowbird
Baltimore Oriole

FIVE

*

AFIELD

*I*WALKED ACROSS THE MCDONALD'S parking lot toward my Jeep, slurping a sweet iced tea and wishing I'd been able to take a shower after my energetic six-hour birding adventure with Hillar and Andy. It would take another forty-five minutes or so to get to Jacksonburg, West Virginia, and I figured that this town, Shinnston, would be my last chance to get a drink and wash up before I met Greg George and his research team at the Lantz Farm and Nature Preserve in the Lewis Wetzel Wildlife Management Area. As I pulled out of McDonald's and onto narrow, two-lane Route 20, I began to suspect that I smelled like dried sweat. I'd been trying out an all-natural, unisex deodorant, and it seemed to have quit working a few hours earlier.

Route 20 winds west through the hollows of Harrison County before crossing into Wetzel County near the village of Folsom. The road follows Little Tenmile Creek for several miles before the stream veers to the south and the road to the north. Near Folsom, the road begins to follow the south fork of Fishing Creek. Railroad tracks also snake along parallel to the windy road. I rolled my window all the way down and let the late-afternoon breeze cool me off. Wooded mountains rose on both sides of the road, but here they were more rounded and less dramatic than in the southern part of the state. I passed several cleared acres along the creek; a garden next to a house held the beginnings of tomato plants and lettuce, and damp laundry swung from a line. Around another curve, a half-dozen beef cows rested under sycamore trees, slowly swishing their tails and chewing cud.

Wetzel County is considered part of West Virginia's northern panhandle region, although it seemed to me that the panhandle actually began above Wetzel's northern border, in Marshall County. To understand the geography of West Virginia, make a fist with your right hand, palm-side facing you. Extend your thumb like you would if you were hitchhiking. Then raise your middle finger as if making a rude gesture. Your hand now makes the shape of the state of West Virginia. Your thumb represents the eastern panhandle, and your middle finger, the northern panhandle. Wetzel County lies just below your middle finger's second knuckle; the county borders Pennsylvania on the northeast and Ohio on the west. Clockwise from the east, it borders the West Virginia counties of Monongalia, Marion, Harrison, Doddridge, and Tyler.

Both the county and its 13,000-acre Wildlife Management Area were named in honor of Lewis Wetzel, a famous frontiersman who lived from 1764 until 1808. According to R. C. V. Meyers's 1883 book, *Life and Adventures of Lewis Wetzel, The Renowned Virginia Ranger and Scout*, the Wetzel family left Lancaster, Pennsylvania, in 1764 when Lewis was just a few months old and moved to an area south of present day Wheeling. This was a bold and dangerous move for the young family. At this point in history, western Virginia (West Virginia would not officially split from Virginia until 1863) was truly wilderness; gray wolves and mountain lions hunted elk and woodland bison in the thick forests, which were dominated by towering American chestnut trees. But the most deadly threat, according to Meyers's profoundly racist and violent text, was the "red-skinned savages" who preyed on innocent frontier families. When Lewis was about thirteen years old, American Indians supposedly attacked the Wetzel cabin. While several versions of this story exist, in Meyers's account Lewis's father was killed and Lewis, along with his brother Jacob, were taken captive. Lewis's mother and his five other siblings somehow managed to hide and evade capture. To make a long legend short, Lewis and Jacob escaped their kidnappers, and when Lewis arrived back in Wheeling he vowed to "kill every Indian that crosse[d] [his] path."

According to Meyers, after Wetzel's famous vow for revenge, not much was known of him until around age eighteen, when he joined a militia whose purpose was to kill local Indians. When the militia was defeated in 1782, Wetzel retreated to the wilderness where he lived for several years, "hermit-dwelling in the woods." He would periodically show up in Wheeling, Mingo Bottom, Marietta, and other settlements in the area—often, said the legend, with Indian scalps hanging from his belt. Meyers describes him as an aloof, socially awkward fellow with dark, matted hair that hung down past his knees: "an unkempt, wild-looking, long-haired man." Before long, young Lewis Wetzel became a local hero, mysteriously emerging from the woods after successful "hunting" expeditions.

The new United States government, however, hoped to reach peaceful agreements with the Native Americans living in this region, and in 1786 or 1787 the army arrested Wetzel for murder. In a somewhat confusing series of events, Wetzel escaped custody, was recaptured, but then was acquitted of this crime when other settlers paid the judge a large amount of gold. After this incident, Wetzel mellowed a bit, and Meyers claims that he started hunting animals instead of humans. His reputation as an expert white-tailed deer hunter grew, and his hides "found ready purchasers." As this region of western Virginia became "tamed"—fewer game animals and fewer Native Americans—Wetzel reportedly ranged further south and west. He died in Mississippi in 1808 at age forty-four.

I hoped that naming the county and its Wildlife Management Area in honor of Lewis Wetzel had more to do with his prowess as an outdoorsman than his reputation as an "Indian hunter." Despite the dozens of Native American deaths Meyers's book attributes to him, it seems possible that Wetzel never killed any humans at all. In his preface, Meyers admits that he created scenes from oral histories told to him by descendants of the Wetzel family and descendants of others "who lived at the time when the hero of [his] work lived." It seems that none of Wetzel's biographers ever spoke to him directly, and since he apparently didn't have any children or close friends, it's possible that none of the events described in the book were true; perhaps Lewis was just an odd, quiet fellow who would occasionally materialize from the trees, dirty hair matted around his shoulders, dragging dead deer to sell to the settlers. If there was an unsolved murder, it would be easy to blame the weird guy who lived in the forest. I know I am being an apologist for West Virginia, but this is the version of Lewis Wetzel's story that I am more comfortable with: not a revenge-seeking homicidal maniac, but a misunderstood loner who preferred nature to civilization. Meyers (somehow) quotes Wetzel as saying, "I cannot breathe in open air. I require the leaves of the trees to break and filter it before it enters my lungs." Yes, I liked Lewis Wetzel better as a tree-hugger.

Whoever Lewis Wetzel actually was, his legend helped shape this region. As I sped along Route 20, I imagined what Wetzel County might have looked like two hundred years ago. While still remote and sparsely populated—about seventeen thousand people currently reside here—the county's wolves, cougars, bison, and elk are long gone. The thriving native population is gone, too; according to the 2000 US Census, 0.1 percent of Wetzel County's population (fewer than twenty individuals) were counted as American Indians.

As I drummed my fingers on the steering wheel—imagining the ghosts of murdered Shawnee and woodland bison alongside the road—I suddenly realized I had almost reached my destination. The speed limit dropped as I entered the small town of Jacksonburg around 5:30 p.m. The road curved between houses.

From inside chain-link fences, dogs barked at my Jeep, and more laundry hanging on lines flapped gently in the breeze. After a volunteer fire department, I turned left, crossed a small bridge, and swung into the long gravel driveway of the Lantz Farm and Nature Preserve. At the end of the driveway, a restored white farmhouse loomed before me. I parked in the small gravel lot in front of the house, near a sign indicating that the property was part of the Wildlife Management Area. Beyond the farmhouse was a barn, and the directions that had been emailed to me told me to go there.

I climbed out of the Jeep, stretched, and noticed a young man with a goatee walking over from the barn. He wore a T-shirt advertising shade-grown coffee and a faded green baseball cap from Hawk Mountain Sanctuary. "You must be Katie," he said, extending his hand.

"Yep, and you must be Greg," I answered. We both smiled, and he told me to go ahead and drive my Jeep through the field and around to the back of the barn to unload my gear.

The 500-acre Lantz Farm can only be described as idyllic. Green fields rolled to the tree line, and beyond them, the horizon was made of forested mountains. Barn swallows cut and dove above the tall grass in front of me, and red-winged blackbirds clung to swaying cattails in a swampy part of the meadow. I pulled around to the back of the barn, which sat about a hundred yards past the farmhouse. Behind the barn, two small lily pad–filled ponds vibrated with life. Insects skittered along the brown water's surface, phoebes buzzed from trees along the banks, and frogs growled a belching chorus. The railroad tracks that I'd followed much of the way here ran through the property, about another hundred feet away, parallel to the farmhouse and barn.

I collected my sleeping bag and daypack and walked up the wooden stairs into the backdoor of the barn. Inside, I was surprised to find that it had been converted into a bunkhouse; where stalls had been, there were now about ten bedrooms, a large common room, and a makeshift kitchen with a microwave and refrigerator. Adjacent to the barn, in a separate building, was a bathhouse, complete with separate men's and women's facilities.

Greg helped me unload my gear and introduced me to the other folks working at this field site. Patrick, a master's student, sat in front of a laptop computer at a small desk along the wall. Aaron, an undergraduate field technician working part-time for the summer, busily prepared himself a Hot Pocket in the microwave. I sat down on a metal chair at the barn's long folding table next to Randy Dettmers, a US Fish and Wildlife Service Senior Migratory Bird Biologist from Hadley, Massachusetts. He smiled warmly and picked at a microwave dinner on the table in front of him. Greg explained that three other field technicians were working at the

Greg George (left) and Randy Dettmers at the Lantz Farm.

site this summer, but two had left the day before to compete in the World Series of Birding in Cape May, New Jersey, and the third drove out from Morgantown every morning instead of staying on-site.

I quickly learned that Randy Dettmers was renowned for his skills as a cerulean warbler nest-finder. A few years earlier, when he'd been working on his PhD at Ohio State (which involved searching for the nests of other forest bird species), he first heard about the cerulean warbler's steep population decline through a presentation by Paul Hamel. The plight of the small blue bird stuck in Randy's mind, and he began to search for cerulean nests. He admitted that many of his early attempts were unsuccessful; then he realized he wasn't searching early enough in the breeding season. He continued to hone his nest-finding skills during his postdoctoral work at the University of Tennessee, and by the time he finished and took a biologist job with the US Fish and Wildlife Service in 1999, Randy was a cerulean nest-finding ace.

I said as much, and Randy laughed. "Well, I don't know about that. There are a number of people who are much better than I am. I just manage to do it," he said.

Greg chimed in that Randy was being modest.

In addition to his nest-searching work as a student and beyond, Randy had other credentials; birding and nest-searching ran in his family. His great-uncle, ornithologist Hal Harrison, literally wrote the book on birds' nests; he authored two texts in the Peterson Field Guide Series, *A Field Guide to the Birds' Nests* and *A Field Guide to Western Birds' Nests*. His son, George Harrison (Randy's uncle, not the Beatle), continued the tradition, and he has authored more than a dozen books on watching birds and other wildlife. I also learned that Randy had traveled from Massachusetts to West Virginia on his own time, to volunteer for a week with the field crew; he had actually taken vacation days to be here.

Greg, too, already had a long history working with birds. After high school he worked at Hawk Mountain Sanctuary in eastern Pennsylvania, counting migrating raptors as they soared overhead. He eventually enrolled in East Stroudsburg University to study biology; after earning a bachelor of science, he continued on for a master's degree, his research focusing on the Louisiana waterthrush. Now he was nearly finished gathering cerulean warbler data for his doctoral work at West Virginia University. He hoped to teach ornithology, as well as continue his research when he completed the degree.

Before everyone headed off to bed for the night, I inquired about a shower, still self-conscious about my potential stinkiness. Greg had warned me that the local water was very sulfuric, so I had brought spring water to drink. Randy joked that I should wait as long as possible before taking a "warm mineral bath," so I decided to tough it out.

The plan for the next day was to leave the farm at 6:00 a.m. for a nearby study plot on a section of the Wildlife Management Area known as Snake Ridge, so named because of its abundant rattlesnake population. Two days earlier, Dr. Wood had explained that this project was one part of a larger, cooperative effort conceived by the Cerulean Warbler Technical Group. One of her former graduate students, Kelly Perkins, conducted her thesis research in 2004 and 2005 in the Lewis Wetzel Wildlife Management Area and surrounding properties. Perkins and her research team surveyed the area, selected study sites, mapped cerulean warbler territories, and logged hours and hours of observations in the field. The data from two field seasons of study seemed to support the anecdotal belief that ceruleans favored gaps in the forest canopy. One possible reason for this, Perkins hypothesized, was that the light entering the forest through the gap attracted the insects that ceruleans eat. Another possibility was that gaps "may serve to enhance song." Regardless of the reason, Perkins's thesis suggested that ceruleans benefited from gaps in the canopy.

In nature, gaps occur when tall canopy trees die and fall to the forest floor, are struck by lightning, or are knocked down by intense storms. Humans create gaps in forest canopies for a wide variety of reasons: hiking or all-terrain vehicle trails, roads, natural gas or oil wells, food plots for game animals, and of course timber harvesting. However, as Dr. Wood had explained to me the day before, another way to achieve this complex canopy structure could be through careful, selective logging. Since Perkins's research showed that ceruleans did in fact seem to prefer canopy gaps, the next step—one of the projects Greg's team was currently working on—was to study the effects different logging intensities had on the local cerulean population. In the Lewis Wetzel Wildlife Management Area, there were four different study plots: an uncut control plot, a light single-tree selection plot, an intermediate cut that left about 40% of the canopy, and an almost clear-cut plot. Uncut buffer plots flanked each study plot.

The field technicians would take point counts to evaluate the presence and absence of ceruleans and other Neotropical migrants and to "spot-map" the area to define the territories of individual birds to determine territory density in each plot. Nesting success would also be monitored. Additionally, researchers were interested in return rates from previous years to help determine individual survival. One important way to monitor this is through bird banding, which I would be "helping" Greg with the following morning.

Around nine o'clock, everyone in the barn began to retreat to his (or her, in my case) room. I unrolled and unzipped my sleeping bag and lay down on a narrow bed in stall #3. The small, particle board–walled room contained two single beds, a wooden chair, a window, an overhead light, and a ceiling fan. I cracked the window so I could listen to frogs in the ponds and other night sounds as I fell asleep. It turned out that one of the prominent "night sounds" was a CSX freight train, which seemed to rumble continuously past my window all night, whining a long, mournful whistle.

I stared at the dark ceiling and couldn't sleep. The train taunted me. The frogs wouldn't shut up. The springs in the bed creaked if I rolled around, so I forced myself to lie perfectly still. I wanted to sleep, but at the same time I was worried— what if I my cell phone alarm didn't work, and I failed to get up at 5 a.m.? I didn't want to be the stereotypical bookish writer; I wanted to show I could hang with the biologists. The discussion of college degrees earlier made me consider the path I'd taken so far, and how different my life could be if I'd made slightly different decisions. I'd begun my college career as a wildlife and fisheries science major at Penn State University; unfortunately, my immaturity (combined with an active social life) led to a failing grade in chemistry and less-than-stellar performances in other "weed-out" freshman classes. Instead of buckling down, getting serious, and retaking chemistry—which was required for the wildlife degree—I spun my wheels for another semester or two before finally switching my major to English. I found that I thrived in the small, discussion-based literature and writing classes where I had floundered in the five-hundred-student lecture hall science courses typical of large universities. While I loved the English major and don't regret my decision to switch, I still carried a small chip on my shoulder about failing as a wildlife biologist before I'd even begun.

So, I lay there on my sleeping bag on the narrow bed, perfectly still, but not sleeping. I checked the illuminated face of my wristwatch every ten minutes or so. Just before four, I heard a song sparrow, and shortly thereafter the twitters and gurgles of barn swallows. Then red-winged blackbirds, and finally everything else. I didn't roll out of bed until I heard Randy shuffling around in the adjacent room. I stumbled through the pre-dawn darkness to the bathhouse, jug of spring water in hand, to get ready for the day.

SIX

★

UP CLOSE AND PERSONAL

HE WHITE, GOVERNMENT-ISSUED BLAZER bumped along the poorly paved road. Through the side window, I scanned the dense, misty woods around us for early birds and found myself wishing I'd gotten some sleep the night before. My eyes felt itchy under my dry contact lenses. Greg and I rode in the Blazer, and the others followed behind us in a white Jeep Cherokee. Earlier, we'd loaded the mist-netting and bird-banding gear into the back of the vehicles, and promptly at 6 a.m. we set out for the study plots on Snake Ridge. The site was about five miles from the Lantz Farm, deep within the Lewis Wetzel Wildlife Management Area.

This day—May 10—would be the first cerulean-banding day of the field season. Most of West Virginia's ceruleans had probably arrived here by the end of April, though a few could still show up as late as the middle of May. Greg and his field crew had been surveying their study areas since mid-April; they'd done their best to identify locations where male ceruleans had begun to stake out territories, and over the last two or three days Randy and Patrick had been searching for the beginnings of cerulean warbler nests. Nest trees would be flagged with orange strips of plastic around their trunks. I tapped my fingers on my knees and stared out the window. The treetops were hidden by thick fog at this early hour, but I knew that cerulean warblers were in there somewhere, waiting to begin a day of staking out territories, wooing potential mates, and gobbling up leaf-hoppers.

The pavement gave way to dirt near a rusted metal gate, which Greg unlocked and swung open. After crawling and lurching along for a few more minutes, avoiding ditches and piles of rocks, we pulled off the logging road at the bottom of a steep, looming hill. Greg explained that we weren't allowed to drive any further up the road, so we would walk to the top of the ridge, carrying the mist-netting equipment with us: two heavy three-foot stakes, two hollow aluminum poles that fit over the stakes, and two much longer hollow poles. I grabbed one of the long poles, tightened the straps of my pack, and began climbing. As we trudged up the hill, birds sang from the thick green forest that surrounded us—scarlet tanagers, black-throated green warblers, ovenbirds. It was obvious that a variety of bird species thrived here; the Lewis Wetzel Wildlife Management Area supposedly had the highest ruffed grouse population in West Virginia, too.

A study by Petra Wood and her colleague Cathy Weakland was one of the first published descriptions of cerulean warbler habitat in West Virginia. They surveyed intact, mature deciduous forests as well as fragmented forests in four West Virginia counties. The results revealed that "more territories occurred in intact forest than expected based on available habitat area. Seventy-three percent of all territories occurred in intact forest, though only 28% of the total area surveyed was intact forest. Territory density was [greater than six times] higher in intact than in fragmented forest." They also found that more cerulean territories occurred on ridgetops than they had expected: "Territory density was [more than eight times] greater on ridges than on either mid slope or bottom; it was almost twice as high as on northeast-facing slopes." Additionally, their study revealed that ceruleans preferred a high percentage of canopy cover within their territories, though they did not avoid small gaps in the forest, such as those caused by roads or trails. In other words, cerulean warblers seemed to strongly prefer to breed within contiguous tracts of deciduous forests on ridgetops.

Habitat within the Lewis Wetzel Wildlife Management Area seemed to match the preferred cerulean environs described in Weakland and Wood's paper. In her master's thesis, Kelly Perkins summarized Lewis Wetzel's specific habitat components. She reported that the elevation of the area ranges from about 800 to 1,500 feet above sea level, and that the forest has been variously classified as mixed mesophytic *and* Appalachian oak. Both types of forest harbor a great diversity of plant and animal species, but mixed mesophytic forests are generally characterized by maples, tulip trees, and basswood, and have "moderately moist" soil; Appalachian oak forests typically consist of a variety of oak species as well as hickories. Perkins identified most of Lewis Wetzel's trees as mature, second-growth hardwoods, including red, black, white, chestnut, and scarlet oak; sugar maple; several species of hickory; white ash; and tulip tree. Snake Ridge, our group's destination, was a dry, steep ridge with rocky soil; the dominant tree species were chestnut and scarlet oak. The canopy trees along Snake Ridge soared to heights of eighty to one hundred feet—as tall as ten-story buildings.

I stumbled over a large stone and almost lost my footing. The dry dirt of the steep road below my feet was packed hard and deeply rutted from heavy equipment. My small pack, which held only two bottles of water, my binoculars, camera, notebook, and a few granola bars, began to make my shoulders ache. I started breathing heavily, then my heart began to drum, and soon I faded to the back of our six-person procession up the steep hill. I didn't want to embarrass myself by being last, but I also didn't want to embarrass myself by having a heart attack.

When we finally got to the top of the ridge, after an excruciating eternity of climbing, I collapsed (as gracefully as possible) on a flat rock to catch my breath. Randy, Patrick, and the field technicians left the mist-netting equipment with Greg and me, and then they dispersed into the forest on the right side of the steep slope to search for cerulean nests. I unsnapped my pack and let it slip from my shoulders as I fought the light-headed feeling that precedes blacking out. I managed to fish a water bottle from my pack and indulged in two or three long swallows. I took a few deep breaths and waited for my heart to stop pounding in my ears.

Once I'd recovered, Greg and I gathered the poles and stakes and continued to walk the road, which ran along the spine of the ridge. Greg had promised to get me "up close and personal" with a cerulean warbler, which was about the only thing keeping my aching lungs and legs moving.

The woods at this early morning hour echoed with birdsong, which I began to appreciate again once my heart rate returned to normal. Red-eyed vireos quipped their *Where are you? Can you hear?* song from above us, while a worm-eating warbler's dry trill rose from the undergrowth. It was brighter here on the ridgetop, and we could look down at the hollows filled with mist below us. Towering oaks ran along the logging road, sheltering delicate wildflowers and tangled brush. A familiar conflicted feeling returned: on one hand, I wanted to tell everyone about the Lewis Wetzel Wildlife Management Area—its old trees, steep hills, abundant birds, and ethereal fog—but on the other, I wanted to keep it that way, and therefore keep everyone else out. *(It's not pretty; don't visit!)*

Greg and I ambled slowly along the ridge road, listening for the song of a male cerulean. It wasn't long before we heard one, the buzzy *ziziziZEEE* coming from somewhere high in the leafy canopy. I perked up a bit and dug my binoculars out of my pack. Greg pulled a portable CD player and two small speakers from his green bag, pointed the speakers in the direction of the bird, and played a recorded cerulean song. Almost immediately, a male swooped into view to investigate "the intruder." The cerulean resembled a falling leaf as he descended, one canopy tier at a time. He finally stopped about fifteen feet above our heads and perched out in the open on the end of a thin branch. I had a much clearer view of this cerulean than the one I'd seen the day before at Cooper's Rock; through my binoculars I watched him quickly turn his head from side to side as he searched the ground for the source of the other male's song. He appeared agitated, rapidly fluttering and twitching his blue wings. He puffed up the soft white feathers of his chest—perhaps to appear larger—and buzzed viciously. He seemed totally consumed by hatred for the intruding, brazen male who must be down there *somewhere*, and he didn't seem to notice the two humans staring up at him. I'm sure that to another male cerulean warbler his display would be quite intimidating, but to me, the puffy, twitching ball of blue and white feathers was adorable.

"He's so cute," I whispered.

Greg smiled and whispered back, "Don't let him hear you say that!"

Since this loveable clump of raging testosterone seemed ready to aggressively defend his territory, Greg decided to set up the mist net.

Different kinds of research—and different bird species—require different mist-netting techniques. Greg used a method called target-netting to capture ceruleans. Target-netting is used when you know where the territory of the bird you want to catch is located, and your purpose is to target that specific bird. This kind of mist net needed to be set up and then taken down for each different target. Greg and I descended a few feet down one side of the ridge, our boots crunching last fall's leaves, and lay the poles and other equipment on the ground of the dry slope. Greg began by hammering the two metal stakes into the forest floor, about ten feet from each other. The two four-foot hollow poles fit over the stakes, and the two longer, thinner poles fit inside those. Greg then took two plastic grocery store bags out of his pack; one bag held two thin ropes, and every few inches a metal ring was attached to each rope. Greg fit the rings over each of the long, hollow poles. The other plastic bag held the mist net itself, which was black and resembled a hairnet. Greg carefully extracted one edge of the net, which he attached to the metal rings with fishing swivels. Inch by inch, he slowly stretched the net to the other pole; he then attached the other edge of the net to the rings. The apparatus worked as a pulley system; the height of the mist net could be adjusted by pulling the ropes, which allowed the net to be raised as high as fifteen feet above the ground. When the net was fully extended and stretched between the poles, its fine black strands were difficult to see.

I commented on the elaborateness of the process and asked Greg if he thought banding these birds would be worth the trouble. "Well, the whole idea," he said, "is that we have a bunch of cerulean warblers, and by banding them, we make each bird an individual as opposed to just a member of a population. It gives us the ability to check the bird over time and identify it to a specific territory and then, over the years, see if we get return of the birds. We can check for longevity and even within-season survival rates." All of this information would be important not only to the growing body of knowledge about cerulean warbler natural history, but also for the development of management or species-recovery plans. In order to preserve cerulean warblers in their breeding range, we must be certain we know exactly what kind of habitat the birds need to thrive and successfully reproduce.

Another aspect of cerulean warbler natural history not yet completely understood by biologists is how individual male cerulean warblers choose their specific territories. Typically, a male songbird will attempt to defend as large a territory as he can, as long as the drawbacks of having such a large territory (expending energy to defend its borders, for example) do not outweigh the benefits (food resources, available nest sites). Several published studies show that the size of a cerulean's territory is variable. Biologists based in Ontario, near the northernmost edge of the cerulean's breeding range, found that the average size of a cerulean territory ranged from about 1.5 acres to 2.5 acres. A study from southern Indiana (also, incidentally, outside of the cerulean's core breeding area) reported a mean territory size of only half an acre. In her thesis research, Kelly Perkins found that the average cerulean territory on Snake Ridge also encompassed about half an acre, while the average territory size across all of the Lewis Wetzel Wildlife Management Area ranged from about three-quarters of an acre to an acre. To put this in perspective, an American football field measures slightly more than one acre in size.

Biologists aren't exactly sure why cerulean territory sizes vary so widely; smaller territories could mean that a greater number of birds are trying to utilize prime habitat conditions, and larger territories may suggest that the conditions are less than ideal. It has also been hypothesized that male ceruleans "cluster" their territories. Biologists Kamal Islam and Kirk Roth studied this behavior in southern Indiana. They reported that territorial clustering might occur for two reasons: one, optimum habitat conditions within an environment, or two, "social" reasons. Male cerulean warblers typically return from migration a few days before females. Once on the breeding grounds, the males begin to set up territories that will, ideally, attract females. Since ceruleans do not return at the same times, it's possible that the first males back stake out the prime sections of habitat for their territories, and then the males who return later cluster together around the first male, since his territory is in the best section of the woods. The second possibility, the "social" hypothesis, is that later-returning males cluster around an early-returning, "dominant" male, following his lead. If "the initial bird identifies a stand of quality habitat which is too large for a single territory," then this copycat behavior could benefit the birds who return to the area later. It could also, however, leave areas of ideal habitat unoccupied by nesting birds. It is also possible that a combination of both factors—social and habitat—contribute to clustered territories. Like many aspects of cerulean life, biologists admit that additional research may be needed to definitely determine the way ceruleans choose their territories. Regardless, since cerulean territory density was known to be high on Snake Ridge, it was an ideal place to try to capture birds.

Once Greg finished setting up the mist net, he balanced a carved, wooden cerulean warbler decoy between tree branches. "Does the decoy have a name?" I asked.

"Not yet," he laughed. "'Chuck.'"

After stabilizing Chuck, Greg positioned the CD player and speakers on the ground below the net. He pressed play, and we retreated about twenty feet and crouched on the road. After the first recorded call buzzed into the forest, the male cerulean swooped down again and flitted from branch to branch near the net, but he kept barely missing it. After a few tense minutes, a second bird—a female cerulean—fluttered down from the canopy and landed on a branch that was actually touching the mist net. This was the first time I'd seen a female. I raised my binoculars and held my breath. Like many bird species, her colors were softer than the male's; instead of bright blue, the female's muted, aquamarine plumage looked washed with a soft yellow. Her subtle movements were quieter and more deliberate than the male's. To our amazement, she began to tug at the mist net with her beak, as if she wanted to use it for nest material. Suddenly she flew directly into the net. Female cerulean warblers are notoriously difficult to capture, and banding her would be a rare accomplishment; Greg and I both knew this, and we leapt to our feet—but then the bird just rolled out and fluttered away. She appeared quite casual about the whole ordeal, like she'd been testing out a hammock. After this disappointment, the male cerulean seemed to lose interest, too; apparently, Chuck was not so tough after all. Greg decided that we should try a different location.

After breaking down the pulley system, yanking the metal stakes out of the earth, and gathering up all our materials, we walked about twenty yards farther down the dirt road and Greg played the recorded call again. Again, a male cerulean swooped lower to investigate. Greg decided to try to catch him, so we slid down the steep slope on the other side of the logging road. Ankle-deep dry leaves rustled under my feet, and tangled greenbrier snagged my jeans. Sweat trickled down my temple, and I peeled off my long-sleeved shirt and tied it around my waist. We went through the same elaborate set-up process, and then Greg and I retreated to a moss-covered fallen log a few feet away. Again, the male cerulean warbler kept swooping either above or below the mist net.

"Well, this is how it is sometimes," Greg said, shrugging. I could tell he felt a bit uneasy about not having caught any birds yet. "Sometimes, you can spend a whole day in the field and not band anybody."

While we dismantled the mist net again, a wave of tiredness washed over me, and I again became self-conscious about my sweaty smell. We'd been in the woods for almost two hours and the temperature was rising. We lugged the equipment up the slope and trudged along the ridgetop road into the brightening day.

When we'd hiked a sufficient distance from our second unsuccessful attempt at capturing a cerulean warbler, Greg again pointed the speakers toward the forest canopy and played the recorded song. Like the previous times, a bird countersang immediately and swooped down, closer and closer, until he perched just a few feet above our heads, twitching his blue wings and buzzing angrily. Greg and I slid down the dry slope, rigged up the net a third time, wedged Chuck between sugar maple twigs, set the CD player on "repeat," and retreated to hide behind the wide trunk of a nearby red oak.

The male cerulean heard the intruder's call and again came down to investigate. After a few passes close to the mist net—perhaps to get a better look at unflinching and unintimidated Chuck—the bird flew squarely into the net's center and became entangled. Greg sprang to his feet and ran a few steps ahead of me to the snared cerulean warbler, who flapped pathetically a few times before giving up and hanging calmly in the net. I fought the impulse to shriek, "Get him out! Get him out! Hurry!," and my heart began to pound as I approached. The bird hung upside down, and although he had stopped struggling, he kept his head turned to watch us closing in on him. A few steps later, and I was eye to eye with him, this beautiful bird, an important member of one of the fastest-declining songbird species in the United States. It took us three tries to outsmart a cerulean, but we'd finally done it. As the tiny creature hung there, helpless, black eyes fixed on us, I felt sorry for him.

"You're so little," I said quietly, "But you're a handsome little man, yes you are...." I caught myself baby-talking to the bird and tried to regain my serious, writerly composure. "So, do you band him while he's in the net?" I asked.

"No," Greg answered, "he comes totally out." He turned his green Hawk Mountain cap backward, bent down to turn off the CD player, and pulled Chuck out of the tree to reduce the netted bird's stress level. Then he began the process of removing the cerulean from the net. Greg kept the bird still by cupping his hands around him while at the same time working to free him. "It's almost like taking off a jacket," he said softly, his face close to the bird. "His feet are essentially undone, so now I'm pulling it off one wing, and now I'll move over and do the other. That wing's done, so now just the head is caught, and it's not caught bad at all." The black net fell away from the bird, and Greg closed his hand around him. His tiny head, about the size of a small grape, peeked out from in between the second and third knuckles of Greg's careful fist. "There you go," he smiled. "One little cerulean warbler."

I wondered (perhaps anthropomorphically) what was going through that bird's mind. He had to be confused. He hears another male cerulean moving in on his territory—maybe on his mate—so he comes down to investigate. Does he wonder why the call is coming from the ground? I think he must, but his hormones and the evolutionary drive to defend his territory are too great. Then he sees the per-petrator, perched serenely in a tree's low branches. The intruder doesn't seem at all bothered by his presence, which infuriates him even more. He swoops. He flicks his wings. He buzzes viciously. *Who is this guy?* He swoops closer, and sudden-ly he's caught in something and can't get out. His wings don't work, and he can't move his legs. Then these two huge, hulking predators lurch over to him, making frightening sounds, and proceed to manhandle his entire body. Or maybe the bird simply has no idea what's going on—humans have probably never hunted cerulean warblers for food. Why would we? A human would certainly expend more energy trying to catch one than the human would gain from eating it. Maybe the bird's experience is more akin to being abducted by aliens.

Greg knelt down, and with his free hand he rummaged in the pack that held the banding equipment. I crouched on the ground to watch more closely.

"Normally I would use a paper lunch sack, but this time I'm going to put him in a sock instead," he told me. "A clean sock."

The sock would keep the bird from hurting himself by flapping around too much but would still allow him to breathe. Greg put his hand and the bird inside the white athletic sock, and then he slowly extracted his hand without the bird in it. While he held the opening of the sock closed, the area near the toes bulged and moved slightly. Greg pulled a thin, tube-shaped scale with a clamp at one end out of his banding pack. He clipped the scale over the open end of the sock and hung the other end on a thin branch. "Perfect," he said. "Later, we'll weigh the sock by it-self and subtract to determine how much he weighs. Now we get the bands ready."

Greg reached into his pack again and pulled out a small plastic canister, the kind used to hold 35mm camera film. An X was cut into the lid, and a thin piece of wire poked through its center. "You want to keep your bands in a sturdy con-tainer," Greg explained. "I can just grab the wire, give it a little pull, and out comes a band."

The aluminum bands that Greg kept in the film canister were each engraved with a unique identification number, a 1-800 telephone number, and the address of the federal Bird Banding Laboratory (BBL) in Laurel, Maryland. The BBL is part of the Patuxent Wildlife Research Center, which in turn is part of the United States Geological Survey, which is part of the Department of the Interior. The gov-ernment took control of all bird banding in the United States in 1920; prior to that, several pioneering scientists banded birds to learn more about their migration patterns and lifespans, which remain some of the primary reasons for banding birds today. The BBL acknowledges Paul Bartsch as one of the first bird banders. In 1902, Dr. Bartsch, who worked for the Smithsonian Institution, banded twenty-three black-crowned night herons. Several other banders followed Dr. Bartsch's example, leading to the formation of the American Bird Banding Association and eventually the government-run BBL. Banding birds now requires a federal permit and an accompanying state permit; according to the BBL, "There are currently only 2,000 Master banding permits and 3,000 subpermits in the United States…. Persons who want to apply for a banding permit must be able to show that they are qualified to safely trap, handle, and band the birds." The BBL also suggests that persons first apply to be a sub-permittee of a Master bander. Greg holds a Master banding permit.

In addition to an aluminum federal band, each cerulean warbler would get three brightly colored hard-plastic bands. "What colors should we give him?" Greg asked, pulling a clear baggie from the pack. The baggie contained tiny red, blue, green, and black bands. "I like red a lot," he continued, "let's definitely put on at least one of those."

Four bands on the cerulean warbler's gray toothpick legs seemed excessive to me; however, the color bands would allow researchers on the ground to identify an individual bird by observing it through binoculars. The four bands also meant 128 different color combinations. Once banded, the movements, breeding, and nesting success of a bird could be determined without having to recapture it.

While Greg and I were discussing which colors to use, another male cerulean warbler flew into the mist net behind us. "That's crazy," I said, scrambling to my feet. "I can take off one of my socks, if you need it."

Greg laughed and stood up, too. "Actually, I do have a paper lunch bag." He bent over the ensnared bird and began to untangle him. "This guy's caught a little worse than the other one. This is what we call 'double-bagged.'" Greg explained that we had left the net a bit slacker than we should have; this had allowed the bird to become wrapped in two folds of the net instead of just one. Even with this difficulty, Greg expertly disengaged the warbler.

I reached into the banding pack for the paper bag when I noticed that the sock, still suspended from the scale and branch, was slack. "Hey, did he get out?" I asked.

With his free hand, Greg felt the empty toes of the sock, then smirked. "He got out."

"Is that him?" I asked, pointing to the bird in Greg's hand.

"This is him. So much for catching two birds," he laughed, gently lowering the cerulean warbler into the brown paper bag. "That just makes this bird unlucky. That happens. Sometimes, working with a bird, you fumble, and 'see ya!' That's why the most important thing to do is put the numbered federal band on. First thing. Everything else can be considered optional."

Greg and I both settled back on the dry leaves. "Let me know if you need any help," I offered.

"Actually," Greg said, passing me a clipboard, "I'm going to have you scribe."

A banding data sheet was attached to the clipboard. The sheet had an acronym key at the top and several lines and columns below. Each bird would be listed on its own line, and all the columns filled in with the bird's information.

Greg picked up the film canister again and a pair of small pliers. "This bird's band number will be 53621," he said, and I wrote it in the sheet's left-hand column. We also recorded capture time, date, and method; Greg's initials and our location; species and sex information; and indicated that this bird was unbanded when we captured him.

After affixing the silver BBL band around the bird's right leg, Greg again picked up the color band baggie and a tool he called a spatula, which is a small aluminum device that the bird's little foot and leg fit inside. "It's almost like measuring for a shoe at the shoe store," Greg said. He put a red band above the silver band and squeezed the tool, causing the band to close around the bird's thin right leg. "This is the first banding day of the year," he told me, "so if we catch any more birds today, we'll keep the red over silver consistent so that I know that the next time I see a bird that has red over silver, it's from this year. Last year I did blue over silver and it was the opposite leg." On the bird's left leg Greg affixed two blue bands. "Over here," he pointed at a line on the sheet, "write 'B/B' for blue over blue, and 'R/X' for red over silver. So he's official now, banded and ready to go. But I'll take a few other measurements while we have him." Greg took a small silver ruler out of the banding pack and lined it up with the bird's wing. "The little wing, this is 66 millimeters," only about two and a half inches long. "And the tail is...40."

I wrote the information in the appropriate spaces and again felt sorry for our bird. I could hear other cerulean warblers buzzing high overhead, and I wondered if less-handsome males were trying to horn in on this guy's territory while he was down.

One of the few spaces left on the sheet was "age." I knew that there was no reliable way to estimate the age of an adult bird by looking at it, so I was curious how Greg would determine it. When I asked, he explained, "The age is based on molt limit. This group of feathers is called the alulas." He held the bird gently in one hand and pointed at tiny feathers near the top of the wing with the other. "I can look at this feather here, which is the carpal covert. Because the alulas are all blue-fringed, and their sheen quality when we get the bird in the sun is all the same, we can say that this bird hatched out a minimum of two years ago."

The elusive quarry captured.

"But," I said, "he could be five or six or even older, right?"

"Right. He could be ten. So just write down 'ASY'—after second year."

I made the notation and noticed one more blank column, under the heading "Fat."

"How we check for fat," said Greg, "is we do a little blow here." He held the bird upside down and blew softly on his chest. The bird's feathers parted, exposing pinkish-gray skin. "See that little indentation area? You can see subcutaneous fat deposits in there when you blow the feathers away. There's no fat, so you can put 'zero.' They won't really start stocking up on fat until premigration, and in that case, we have codes 0, 1, 2, and 3. Three is when that indentation is full. Full and bulging."

"That sounds kind of gross," I said.

"Yeah," Greg agreed, "but they need energy stores."

I tried to imagine the journey this cerulean warbler had made just a few days or weeks earlier. Those two 66 millimeter–long wings had carried him above the Andes Mountains, the Panama Canal, all of Central America, and then the raging waters of the wide Gulf of Mexico. How did he have the strength to migrate so far?

"It's hard to believe," I said, leaning closer to the bird, "that this little thing went from the Lewis Wetzel Wildlife Management Area in West Virginia all the way to

South America and back. This tiny thing." I suddenly felt like I was going to cry.

"Yeah," Greg nodded, "and potentially, a lot of that's over open water. You hit a storm front—done. Not only that, but if these birds live ten years, and they go twice a year, that's twenty trips. Can't get a car to do that."

"And I had trouble walking up that hill," I said. My legs could barely carry me up a steep logging road, but this tiny bird had just completed a 3,000-mile trip despite tremendous odds—perhaps dodging storms, evading predators, and dealing with shrinking habitat the entire way. Since this bird was more than two years old, he'd made that journey at least *six* times. I admired our little cerulean a great deal. He was much stronger than I was. A bird equivalent of me would have dropped into the Gulf after only a few feet.

Greg asked if I wanted to hold the cerulean warbler. This was a silly question, of course, and he passed the bird to me. He showed me how to hold the bird in the "photographer's grip"; the cerulean's thin gray legs went between my second and third fingers, and my thumb held them in place. I put my free hand on the bird's back to help support his small body. I noticed how his sharp toenails curled gently at the ends of his delicate feet. He barely felt like anything in my hand, and it seemed like I would break him if I squeezed too hard. Subtracting the weight of the paper bag revealed that this bird weighed just ten grams—about the weight of two standard United States nickels.

The warbler cocked his head and looked at me with a clear black eye. A month earlier, he may have stared at scarlet macaws and other tropical birds during migration. He could have looked down at oil rigs in the Gulf of Mexico. And now, he peered at me. I swallowed, tried not to cry, and instead focused on memorizing all of his intricate markings and colors. The bird's thin, pointed bill—which was longer than I had imagined—was a dull black. Above his bill, his feathers were sky blue. A faint black stripe ran from the corner of his mouth to his eye and past, fading out on the back of his head. A few tiny, black, whisker-like feathers sprouted around his bill. The bright, brilliant white of his chin and throat were collared by a thin blue-black necklace. He had a few stray flecks of black and dark blue on his white stomach and breast, and his electric-blue back was occasionally streaked with black. The long, pointed flight feathers of his wings appeared black, as well, while two parallel white bars crossed each shoulder. His tail's base was dark, but each long tail feather had a white splotch near its end and then a small black blotch on the very tip, almost like it had been sloppily dipped in black paint.

"I love you," I told the bird, and gently handed him back to Greg. Greg turned the bird upside down in his palm and uncurled his fingers. The cerulean lay still on his back for a few seconds, displaying his four new bands. After I snapped a picture, Greg swiftly flipped him right side up, and the bird zipped away, disappearing into the green canopy.

I thanked Greg, and he said, "I love showing people this stuff. Especially if you're going to be able to pass the word on a little bit about ceruleans and neotrops in general."

"That's my plan," I assured him.

"Then I'll bring you out here every day," he said, and smiled.

I smiled too, and we began to take down the mist net.

SEVEN

★

CERULEOMORPHIZING

"**B**UDDY, YOU HAVE GOT lots of red," Greg said to the warbler in his hand, as he squeezed the last of the three red plastic bands shut. "We'll be able to see you from a quarter-mile away."

This bird—53623 R/R R/X—was our third cerulean of the morning. The first bird was 53621 B/B R/X and the second, 53622 G/G R/X. "Do you think the lady cerulean warblers will notice all that red?" I asked.

"You have to wonder," Greg answered, pulling the small silver ruler out of the banding pack. "I wonder if I put all blues on, if the females would be like, 'Ho, ho! Look at THAT one!'" he laughed. "Sixty-seven for wing."

I made the notation on the banding sheet and silently felt sorry for R/R R/X. What if the red bands made him more visible to predators? Or what if bands in general slow the birds down during their migration? The bands don't weigh much, but neither do cerulean warblers—the first bird tipped the scales at just ten grams, and the second and third both weighed nine. Hopefully, the importance of the data gained from banding the birds will outweigh any possible detrimental effects.

Greg held the ruler alongside the bird. "This is a long tail. Forty-three."

"Wow," I said, writing the number down, "he's sort of a freak."

"Yeah, he's an outlier." Greg bent his head closer to the bird. "Another ASY for age. That's what we expect. And fat..." he paused and blew on the warbler's chest, "zero."

We double-checked the sheet to make sure all the bird's information had been properly recorded, and then we stood up. My legs had already begun to ache from the morning's climb up the steep road. We took a picture of the bird's bands, and Greg handed him to me. He squirmed a bit in my palm while I adjusted him. "He's not happy with you," Greg said. "He's pretty mad."

"No," I cooed, "he loves me. I'm his mom." I could feel the bird's lungs expanding and contracting as he twisted his head to keep his black eyes focused on me. The bright electric blue of his crown contrasted sharply with the white under his chin. In my opinion, there's not a more beautiful bird than the cerulean warbler anywhere in the world—and no other habitat as diverse and spectacular (and underappreciated) as an Appalachian hardwood forest. I took a step backward so the bird and I were under the shade of a towering red oak.

"Hold on one second before you let him go." Greg turned and lowered the net so we didn't recapture him.

Before I released the cerulean, I gave him a quick kiss on the top of his head. When I opened my hand, he zipped up to the nearest tree branch and began to preen. "I don't think he liked his little kiss," I told Greg.

"I bet not," he laughed. "'She's going to eat me!'"

We continued to laugh as we packed up the banding bag and disassembled the mist net. The hot sun beaming through tree branches burned my forearms; it was almost noon. Gear in hand, we scrambled up to the logging road and continued to the next location. "Those are the ones you hope for," Greg said.

"Yeah, that was a good one," I agreed. "He just flew right into the net, and you got him right out, and then we released him and he flew away."

"Hey," Greg said, pointing with a metal stake, "there's Randy."

About fifteen feet down the slope of the ridge, Randy Dettmers leaned against a tree trunk, clipboard in hand, and stared up into the canopy, his graying hair barely visible beneath the back of his navy blue baseball cap. Greg and I set the mist-net poles on the ground and joined him. The tree Randy was watching held the beginnings of a cerulean warbler nest; he had somehow spotted a female constructing it high up in the tree. While I watched the leafy branches where Randy said the nest was located, a bluish-green female swooped in, hopped around a branch, and stuck something into a small clump of fine, tangled material. The clump was wedged between a small bend in the branch and the nub where it looked like a twig had been before it broke off.

Cerulean warbler nesting biology is still somewhat of a mystery. Several factors make this kind of research difficult, not the least of which is the fact that ceruleans usually build their nests at least eleven meters—more than thirty feet—above the ground, and have been found as high as forty-nine meters (160 feet!). To say that this height makes observation of the nest contents challenging is an understatement; because of ongoing research, however, some nest-site characteristics are becoming a bit clearer. According to Paul Hamel's account in *The Birds of North America*, in addition to being placed on a lateral limb of a deciduous tree, cerulean nests are often constructed over "open spaces...often 5–20m [16–65 feet] from nest to nearest vegetation below," and about eleven feet from the bole, or trunk, of the tree. Those characteristics seemed to hold true for this particular nest; it was several feet above the nearest thin branch, and the area below the nest was, generally, open the entire way down to the forest floor. Female cerulean warblers have been observed "bungee jumping" from their nests down into this open area below; the female birds suddenly "fall" from their nests headfirst toward the ground before zipping away into the undergrowth just before impact. Some biologists think the females may be imitating falling leaves in an attempt to depart from their nests unnoticed.

"This nest," Randy told me quietly, "is fairly typically placed in terms of the lateral branch with some sort of a little crook or fork in it. That makes a good location to attach nest material." I glanced down at the clipboard and noticed that Randy had sketched a diagram of the tree and the nest's location on the branch.

"I'm not very good at identifying tree species," I admitted, "especially trees with oval leaves."

"I think that's a black gum tree," he said.

Black gum, also known as black tupelo, produces a small, bitter fruit eaten by game birds common in the Lewis Wetzel Wildlife Management Area, like ruffed grouse and wild turkey. Ceruleans have been known to nest in more than a dozen other tree species, including sugar maple, red oak, and black walnut. Some biologists think that the choice of a nest location has less to do with a deciduous tree's species and more to do with its height, width, and placement in the forest.

Through my binoculars I watched the female work on the nest and tried to determine what kind of material she kept collecting and adding to the clump. "Are those spider webs?" I asked.

"Yeah, it looks like she's starting off by weaving spider webs around that little crook in the branch," Randy answered, making a notation on his clipboard. He raised his binoculars. "She's making some progress on it. It's starting to look like you'd imagine the base of a bird nest, a little cup."

"It's so small," I said. The bright blue male joined the female, hopped around next to her on the branch, then flitted away.

"The nests are actually amazingly small," Randy agreed, nodding. "If you had one in your hand, it would *maybe* cover the palm. And maybe not that big." Biologists in Tennessee collected several cerulean nests and found the diameters of the inside of the cups to be between 4.57 centimeters and 5.15 centimeters (about 1.8 inches to two inches), and 3.03 centimeters (about 1.2 inches) deep. To put this in perspective, an average teacup has a diameter of about nine centimeters and a depth of about six centimeters; a cerulean warbler nest is, therefore, approximately half the size of a teacup. Locating a well-camouflaged, half-teacup-sized clump of spider webs more than three stories up in the forest canopy must be a skill acquired only after years of practice; it seemed amazing to me that researchers had found even one nest—ever—let alone several over the course of a few days, as Randy had done. I was in the presence of a nest-finding Jedi master.

We watched through our binoculars as the female used her bill to wind the spider webs around the nub before flying away again.

"Randy, do you mind if we try to band right here?" Greg asked. Randy shook his head, and Greg began to set up the mist net behind us.

The male returned to the nest site again, cocked his head and looked at the clump; he seemed to be checking the female's work. Female cerulean warblers build their nests without the assistance of males; one nest could take between three and eight days to finish. Once the nest is complete, the female alone will incubate the eggs, keeping them warm beneath her body for eleven to thirteen days. As the female crouches firmly over her eggs, she is vulnerable—the cerulean warbler version of a "sitting duck." Thankfully, the male feeds her as she incubates so she doesn't have to expend energy foraging, and so the eggs aren't exposed to the cold or to predators.

How is a female cerulean warbler persuaded to take on the difficult roles of general contractor, construction crew, and stay-at-nest mom? Like the other aspects of cerulean breeding and nesting biology, until recently little was known about how the male and female of a mated pair interacted with each other. A research article, "Within-pair Interactions and Parental Behavior of Cerulean Warblers Breeding in Eastern Ontario," discusses a vocalization called "the whisper song." The whisper song is similar to a male cerulean's typical call, but it is quieter and apparently meant for only the female to hear. "When females are nest building," the article states, "males tend to follow very closely (often within 1-2m) and regularly sing whisper songs directed at the female. ... [W]hisper singing with occasional female response presumably functions in pair-bond maintenance." I imagined young women swooning over Frank Sinatra or Elvis as they crooned seductively. The article also states that researchers "made 28 observations of males feeding females (i.e., courtship feeding) during nest building. Over half of these feeding events were followed by copulations. In all cases, the food item presented was a larval lepidopteran [a caterpillar]." How typically male—a man takes a woman out for a nice dinner and hopes to score afterward; cerulean warbler males, it seemed, were

A clump of spiderwebs half the size of a teacup, three stories up.

not so different from human males. Instead of anthropomorphizing, can we call this "ceruleomorphizing," since the birds were certainly behaving this way before humans walked upright?

I lowered my binoculars and asked Randy if he'd heard any whisper singing that morning. "There was one male earlier," he said, lowering his binoculars as well, "that was whisper singing almost constantly, following the female around and singing really softly. We thought, is that a bird way over on the next ridge, or a bird right up above us?"

The female swooped back to the nest site with more wisps of spider webs in her beak. She added them to the growing lump on the branch and hopped around the area before flying away again. It suddenly occurred to me how very fortunate I was; few people have had the opportunity to even *see* a wild cerulean warbler, let alone witness one of their nests in mid-construction. Though ceruleans were not officially recognized by the US government as "threatened," the species' decline made each and every potential nest important to their survival.

The female returned, peered at the clump, hopped around it, and flitted away. Petra Wood had told me to ask Randy about a behavior he called "the sit-and-spin"; I asked him if that hopping motion by the female was it.

"No," he answered, "I've seen the sit-and-spin more when the females are still trying to decide where they want to nest." The female returned to the branch above us and resumed weaving with her bill. Randy continued, "You'll see them go to different spots, sort of like that lateral branch. They'll look for a little fork or something, and you'll see them go in there and actually kind of get down, and hunker down—" Randy demonstrated by bending his knees and twisting his hips.

"And they'll do the Twist?" I laughed.

"They'll do the Twist, yeah," said Randy, smiling. "And maybe they'll spin around a little bit, and sit and spin a little bit more, and sometimes the males will come in, either before or after them, and sort of say, 'Hey, look, isn't that a good spot?'" We laughed, and after pausing to check on the nest progress through his binoculars, Randy continued. "At first we thought the sit-and-spin was an indication of where they were going to build their nests for sure, but I think we've learned over time that it's just more of a precursor to actually beginning nest building. The investigatory phase. Searching out the best spot. Trying out some places—'How would this feel?'"

"That makes sense," I nodded. "Sort of like going to the mattress store and testing them all out."

We watched the nest for a few more minutes. The male cerulean warbler landed on a branch near where the female was working, checked it out again, then flew away. "When they do start nest building," Randy said, "and they have some material that they want to get firmly in there, they'll kind of get down and do a little wiggle in there."

I laughed and lowered my binoculars, which looked out-of-date and inadequate (or maybe just cheap) compared to the ones Randy and Greg carried. The use of spider webs as nest material amazed me. How did a female cerulean warbler ever figure that out? It's an example of different species unknowingly helping each other survive—ceruleans and spiders, two small parts of a complicated puzzle. The spider spins a strong, sticky web to catch insects and to protect her own egg sac. The cerulean warbler helps herself to some of the web. The work of the spider helps cushion the cerulean's eggs and young, as well as holding her nest together. The tree species that this pair of ceruleans had chosen to nest in—black gum— provides food for game birds, which in turn provide food for predators like bob- cats, hawks, and humans. Black gum lumber is used to build furniture and is often pulped for paper.

It isn't difficult to see the fragile links between species. What if, for some rea- son, the number of black gum trees began to decline? That could mean less food for game birds, less food for humans, less paper for our books, and fewer nest-site choices for songbirds. What effect might the loss of a woodland spider species have on the cerulean warbler? The birds might find something else to use in their nests, but at what difficulty? These thoughts alarmed me, and suddenly all of our places in the world seemed very vulnerable. Subtle changes on a global scale—a rise in the Earth's temperature, for example—could start a disastrous domino effect. What if changes happen too quickly for a species to adapt? "What else does she use in her nest besides spider webs?" I asked Randy nervously.

"You'll see them pulling strands off of grapevines, grapevine bark, getting little strips of that, or other dead trees that have flaky material on them. They'll grab that and bring it in there. Sort of thin, fibrous, stringy material." Randy watched the nest for a moment, then continued. "In other places, I've seen them bringing in lichens and using them as part of the nest or nest lining."

Lichens are another example of several different species working together. A lichen is formed when a fungus and an algae or a cyanobacteria merge. I don't quite understand how this works scientifically, but the resulting organism grows on rocks, tree trunks, walls, and other structures. Lichens don't need soil, but they do require sunlight and are sensitive to pollutants in the environment. From a high school science class, I remembered that reindeer eat lichens.

Sometimes, other bird species unwillingly help cerulean warblers construct their nests and vice versa. Biologists have observed ceruleans as both victims and perpetrators of "kleptoparasitism"—birds stealing nesting material from other birds. The thief often hops onto a branch near the nest (which sometimes is unattended, but sometimes has an incubating female sitting in it), jumps in and grabs a little strip of bark, grapevine, or other material from the nest. Then the offender high-tails it for deeper woods, often with the nest's owner in hot pursuit. Red-eyed vireos, American redstarts, blue-gray gnatcatchers, black-throated green warblers, and others have been observed stealing from cerulean nests. Ceruleans are not innocent, though; biologists have observed ceruleans snatching nest material from red-eyed vireos and blue-gray gnatcatchers, too. Scientists hypothesize that perhaps the benefits of stealing material from other nests outweigh the risks; a bird doesn't have to fly down to the ground and search for appropriate material if another bird has already done it. Additionally, if a bird's first nest blew down in a storm or was otherwise destroyed, time for another clutch of eggs could be short; stealing nest material instead of searching for it could save precious hours. This bird behavior also reminded me of human behavior; breaking into someone's home and stealing a television or jewelry saves the burglar time spent working and waiting for a paycheck. And, in the case of a natural disaster such as a hurricane, flood, or earthquake, humans have engaged in looting—or, perhaps we should say, "kleptoparasitism."

Above us, the female cerulean warbler returned to the branch yet again. "How many eggs do they usually lay?" I asked.

"Three or four is normal," Randy said. "In the early part of the season, they're pretty likely to have four eggs." This seemed impossible; how could *four* eggs—and a female cerulean—fit into a nest smaller than a teacup? The fragility of the entire process sounded almost insurmountable. Randy continued, "If for some reason they get a late start or their first nest fails and they try for a second nest, they're more likely to lay three eggs."

Myriad reasons could cause a cerulean warbler nest to "fail." Most researchers define a nest as "successful" if one or more cerulean babies fledge. A nest fails if no young leave the nest, or if the young bird that fledges is that notorious nest parasite, the brown-headed cowbird. A cowbird female will lay an egg in another species' nest for someone else to incubate and care for. Usually, she lays the egg in the nest of a smaller bird species. Because the cowbird chick is larger, it demands the most attention from the foster parents. The other nestlings often don't survive—they either starve or are pushed over the side of the nest by the bullish cowbird baby. In recent decades, the cowbird's range has expanded; cowbirds once followed herds of bison as they migrated across the Great Plains, feeding on insects and seeds stirred up by their hooves. When bison herds declined, cowbirds adapted to follow herds of domestic livestock, and they can now be found throughout most of North America. As contiguous forest continues to be fragmented by humans, creating more open spaces and "edge" habitats, cowbird parasitism could increase. Some researchers believe that cowbirds have taken a toll on cerulean warbler populations, and some even list the cowbird as one of the primary reasons for the cerulean's decline. While this is subject to debate, undoubtedly some cowbird parasitism occurs with cerulean warblers. In addition to cowbirds, cerulean nests are at risk from predators as well; blue jays, crows, hawks, black snakes, and, in some places, fox squirrels and chipmunks eat the chicks outright.

The article that discusses the whisper song also documents some of the more unusual cerulean warbler breeding situations observed by the authors, including brood adoption by a male who was not the biological father, "extra-pair copulations," and bigamy—scandals that sounded just as racy as an episode of *The Young and the Restless*. I asked Randy about bigamy.

"Yeah," he nodded, "that's another thing that's been documented—a male being mated to more than one female. Certainly some of the males are super-studs and are able to convince more than one female. There will be a male singing over there, and there will be a female he hangs around with, and then he'll go and sing over there, and there'll be another female."

I laughed, and while I had been doing my best to avoid anthropomorphizing, it was difficult not to compare cerulean warbler breeding behavior with human breeding behavior again. "Brood adoption" by a parent who is not biologically related to the offspring is very common in humans. So, of course, are "extra-pair copulations." A male human "mated" to more than one female—and having families with both of them—might be less common, but still occurs. I smiled to myself and glanced over my shoulder. Greg had almost finished setting up the mist net, so I thanked Randy and went to help prepare for banding. As Greg and I readied the decoy and the recorded call, Randy moved off further down the ridge in search of more nests.

Greg and I had barely scurried off to hide when a male cerulean warbler—probably the one whose nest was being constructed above us—flew into the net. We rushed over, and Greg began to untangle the bird. "Now we're making this look too easy for you," he said, smiling.

I sat down on the dried oak leaves and picked up the clipboard. Once the bird was free of the net, Greg sat down too, slipped the bird into the brown paper lunch bag, and attached the scale. "Nine point five grams for the weight," he told me.

"He's a little bit chubby," I said, making the notation.

"Yeah, he's a decent size," Greg agreed, readying the band and banding pliers.

"You're monstrously huge," I told the bird. The warbler twisted his head around and began to nip at Greg's fingers. "Watch out," I warned, "he'll bite you."

"He's ferocious," Greg chuckled. "His number is 53624. For the color bands, I'll do red over silver again, and red over blue." Greg gently squeezed the bands around the bird's thin gray legs. "And his age...ASY." He took the small silver ruler out of the bag. "Wing, 67. And the tail's 40. Fat...zero. What else we got?"

I scanned the rest of the form. "Um...that's it."

"Good. Done. You want him?"

"Sure," I said. Greg passed me the bird. After posing for a quick picture, I opened my hand and the cerulean warbler flew up into the trees, in the direction of the partially built nest.

"Easy!" said Greg cheerfully. The entire process—capturing, untangling, weighing, banding, measuring, releasing—took just ten minutes.

"Well," Greg sighed, unhooking the net from the rings on the rope, "Want to call it a day? It's one o'clock already." Ceruleans, like most other diurnal bird species, become less active in the heat of the afternoon and therefore more difficult to capture.

"Sure," I said. In the excitement of watching the nest and banding the bird, I'd forgotten my tiredness, stinkiness, and general soreness. Since we'd be returning to Snake Ridge the next morning to band more ceruleans, we left the banding poles near a fallen tree along the logging road and made our way triumphantly down the mountain.

EIGHT

★

MADE IN THE SHADE

REG AND I PULLED INTO the gravel parking lot at Lantz Farm around two, and I suddenly remembered that I had a six-pack of beer in the cooler in the back of my Jeep. I'd bought it on my way to Jacksonburg the day before in the hopes that it would endear me to my hosts. I popped the tailgate and slid the top off the cooler; amazingly, a few cubes of ice still floated inside and the bottles were frosty. "I don't know if you drink beer, but I brought some," I said, pulling the six-pack out of the cooler.

Greg's face lit up. "I drink beer," he said, "but there's a rule that I strictly follow about not transporting alcohol in state vehicles, so there's not usually any out here."

"Well, I didn't come in a state vehicle," I shrugged.

"No, you didn't," he said, smiling, and we walked across the field to the barn.

The beer went in the refrigerator, and I finally went to the shower for a "warm mineral bath." I turned on the water, which was scalding hot and smelled strongly of sulfur. The cement around the bottom wall of the shower was stained orange. I hoped the local residents of Wetzel County didn't drink that water; I'm not sure what sulfur does to a body healthwise, but its smell and taste were highly unpleasant. It was wet, however, and I would have bathed in the pond out back if it meant rinsing several days of dried sweat from my body.

The faucet in the shower confused me, and as I stood under the spray, the water grew hotter and hotter. This sort of thing happens to me with surprising frequency—because I was too embarrassed to go back inside and ask how to work the shower, I fumbled around, getting scalded, until I gave up and decided to suffer. I somehow managed to wash myself and my hair before my flesh burned off.

Back inside the barn, I heated a cup of miso soup in the microwave and sat down at the long folding table in the common area. Greg sat across from me, his banding bag open in front of him as he organized the equipment inside. Dr. Wood had told me that Greg had an interest in Latin America, and that I should ask him to talk about some of the problems ceruleans face on their wintering grounds.

"Well," Greg began, "I'm concerned about the habitat in the tropics because ceruleans already live in relatively narrow bands down there."

I sipped my soup slowly and folded one of my sore (but relatively clean) legs under me. "The habitat is in danger because of coffee production, right?"

"Yes," Greg nodded. "Full-sun coffee is bad. As quickly as I can say that."

As the demand for coffee rises, more and more small-scale, traditional farms are converted to full-sun plantations. According to the Coffee Research Institute, coffee plants (which are native to Ethiopia) were brought to the Americas for cultivation in the early 1720s. Until recently, in South America these coffee shrubs were grown in the shade of the primary forest's canopy. In Colombia, Venezuela, Ecuador, Peru, and Bolivia, most Arabica coffee is grown on the slopes of the Andes Mountains at elevations of four thousand to six thousand feet—in the same approximate elevation range as wintering cerulean warblers and other Neotropical migratory birds. Biologists in Colombia estimate that at least 60 percent and perhaps more than 90 percent of the cerulean warbler's original wintering habitat has been lost. Ceruleans are known to forage in the canopy's tall trees that provide shade for coffee shrubs; if these trees are cleared to make way for full-sun coffee farms, the birds lose their winter homes.

In the last twenty-five years, many shade-grown coffee farms have been converted to full-sun because the coffee plants can be grown more quickly and produce more beans. But since the beans are not allowed to remain on the plant for as long a period of time, the result is weaker-tasting, less-acidic coffee. Besides the coffee's flavor, the conversion to full-sun plantations has other detrimental effects. The Coffee Research Institute warns that on a full-sun farm "production is higher, but fertilizers, pesticides, and herbicides are often used." In a heavy rainstorm these chemicals can be carried down mountain slopes to the rivers, streams, and towns below. Handling dangerous chemicals could also put the workers—often peasant farmers, or *campesinos*—at risk.

Fortunately, American consumers still have the option to purchase coffee grown and harvested using more responsible methods. Several certifications exist for coffee—organic, Fair-Trade, Equal Exchange, shade-grown, Bird Friendly, Rainforest Friendly, and others—and while the certifications differ, many coffees are double- or triple-certified. In general, buying coffee with *any* certification is more socially and environmentally responsible than buying coffee without certification.

"As long as it's certified by someone," Greg said, "for the most part you can find out about who certified it and what their qualifications are on their webpages. There are folks who try to market shade-grown coffee that's not necessarily certified, in which case you have to wonder, what's it shaded by?"

"What do you mean—the coffee shrubs might be shaded by a big umbrella or something?" I asked.

Greg laughed. "It can actually be worse than an umbrella. The coffee can be shaded by eucalyptus trees, which are an introduced species. Eucalyptus grows very fast, which makes it a great second resource for farmers because they can cut the eucalyptus down and sell that, too, but the trees suck all the nutrients out of the soil because they grow so fast. And since they're an introduced species, there are not a whole lot of insects that like to hang out on them. So they're really not the best trees for birds. You could claim that coffee shaded by eucalyptus is 'shade-grown,' but is it part of a functioning system? No.

"There are other situations," Greg continued, "where there are multiple layers of different sorts of marketable produce. Maybe coffee on the bottom, then papaya over that, and over that, bananas, and over that, some sort of tree species." While this kind of agriculture is better than full-sun or eucalyptus, it still isn't as desirable as primary forest. "But I think one of the biggest problems," he said, "is that if you walked up to the average American and asked, 'Have you ever heard of shade-grown coffee?' they'd probably say, 'No.' So a lot of this comes down to education. If people don't know about shade-grown coffee, they're not going to buy it."

I nodded and sipped my soup.

Greg leaned back in the folding metal chair and continued. "It also comes down to who's responsible for this sort of thing. You have the coffee farmer, the person who's marketing the coffee, and the person who's consuming it. For the most part, in my opinion, the responsibility falls on the consumer. The farmers—they don't have much of a choice. They're poor, they're doing the best they can to get by, and they don't have the ability to make a whole lot of choices as far as what they can and cannot change. And then, to some degree, the marketing folks, they might have something to do with this, but the marketing folks are driven by what the consumers want. It all seems to fall on the consumers."

"So," I asked, wiping a drip of soup from my chin, "where do cerulean warblers fit in? Who cares?"

Greg smiled, then looked up at the plywood ceiling and thought for a moment. "Well, in the end, I think it's our responsibility to do the best we can to maintain what we already have. The interconnectedness of all these different species needs to be maintained. If we start dropping off species here and there, in the beginning it might not seem like much, but you got to kind of wonder where you hit a tipping point. Where you disrupt something."

"It's like Jenga," I said.

"Totally," Greg agreed, nodding. "You got to wonder how many of those blocks you can pull out…"

"Before the whole thing falls down," I finished.

"Yep. Exactly. And with shade coffee, we're working toward a balance between people, economics, and conservation. This species could show how we could pull in experts from different areas and make things better for everyone. I think it's very possible to make habitat on the wintering ground—and on the migratory route for that matter—much more secure for ceruleans and, at the same time, make things better for the farmers who are working those lands. And, at the same time, also making folks on the breeding grounds happy by maintaining high population numbers. Potentially, then, the species would not have to be put on the endangered species list, and therefore would not affect thousands of people who are working in the mountains of Central Appalachia. I think it's a win-win-win situation all the way around." Greg smiled again. "It's just a matter of getting the word out to folks about what's going on and how easy it is for everyone to chip in a little bit. Buy shade-grown or 'songbird' coffees."

Songbird coffees—widely available online and at many nature and garden stores—are usually certified as shade-grown and often organic or Fair-Trade as well. These coffees are marketed specifically to consumers who care about conserving migratory and wintering habitat for songbirds. The Wild Birds Unlimited franchise sells its own line of songbird coffee, as does the National Audubon Society. The Smithsonian Migratory Bird Center certifies coffees as Bird Friendly. The American Bird Conservancy, in cooperation with the American Birding Association and Fundación ProAves Colombia, offers twelve-ounce bags of Cerulean Warbler Conservation Coffee. Its bright-blue foil package sports a photograph of an equally bright-blue male cerulean warbler. The text on the back begins, "Let's Save the Cerulean Warbler," and goes on to explain the reasons for the bird's shrinking Colombian habitat. The label promises that purchasing this coffee will help "ProAves Colombia protect bird habitat and the cultural heritage of the region, ensuring a warm winter welcome for the Cerulean Warbler."

Colombia is famous throughout the world for its rich coffee; the image of Juan Valdez and his mule, "Conchita," is familiar wherever coffee is consumed. It is perhaps less well-known that Colombia also harbors more bird species than any other country in the world; it boasts a total of more than 1,800 resident and migratory species, including many Neotropical birds that spend the winter in Colombia's varied habitats. In addition to the cerulean, Colombia's Andean *intermontane* region shelters wintering Canada warblers, Blackburnian warblers, rose-breasted grosbeaks, black-and-white warblers, summer tanagers, and a host of others. In 2002, the conservation organization ProAves Colombia established the Cerulean Warbler Bird Reserve in Colombia's Santander province; the Reserve is surrounded by shade-grown coffee farms. The ceruleans we'd banded earlier linked me, Greg, the state of West Virginia, and indeed the entire Appalachian Bird Conservation Region with those coffee farmers on the slopes of the Andes in Colombia.

I finished my miso soup, tore open a granola bar for dessert, and Greg and I went out the back door of the barn to watch the ponds. The beer chilling in the refrigerator tempted us, but we decided to be polite and wait for the others to get back from the field before drinking it. We sat on the back stairs of the barn and watched barn swallows skim the surface of the brown water. I heard a trilling birdsong that began slowly but gained speed. "Field sparrow?" I ventured.

Greg shook his head. "No, prairie warbler."

"Hmm," I mumbled. I hated to be wrong about birdsongs (if I indeed had been wrong!).

We watched an orchard oriole working on a basket nest in a small maple tree along the pond. Soft-shell turtles poked their noses out of the water while a white-eyed vireo's strange notes burbled from thick shrubs across the field. The exhaustion that I'd forgotten about returned suddenly, and I went back to my room to "read." I woke up a few hours later when Patrick and Aaron returned to the barn. They'd left Randy on Snake Ridge because he'd wanted to continue searching for nests. Patrick would pick him up at seven—after Randy had spent a total of thirteen straight volunteer hours in the field. Aaron had to drive back to Morgantown that night for West Virginia University's graduation, so he left shortly after returning to the barn.

By 7:30 or so, Greg, Randy, Patrick, and I were seated around the barn's folding table, happily sipping pale ale and talking about cerulean warblers. Randy had found three cerulean nests and a score of other birds' nests, as well. Patrick imitated an agitated male cerulean warbler, flapping his arms stiffly while saying, "You wanna piece of this?" Halfway through my beer I began to giggle, and by 8:30 we all decided to call it a night. I lay down on my narrow bed, still exhausted despite my nap.

I opened my eyes just before my alarm was set to go off at 5:00 a.m. I stretched out and yawned. My arms and legs were sore, but it was a good, healthy sore. I blinked a few times and realized that I'd heard no frogs and no trains all night long. I hadn't thrashed around in bed or checked my watch. I swung my legs over the side of the small bed, turned on the light, and began to quietly stuff dirty laundry

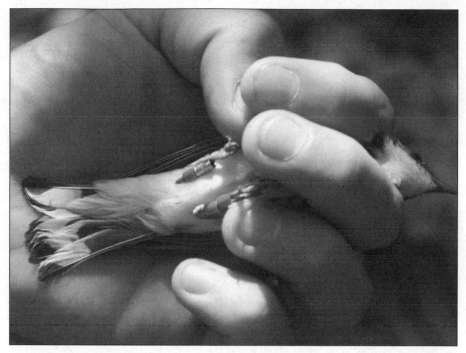

A banded cerulean.

into my bags. I would accompany Greg and the others into the field this morning, but I would leave my Jeep at the entrance to the Wildlife Management Area. After a few hours of banding, I planned to walk back down the steep road to my Jeep and head back to Virginia.

I ate a breakfast bar, swigged some warm spring water from my jug, and loaded up my gear. I followed the other vehicles, parked my Jeep by the gate, and then rode in the Blazer that Greg drove. The other folks followed in their government Jeep, but then they parked it along the road and all piled in the Blazer. The day before, as Greg and I had walked down the incredibly steep hill after our morning of banding, a pickup truck had rumbled up past us—so much for not being allowed to drive, Greg figured, so today we would ride all the way to the top of Snake Ridge. It felt a bit like climbing a hill on a roller coaster, and at times I couldn't see over the Blazer's white hood because of the steep angle.

When we finally reached the top, we all got out, and like the day before, the others prepared to head off to search for nests while Greg and I would band. I said my good-byes to Randy and Patrick, and Greg and I went off to find the mist-net poles that we'd hidden by the fallen tree. Well-rested, alert, and generally more confident, I marched through the woods behind Greg with a smile on my face and a buzzy cerulean song in my heart.

AFTER A FEW HOURS IN the field, I strode back down the steep logging road, talking to myself and listening to the birds all around me—black-and-white warbler, scarlet tanager, ovenbird, and the ubiquitous red-eyed vireo. The woods smelled of warm, dry leaves, and wild geraniums grew along the road. Greg and I had banded two male ceruleans that morning before it was time for me to leave, for a total of six ceruleans during my visit—BBL numbers 53621, 22, 23, 24, 25, and 26. Each had a red band over a silver band on the right leg and various color combinations on the left.

I smiled at the trees and the unseen birds, and the happiness that had filled me at Cooper's Rock crept slowly back. My legs ached, my hair smelled like sulfur, and I had a four-hour drive ahead of me, but at that moment, I was the only human in sight. The birds and trees outnumbered the people. The handful of humans who *were* up here on this ridge loved cerulean warblers, even if they weren't allowed to say that for fear they'd be risking their scientific objectivity. But love was obvious in the gentle way that Greg handled the delicate birds while banding them, and in Randy's smile when he described the sit-and-spin and the whisper song.

The peace of the forest was abruptly cut short, however, by the buzzing of a small engine somewhere ahead of me and off the road to the right. It became louder and louder, and finally a four-wheeled all-terrain vehicle rumbled out from a side trail and stopped on the rocky road just ahead of me. The driver was a thin, elderly man wearing a red-and-white flannel shirt and jeans despite the heat. The ATV had what appeared to be a homemade roof—sort of a blue tarp tied to a frame.

"Goin' down to the gate?" the man asked over the rumble of the engine. "Wanna ride?" He slid forward on the seat to make room for me. I noticed a small black poodle-like dog strapped to the seat behind him. The dog wagged his tail and wiggled as I got closer. Anyone who took his poodle for rides on his ATV had to be alright.

"Sure," I said, swinging my leg over the seat. "Thanks." The little dog squirmed behind me and proceeded to lick my ears as we started down the hill. I peeked over the man's shoulder and noticed how gnarled and wrinkled his fingers were as he gripped the handlebars. His brown leather work boots were crusted with mud, and the back rim of his black baseball cap was ringed with dried sweat. He spoke over his shoulder to me, but because of the rumble of the engine and his thick accent, I couldn't understand much of what he said.

"The boys are putting in pipes," I think he told me as we passed an idle construction vehicle parked alongside the dirt road. He cackled and steered around a large rock. I think he continued to tell me about the pipes, but I said very little other than an occasional "Oh?" or "Yeah?" I had no idea what he was talking about.

"Is my buddy giving you enough room?" he shouted over his shoulder, and laughed again.

"Yep," I said, "I'm fine."

"You looking for birds?"

"I am," I told him.

"Got lots of birds here," he said, "lots of rattlesnakes, too. I got lots of birds at my feeders. I got this one bird who comes, he has a red ring around his neck and a red spot on his head."

"I'm looking for cerulean warblers," I said, leaning to one side so he could hear me better. "Little blue birds with white chests."

"Oh yeah, I got lots of those blue birds at my feeders, lots of them," he nodded.

"Yeah," I said, though I knew he was probably referring to blue jays or maybe indigo buntings. Since cerulean warblers eat almost exclusively insects, they have no reason to visit bird feeders. I didn't think it would be possible to explain that over the growl of the engine, so I didn't try.

When we reached the gate and my Jeep, the man slowed the ATV to a stop but left the engine running. He spryly hopped off and turned to help me. As I swung my leg over the seat, a second ATV rumbled out of the woods and pulled up next to us. Its driver, a burly, flannel-shirted man with a thick brown beard, nodded at the old man and then said to me, sternly, "If you're walking around up there, you better watch out for them rattlesnakes."

I assured him that I would, and that I hadn't seen any. I noticed that the man's left eye was squinted slightly and ringed with a deep, purple bruise. I wondered what the other guy looked like.

"Rattlesnakes sure are pretty," said the elderly man, smiling and winking at me, "but deadly. Last summer I killed one seventy-two inches long."

I decided not to try to persuade him to allow rattlesnakes to live, and as the two men began to discuss the progress on the mysterious pipes, I said good-bye to the black poodle on the seat of the ATV. He wiggled and wagged his tail and stood up on his hind legs to lick my face. When the old man noticed, he turned to us and laughed. I thanked him, and as I began to walk to my Jeep, he called after me, "If you ever need a ride up or out of these mountains again, just holler for me and my buddy!"

I waved and pulled onto the road. As I left the Lewis Wetzel Wildlife Management Area behind me, I smiled. There were still a lot of decent people in the world—people who cared about the poverty of other people half a world away. People who volunteered long hours because they enjoy what they do. People who, out of simple kindness, offered rides out of steep places. People still loved their dogs and their bird feeders, and worried about strangers stepping on rattlesnakes.

NINE

*

ALMOST LEVEL

ESSE PULLED OUR COMPACT SILVER car into a parking space at the West Virginia Welcome Center near the town of Princeton. It was a cloudless Saturday morning in late May, one week since my trip to the Lewis Wetzel Wildlife Management Area. Earlier this morning, Jesse and I had loaded up our dog, Mr. Bones, and our camping gear and headed back to West Virginia's mountains. Jesse had been working long hours in the veterinary teaching hospital, and this was his first weekend without a patient in the Intensive Care Unit. This would be our first camping and birding trip together this spring, and our last for at least a few weeks; Jesse would be spending his next three-week rotation at a wildlife disease laboratory in Georgia, and I would be staying at home in Virginia.

After buying a *Best of the Mountain Stage* CD at the Welcome Center, we merged onto Interstate 77. Our destination was the Kanawha State Forest, located just seven miles south of Charleston, West Virginia's state capital and largest metropolitan area. According to the Cornell Lab of Ornithology's Cerulean Warbler Atlas Project, the Kanawha State Forest harbored the second-highest density of breeding cerulean warblers in the state, just behind the New River Gorge's Garden Mountain Area and tied with Guyandotte Mountain and vicinity. Like the Lewis Wetzel Wildlife Management Area (which held the third-place spot, according to the Atlas), the Kanawha State Forest provided critical cerulean habitat in the heart of their core breeding range. After my experience in Lewis Wetzel, I felt confident that I knew how to find ceruleans, and I looked forward to showing off my new skills; Jesse and I had something of a healthy birding rivalry between us, and he usually emerged victorious. Perhaps this time things would be different.

After passing the exits for Ghent and Flattop Mountain (areas notorious for ice and blowing snow in the wintertime), we pulled off the interstate near the town of Pax in Fayette County. My great-great-grandfather William Hosey, an immigrant from Ireland, settled in the town of Dothan, about ten miles from here, in 1911 or 1912, to work in one of the region's many coal mines. He moved here after his first wife, Julia, had tragically died in a kitchen fire. Shortly after arriving in Dothan, William married a local woman, Angeline Hurt, and the two lived in coal-company housing along the Lick Fork of Paint Creek. According to our map, this smaller road—County Route 5—followed the Toney Fork of Paint Creek, and would lead us through some of southern West Virginia's most notorious coalfields and near several mountaintop removal mines. Mountaintop removal represented one of the biggest threats to cerulean breeding habitat, and this was the part of West Virginia where it was most widespread. We planned to follow Toney Fork Road until it met Clear Fork Road (County Route 1) in the town of Clear Creek. Then, near Whitesville, we'd turn onto the larger Coal River Road, which we'd follow through Boone County until it met Highway 94. We'd head north, and just before Hernshaw we'd take a left up County Route 42 to the back entrance of the Kanawha State Forest.

Six months earlier, in October, I'd toured mountaintop removal sites in southern West Virginia. The tour, sponsored by the Ohio Valley Environmental Coalition, began with a visit to Kayford Mountain—a massive mine site about thirty-five miles from Charleston. Afterward, I flew over the area in a small four-seat airplane operated by a pilot from the nonprofit organization South Wings. The secondary roads Jesse and I would take to get to the Kanawha State Forest wound through the areas I had flown over. From the air, it looked as if bombs had been dropped on southern West Virginia; from the copilot's seat of the plane, I had looked down on massive brown ditches; flattened, grass-covered "reclaimed" mountaintops; and ominous black lakes of coal slurry. It was horrifying and far more pervasive than I had realized. I was curious to find out how mountaintop removal looked from this different perspective—from the public roads and nearby towns.

Shortly after veering away from the interstate, County Route 5 narrowed to a one-lane dirt road curving between modular homes and well-kept trailers. West Virginia's state flower, the rhododendron, bloomed around many front porches, its round globes of purple blossoms and waxy, dark-green leaves brightening the roadsides. An elderly man pushed a lawnmower over the spring grass of his fenced-in yard. After only a mile or so, the road turned sharply and began to climb the mountain. Jesse downshifted, and as our small, fiberglass, manual-transmission car skidded on the road's dry dirt, I began to wish we'd brought the Jeep instead. The road continued to climb and switch-backed again; the forest thickened and tree branches stretched above us. Jesse stopped the car often (more often than I liked) to stick his head out the window and listen to birdsong. No matter how many times I asked him to *please* not stop the car in the dead center of the steep, winding, narrow road, he refused, and accused me of being too careful, warning me that I'd miss out on things if I didn't take chances now and then. I reminded him of the distinct difference between "taking chances" and plain stupidity.

When the road finally leveled out a bit, we arrived at a four-way intersection, which was curious because our map didn't show any adjoining roads. We pulled over to the side this time (instead of just stopping in the middle) to investigate. One of the dirt roads led up the mountain to our left; a sign near this road announced Island Fork Construction, LTD, Mt. Top 4 Mine, and listed three permit numbers—one for a surface mine, one for a haul road, and the third from the Mine Safety and Health Administration. Another sign instructed all persons entering the property to first check in at the mine office. Across the intersection, near the other dirt road, stood a sign for Pioneer Fuel Corporation's Simmons Fork Mining, Inc. This sign listed permit numbers, too—two of the permit numbers corresponded to the Ewing Fork Number 1 and Number 2 Surface Mines. Certainly I could have seen these mines from the air, but from where we stood at the intersection, we could only see dirt roads leading into the forest. A Northern flicker swooped in front of us and disappeared into the trees. How far could that bird fly before reaching the edge of a surface mine? Jesse and I climbed back in the car and continued on County Route 5, which wound down the other side of the mountain. We crossed into Raleigh County and turned onto Clear Fork Road. Just a few miles to the south and west was Raleigh County's most famous public school— Marsh Fork Elementary.

During my flyover of this area, the pilot had circled Marsh Fork Elementary several times so I could appreciate the danger that faced the more than two hundred children who attend school there. The school sits in a hollow along the Marsh Fork of the Big Coal River, next door to a Massey Energy coal processing plant, where recently mined coal is washed and separated from rocks and dust. The plant's coal loading silo looms just 225 feet from the school's playground, where children climb across monkey bars, swoosh down sliding boards, and chase each other during recess. After the coal is ground up and washed at the processing plant, the resulting liquid waste—toxic black "slurry"—is stored behind a dam of compacted dirt, rocks, and soil constructed in a valley just 400 yards from the school. While its exact components can vary, some coal slurry contains mercury, selenium, arsenic, and other potentially harmful chemicals.

Earthen dams like the one near Marsh Fork Elementary sometimes fail. A tragic example occurred in nearby Logan County, West Virginia, in 1972; dams near the town of Buffalo Creek—holding back 132 million gallons of coal slurry—collapsed after heavy rains. In just three minutes, 125 people were killed, more than a thousand injured, and 4,000 left homeless. According to Shirley Stewart Burns's important book *Bringing Down the Mountains: The Impact of Mountaintop Removal on Southern West Virginia Communities*, "more than one hundred similar impoundments exist all over West Virginia." Burns reports that, since the 1972 disaster, at least eighty miles of streams in the state have been compromised by slurry spills. She states that one slurry impoundment here in Raleigh County "is more than nine hundred feet tall. That is more than two hundred feet higher than the Hoover Dam."

The earthen dam behind Marsh Fork Elementary holds back as many as three billion gallons of coal slurry—twenty-two times *more* slurry than the amount that deluged Buffalo Creek. Behind Marsh Fork's slurry lake is an active mountaintop removal mine. I cannot claim to be a mining engineer or expert on mine design; however, common sense dictates that blasting apart a mountain a few hundred yards behind an earthen dam is a bad idea. Could explosions on the mountain destabilize the dam? If that dam broke, how quickly would three billion gallons of coal slurry engulf the elementary school, drowning all those little children? Parents and relatives of the students protested and petitioned their elected officials for help, and they have been promised a new school three miles from its existing location; construction should be completed by 2012.

One of the men responsible for the new school is Ed Wiley, a former West Virginia coal miner whose granddaughter attended Marsh Fork Elementary. I had the pleasure of meeting Mr. Wiley at an event sponsored by the Ohio Valley Environmental Coalition. Tall, fit, and wearing a camouflage hat advertising a turkey hunting organization, he recounted picking up his granddaughter (whom he affectionately called "Possum") from school because she frequently became nauseous and lightheaded. When he realized that other children often went home sick from Marsh Fork Elementary, Wiley started asking questions about the nearby coal processing plant and slurry impoundment. He quit mining coal, met with West Virginia's governor and other elected officials, and in 2006 he walked 455 miles from Charleston to Washington, D.C., to raise awareness about Marsh Fork Elementary School. When Mr. Wiley tearfully said that, "The first ones to get it will be our little children," he made me cry, too, and his frustration was contagious.

Unfortunately, the health problems of coalfield residents don't stop with nausea and lightheadedness. A recent study analyzed medical data gathered from West Virginia University, the West Virginia Geological and Economic Survey, and the West Virginia Department of Health and Human Resources. The study, published in the *American Journal of Public Health*, found that in West Virginia "as coal production [in an area] increased, health status worsened, and rates of cardiopulmonary disease, lung disease, cardiovascular disease, diabetes, and kidney disease increased." People in the coalfields have a 70 percent increased risk for kidney disease, have a 64 percent increased risk for chronic obstructive pulmonary disease (COPD), and are 30 percent more likely to have high blood pressure. What permanent health risks do growing children face by attending school next to a coal processing plant?

I do not believe that a situation like the one at Marsh Fork Elementary could occur in another part of the country. In addition to consistently finishing near the bottom of state-by-state comparisons economically, West Virginians are forced to combat stereotypes at every turn. While prejudice affects everyone at some point, it seems that mainstream American culture has exempted West Virginia and the rest of Appalachia from equality and political correctness; for some reason, hillbilly jokes are not generally considered offensive, and twenty-first century Appalachian poverty is laughable. Movies like *Wrong Turn*, *The Descent*, and of course *Deliverance* depict the region's residents as disfigured, dangerous inbreds who rape, murder, and sometimes even eat unfortunate tourists. Dehumanizing people makes it easier to ignore them, even when they're in dire need of help—like Possum and the other innocent children who attend Marsh Fork Elementary, who risk their lives everyday for our nation's "cheap" electricity.

JESSE CONTINUED TO DRIVE ALONG Clear Fork Road, past small farms surrounded by pink peonies in full bloom. We approached the town of Dorothy, population 300. According to our map, Kayford Mountain was just to our north, on the right side of the road as we drove west through a valley. Amazingly—but not surprisingly—no signs of mountaintop removal coal mining were visible from the road. Folks sat on porches, mowed lawns, and tended gardens. The mountain that rose to our right, above the peaceful homes, looked forested and stable. But this was a lie, an illusion.

I will never forget standing at the wooded edge of local resident Larry Gibson's property last fall, and staring down into a vast hole that used to be part of Kayford Mountain. Far below me, massive earth-moving machines had rumbled across a barren, grayish-brown expanse. The mine site looked like a freakish amphitheater roughly carved by a colossal ice cream scoop. Behind me, red maples had quivered in the October breeze as their leaves floated down around my shoulders. A blanket of tiny white asters bravely grew close to the rocky edge, clinging to ground that in

This vast hole used to be part of Kayford Mountain.

a few months would probably be gone. I remembered hearing a small flock of cedar waxwings behind me; they flew beyond the treetops, into the empty air above the barren hole, and, seeming shocked, quickly turned and headed back for the tree line. I knew how they felt. Seeing Kayford Mountain up close made me realize that the term "mountaintop removal" is far too gentle; it reminds me of "pest removal" or "unwanted hair removal." Not only is the *mountain* removed, but everything on, in, and around it: forests, birds, bears, deer, homes, cemeteries, flowers, butterflies, streams. Mountaintop removal coal mining is like using a baseball bat to remove a tooth—it may be cheaper and quicker than the dentist, but it can leave behind quite a mess.

While visiting Kayford last October, I'd collected some of the leaves that had fallen near the mine's edge—sugar maple, tulip tree, and red oak. On the walk up to the precipice that day, I heard the *Hey there, Sweetie* call of a Carolina chickadee and the frantic laugh of a red-bellied woodpecker. Goldfinches flitted across the path ahead of me. Surely cerulean warblers had once lived on Kayford Mountain; I imagined their confusion when they arrived back in West Virginia after an exhausting three-thousand-mile flight, hormones revving up for the breeding season, only to find that their entire mountain, the territory they'd evolved to return to year after year, was *gone*. Completely and inexplicably missing.

I remember peering down into the gray pit below me at Kayford Mountain and watching the earth-moving machines at work. From the mine's edge, hundreds of feet above the floor of the active site, they appeared small. One piece of equipment, which resembled a bulldozer, slowly crawled up a makeshift road and disappeared behind a gray hill. Oversized dump trucks rumbled in and out of the site, leaving clouds of gray dust in their wakes. Regular-sized pickup trucks, parked near a green porta-potty, looked like Matchbox toys next to the mining equipment. I remember that I toed the loose rocks and gravel at the edge of the hole with my boot and noticed that some of the stones around my feet were black; I bent down and picked up a dull chunk of coal. I rubbed its smooth, cool surface with my thumb before closing my fist around it. Below me, over the constant growl of the equipment, I heard the repeated beep of a truck in reverse. As I stared down at them that October morning, I thought about the urban legend that involved dropping a penny from the top of the Empire State Building; I wondered what kind of damage my lump of coal could do if thrown from there. I watched the machines creeping below me and thought of their tires, their gas tanks, their engines, and all of their breakable parts. Luckily, though, I silenced my inner Edward Abbey, and that chunk of coal from Kayford Mountain now sits on a bookshelf in my office.

As Jesse and I drove along Clear Fork Road through Dorothy, I gazed up at the seemingly intact side of the mountain. If the mine had been readily visible from the road, every out-of-towner and tree-hugger with a camera (like me) would be snapping pictures of it, which was probably why they kept it hidden. Seeing the mine everyday would also be incredibly unnerving for local residents; how scary and disheartening would it be to live at the base of a carved-out mountain? If it's not visible, then perhaps everyone could pretend it wasn't there. As we passed well-tended gardens and porches hung with American flags, I was reminded of the famous short story "The Lottery," in which the fictional town's residents happily gather to stone to death one of their own because of "tradition." Jesse and I drove on in silence.

NOT FAR PAST DOROTHY, CLEAR Fork and Marsh Fork merge to form the Big Coal River. Clear Fork Road ends at the larger Coal River Road (State Route 3) near the rivers' junction. Jesse and I turned north toward Whitesville, following the river into Boone County. The Big Coal flows north until it empties into the Kanawha River near Charleston; then the Kanawha flows west out of Charleston until it reaches the Ohio River, their confluence occurring near the town of Point Pleasant, made famous by the legendary "Moth Man." According to the West Virginia Coal Association, Boone County is West Virginia's leading coal producer from both surface and underground mines, and it holds more coal reserves than any other county in the state. Coal also employs more people in Boone than in any other county in West Virginia; in 2005, 3,063 of the county's approximately 25,000 residents worked in its coal mines. In many ways, Boone County is capital of the coalfields.

Jesse pulled our car into the One Stop convenience store near the intersection. A large blue and white "Friends of Coal" banner hung on a chain-link fence by a dumpster nearby, and the parking lot and gas pumps were surprisingly crowded. As I slammed the car door shut, I was suddenly glad we hadn't taken my Jeep, with its "Friends of the Mountains" sticker on one side of its back window and "For the Birds" sticker on the other. After using the store's restrooms, Jesse selected an egg salad sandwich from a rack of plastic-bagged choices, and I bought a gooey Milky Way bar. As we got back in the car and prepared to continue on our way, I noticed some anti-George Bush graffiti spray-painted on a silver guardrail. West Virginia's contradictions never failed to amaze me; in both 2000 and 2004, the state voted to elect a Republican president, but during those same years, it elected a Democratic governor. Many politicians in West Virginia, both Republican and Democrat, repeat the "coal is our heritage" mantra to win votes and industry endorsements, yet, according to the West Virginia Coal Association, the top three coal-producing companies in West Virginia are headquartered out of state—tops is Richmond, Virginia–based Massey Energy, followed by Pittsburgh's CONSOL Energy and St. Louis's Arch Coal. How long do you have to do something for it to become "heritage," anyway? Fifty years? A hundred? Five hundred? Have non-American Indians lived in

North America long enough to claim anything we've begun here as "heritage"?

I pondered these questions as Jesse and I headed north up Coal River Road, which now seemed to be called Boone Street. We soon found ourselves in the town of Sylvester, population 195, home of the "Sylvester Dustbusters." In November 1997, Elk Run Coal Company, owned by Massey Energy, applied for a permit from the West Virginia Department of Environmental Protection to build a coal preparation plant just outside the Sylvester town limits. Despite protests from the mayor and town council, the permit was issued, and within five months the plant began operating. The townspeople soon noticed coal dust on their windows, porches, cars, and finally, inside their homes. Trucks with coal piled high in their beds rumbled through the small town, cracking the pavement of Sylvester's streets under their weight.

During last October's tour I met two of the Sylvester Dustbusters, Pauline Canterberry and Mary Miller. These inspiring women—both in their seventies— took the coal-dust matter into their own hands. Pauline Canterberry said, "Our 'golden years' have become black years." In an effort to save their community, they began to document Sylvester's new problems. They videotaped billowing clouds of dust, dust-covered homes, and people sweeping their sidewalks and hosing off their cars. For two years, the women went from house to house wiping coal dust from railings, porches, and windows; they even saved the dirty paper towels they used to collect this evidence. These two Dustbusters, along with the majority of the town's residents, complained to the West Virginia Department of Environmental Protection. After several years of complaining and presenting their evidence without satisfactory results, the people of Sylvester stepped up their efforts. They contacted national news media, joined environmental organizations, and participated in marches and public protests against Massey Energy. Then, in 2001, more than half of the town's residents sued Massey for violating the West Virginia Surface Mining Act by not controlling the coal dust. In 2002, the West Virginia Department of Environmental Protection ordered Massey to construct a large nylon dome over the mounds of coal at the plant. In theory, this dome would stop the dust from billowing over Sylvester. But the dome didn't stop the town's problems; residents still complained about air and noise pollution from the processing plant. Finally, in 2003, a jury sided with the people of Sylvester, and ordered Massey to pay the plaintiffs almost $473,000 in damages. But the legal battles continue.

Jesse and I rolled through the picturesque town, discussing the Dustbusters, when we rounded a bend and saw it—on the left side of the road, beyond a house, the freakish white nylon dome rose above the tops of the trees that surrounded it. Our car swerved as we craned our necks to look. Jesse pulled off onto a side road and stopped the car.

"It kind of reminds me of the Biosphere," I ventured.

"Yeah," Jesse agreed, "the same geometric shapes."

An American flag flapped from a telephone pole alongside the road, and the irony of that scene—a home at the base of a dome (which covered massive piles of coal) and the symbol of our nation snapping smartly in the breeze in the foreground—warranted a photograph. So after snapping a few pictures, we pulled back onto Route 3 and drove slowly north, past the infamous coal processing plant. CSX railroad cars, heaped high with coal, waited on the tracks that ran along the banks of the river. As we passed more houses and local businesses, it became obvious to me why the Dustbusters had worked so hard to try to save their town. In addition to being tucked in a river valley between beautiful mountains, I imagined that in Sylvester kids can go trick-or-treating without having to worry about razor blades in apples, and the elderly probably didn't lock their front doors at night. I'd be willing to bet that neighbors knew each other's names. It seemed like a nice place to live—except for its coal plant and proximity to strip mines, of course. I wondered what effect all the billowing coal dust had on the area's non-human animals—deer, bear, and of course, cerulean warblers.

We left Sylvester behind us and continued to follow Route 3 north. We passed through several small towns nestled in the narrow river valley. Purple and pink rhododendron blossoms bloomed in many yards and grew wild alongside the road. Three or four coonhounds slept inside a chain-link pen next to a small house. Another house had a "Support the Troops" sign displayed in the corner of its freshly mown lawn. Large oak branches overhung the road, and the Big Coal River slugged along beside us, at times dwindling to the size of a small creek. The CSX railroad tracks ran along the river's opposite shore.

I rested my elbow on the open car window. "I think it's great," I said to Jesse, "that there are environmental activists in Boone County, West Virginia."

"Yes," Jesse agreed. "Their experience made them environmentalists because they felt their community was in danger. And then when the company wouldn't do anything about the pollution, that made them activists."

The Dustbusters' story inspired me—a few senior citizens in the rural West Virginia coalfields forced one of the nation's largest and most powerful energy companies to address the damage its processing plant had caused the town's residents. I smiled and tried to stretch my legs out in front of me. We didn't have much farther to go before reaching the Kanawha State Forest, and I was anxious to get out in the woods and start looking for ceruleans.

As we passed the Boone County Dog Pound, I reached back to pet Mr. Bones, who was curled on the floor behind my seat. Every time I see an animal shelter, I'm reminded of the day—almost a decade ago—that Jesse and I adopted a beagle-mix puppy from the Marion County Dog Pound near Fairmont, West Virginia. He sat in the back of his cage in the puppy room with his littermate and yipped at us. The pound's employee told us that someone had found a mother beagle and her pups in a box near a dumpster. We played with the two puppies and decided to take the one with the white tip on his tail. We didn't realize it at the time, but we had adopted (in my opinion) the smartest, most handsome, most snuggly dog in the entire world.

We rounded another bend and a four-wheeler headed toward us, speeding down the double yellow line in the center of the highway. The driver wore a black hooded sweatshirt with TOOL across the front, but no helmet. We sped past church after church—the Amazing Grace Fellowship, the Healing Stream Baptist Church, the Church of Christ, the Church of God of Seth, Comfort Presbyterian Church. Another four-wheeler, this one carrying two helmet-less passengers, drove the wrong way in the highway's left lane. We were going fifty miles an hour, and the ATV's driver kept up with us until we finally passed them. The driver had barbed wire tattooed around one bicep. The CSX train tracks continued to run alongside the highway as we passed Food Marts, used car dealerships, a pork barbeque stand, and yard sales. Dogs barked from fenced backyards, and people weed-whacked bushes around their porches.

Jesse and I realized we'd been driving in Boone County for quite some time and still hadn't been able to see any mountaintop removal mines from the road, but we knew they were all around us. Any user of the Internet can see satellite images of the vast mines and slurry impoundments by logging on to Google Maps and doing a bit of searching. While it may have been the original reason that communities like Sylvester and Keith sprang up, coal is a finite resource—sooner or later, it will all be gone, and what will be left of these ancient Appalachian Mountains in Boone County? Unless the Appalachian Regional Reforestation Initiative's efforts gain widespread acceptance and funding, Boone County could someday consist of flattened hills covered with hydro-seeded non-native grass species, polluted ground water, and diminished wildlife and natural beauty. Why—and perhaps more importantly, how—could anyone stay and make a living in a polluted, flood-prone area devoid of its supporting natural resources? If our country must mine, burn, and export coal, we should at least attempt to do it in a way that is sustainable and safe. Unless a pandemic or some other catastrophic disaster hits, the world and humans are probably going to be around for a long time. What happens when we use everything up?

"What's going to be left," said Jesse, downshifting as the road curved again, "is a flat, non-West Virginia kind of place, where no one can live and no one wants to visit."

Boone County's green mountains—imperiled and probably filled with coal—folded around us as we sped north.

TEN

★

ALMOST HEAVEN

The green rolling hills of West Virginia
Are the nearest place to heaven that I know.
Though the times are sad and drear,
And I cannot linger here,
They will keep me and never let me go.
—Bruce "Utah" Phillips

S JESSE AND I APPROACHED the Boone County town of Racine, we veered away from the Big Coal River onto Route 94. The mountains crowded the road, and it felt as if we were driving along the fold of a giant bedsheet. Just before the town of Hernshaw, we turned onto smaller County Route 42. The pavement gave way to dirt, and a brown sign indicated that we were four miles from the Kanawha State Forest, one of West Virginia's densest cerulean warbler breeding areas. Well-kept houses and trailers lined the road, several with trampolines in their backyards. We rounded a curve and suddenly were face to face with the dusty grill of an oncoming truck. I screamed and Jesse skidded onto the road's shoulder as the heavy truck roared past us, shaking our little fiberglass car. I spun in my seat to see if I could get the license plate number, but it was obscured by a cloud of dust. As the truck rounded the bend, I saw that its bed was heaped with coal.

After shouting obscenities that only we could hear, Jesse righted the car and drove on, and I grew even more anxious to get to our destination. Soon, another small dirt road veered off to the left, and as our County Route 42 steepened and began to climb up the mountain, we looked down at the other dirt road below us in the hollow; we saw drive-over truck scales and a few scattered piles of spilled coal on the ground. We guessed that the other road must lead to a mine, and that the truck that almost hit us was hauling coal a few miles north to Charleston and the Kanawha River. From there, the coal would probably be loaded onto barges or trains to be shipped elsewhere—perhaps to one of the thirty-three US states or twenty-five foreign countries that purchase West Virginia's coal.

Route 42 continued to climb, and as we left the houses and speeding coal trucks behind us, the foliage on both sides thickened. Jesse drove more slowly and stopped the car frequently to listen to birds singing; this didn't bother me as much as it had earlier, since I knew this road ended at the state forest and it seemed unlikely that we'd encounter any more traffic. The dense woods alongside the road were filled with towering, mature hardwoods; I recognized chestnut oak, red oak, and sugar maple. A pileated woodpecker swooped in front of our car, and an ovenbird chirped from the undergrowth.

We crept along, windows down, and almost on cue we heard the buzzy *zhr-zhrzhrZEEEE* of a male cerulean warbler. Jesse stopped the car and we held our breaths, listening for the bird. I tensed my entire body, as if that somehow would encourage the bird to sing again. Mr. Bones panted loudly behind me, and stood on the edge of the back door to stick his face out the open window. After a few moments of silence, the cerulean buzzed loudly again, and I whispered to Jesse, "It sounds like he's right above us."

"He probably is," Jesse whispered back. He put the car in gear, and we proceeded to crawl. The dusty road became steeper as we rounded a hairpin switchback. I looked beyond Jesse—out his driver's side window—and there, through a break in the trees, I could see the ridge opposite the one we were climbing. And I could see the brown, rocky edge of a strip mine.

"Stop!" I squealed, grabbing Jesse's arm. He hit the brakes, causing Mr. Bones to fall into the back of my seat. I pointed.

"Wow," said Jesse, putting the car in neutral and setting the emergency brake. "There it is, finally."

We stared at the opposite ridge's brown, flattened edge, devoid of greenery. I scrambled out of the car with my camera and hurriedly took pictures, as if the mine would disappear before I documented its existence. While I stood there in the shade of a towering red oak, clicking picture after picture of the barren ridge on the horizon, I heard the quick, buzzy cerulean song again, and my arms goosebumped in spite of the afternoon sun. It was tragically poetic—as I stood staring at a mountaintop removal mine, the fastest-declining warbler in the United States sang above me. How many ceruleans had once claimed territories on that opposite ridge? Where were they now? Had they returned from South America only to find their instinctual breeding grounds completely gone, destroyed by the very mine I was photographing?

In addition to destroying the ridge and forest, mountaintop removal mines fragment the remaining forest and create large-scale "edges." Petra Wood has conducted several studies documenting the ways "hard edges"—like the ones caused by mountaintop mining and the subsequent reclamation—affect cerulean warblers. Her research article, "Cerulean Warbler Abundance and Occurrence Relative to Large-Scale Edge and Habitat Characteristics," reports that "cerulean warbler abundance increased significantly with distance from the edge of reclaimed mines, with the edge effect extending 340 m [more than 1,000 feet] into the forest." Mountaintop removal mining not only displaces ceruleans, but degrades the surrounding habitat. Wood's article continues: "Remaining forest tracts are rendered less suitable due to edge effects, further reducing populations over and above forest loss to the mines themselves." How many cerulean warblers did this particular mine affect? Jesse and I had almost arrived at our destination: how many acres of cerulean warbler habitat within the Kanawha State Forest had this mine also rendered less desirable for use by breeding ceruleans?

Nearby, the male cerulean sang again. "This is absurd," I stammered to Jesse. "I can't believe what I'm hearing and seeing at the very same time."

I had been too horrified and intrigued to notice that a stocky man walking a large, fluffy black and brown dog was approaching. As he drew nearer, I smiled and gave him a customary nod. I figured he'd nod back and keep walking, but instead he stopped. He caught his breath, and then asked, winking, "You like them strip mines?"

I looked at him hard for a moment before answering. Beads of perspiration ran down his red face, and sweat stained his white T-shirt and navy blue jogging pants. He stood about five-foot six-inches and probably weighed close to 250 pounds. A gray mustache covered his upper lip and drooped down to the corners of his mouth. His tan baseball cap was turned backward and short white hair stuck out from beneath it. I wasn't sure what to make of him—this was Boone County, after all, the biggest coal county in West Virginia. I figured the chances were good that we'd disagree about strip mines, but I was angry. I shook my head and said, "Nope, I don't like them."

The man laughed. "I guess if you liked them you wouldn't be taking pictures."

Mr. Bones had squirmed out of our car's back window by this point, and he and the larger dog were happily wagging their tails and sniffing each other's butts. Jesse got out, too, and the man began talking. It took me a moment to process what he was saying, because what came out of his mouth was *not* what I had expected, given our current location.

"If you want a better view of that mine," he said, wiping his forehead on his sleeve, "keep going up this road, and just before the state forest, park your car on the right and walk up the four-wheeler trail. You'll get better pictures from up there." The fluffy dog began nosing me, and I bent down to pet him as the man continued. "If anybody ever tells you those strip mines provide jobs, they're lying. They're not supplying anybody with jobs, but that's how they justify it," he grunted, gesturing toward the opposite ridge. "Each crew is only eight red hats, and probably not more than thirty men work during a twenty-four-hour day."

I shook my head and sighed as the cerulean warbler buzzed again from somewhere nearby.

The man wiped more sweat from his cheek and pointed at the Virginia license tag on our car. "What happened to old Jerry?" he asked, winking at me again and smiling. I didn't know who he meant at first, but when he began talking about the religious right, I realized that he meant Jerry Falwell, founder of Liberty University in Lynchburg, Virginia, who had recently died. "He got that atheist Reagan elected by firing up all the religious people," he growled, his smile fading. "The Republican Party's wrecked a lot of good people. They're hypocrites. Look at what they did to Colin Powell..."

As the man continued a curse-filled rant, I couldn't stop a smirk, and then an all-out grin, from creeping onto my face. He threw up his hands, and his face got even redder. "Those Republicans," he said, "they're in bed with Massey, that *scab* outfit."

Massey Energy, while notorious for many things throughout Appalachia, was also known for hiring almost exclusively non-union coal miners. According to data presented in *Bringing Down the Mountains*, in 2003, only 193 of Massey's 4,428 employees were members of the United Mine Workers of America. With the rise of mountaintop removal mining and the decline in the number of employees needed, union miners often found themselves out of work. According to the West Virginia Coal Association, 106,590 people labored in the state's coal mines in 1934; by 1984, that number had dropped to 39,950; and by 2007, only 19,213 people worked as coal miners in West Virginia.

For many coalfield residents—including our new friend—the practice of hiring non-union miners was unacceptable. Several mine wars, pitting striking workers against the hired guns of the coal companies, were fought in Appalachia's mountains. Blood was spilled for labor's right to organize in order to demand safety and competitive wages. My great-great-grandfather William lived near the site of West Virginia's first mine war, known as the Paint Creek/Cabin Creek

War, which lasted from April of 1912 until July of 1913. Striking miners, seeking the right to organize, accurate scales, fair pay, and several other reasonable demands, clashed with coal company owners and their well-heeled thugs. Several striking miners and coal company guards lost their lives. William, who lived on the Lick Fork of Paint Creek during that time, would have been involved in the struggle. Eight years later, as a union miner in southern West Virginia, William probably participated in the Battle of Blair Mountain, the violent clash between ten thousand striking coal miners and deputized agents of the coal companies. The five-day gun battle ended when the US Army arrived and quelled the strike.

I stared out at the brown edge of the opposite ridge. What must it be like to live near a mine that size? Imagine: you live in southern West Virginia, amid clear mountain streams, thick forests, and towering green mountains, in a town with a low crime rate and friendly neighbors. Coal mining never really bothered you too much until they started blowing up the mountains around your house. *That's when I'd move*, some people would say. Well, let's put aside the fact that this is your home and you don't want to move. What does relocating require, first and foremost? Somewhere else to move to, right? How do you get that somewhere else? With money, of course. So, you'll need to sell your old home in southern West Virginia. But there's a problem; no one wants to buy a home next to a giant strip mine. Your property value has plummeted. The coal company offers to buy your house at "fair market value," but it's not enough. So what can you do, while each day more and more of the area around your home is destroyed, as your house shakes from the blasting, as your well water turns orange, and each rainstorm brings the threat of a flood?

Thinking about this hypothetical situation in southern West Virginia made me feel selfish and lucky. At one time my family also depended on coal for survival. William's son, my great-grandfather Ignatius, also worked in an underground coal mine. Ignatius was elected president of his local UMWA chapter at age nineteen, but after losing an eye in a mining accident he retired and worked as a police officer in Plymouth, Pennsylvania. According to my mother, he hated going down into the mines, and he vowed that none of his children would ever work underground. And none of them did. When World War II struck, all four of his sons, including my grandfather, joined the military. My father's father, Touffy Sallitt, who immigrated to the United States in 1923 from Syria, worked in eastern Pennsylvania's coal industry almost from the moment he set foot in the country. At the age of twelve, he took a job as a "breaker," separating useable anthracite coal from waste material as it came up from the mines; now, this work is done primarily by machines at processing plants like the one in Sylvester. I can't deny that the coal industry played a significant role in the financial beginnings of both sides of my family, and on some level, I wouldn't be here without coal. But that doesn't mean I

Mr. Bones guards the tent in the Kanawha State Forest.

have to like it, and our story shows that it's possible to leave the coal industry and do something else, even if it's your family's "heritage."

The fluffy dog sniffed my boot as his owner, seeming glad to have this enthusiastic audience, told us about a recent mining accident that killed two underground miners at a Massey operation. "I worked underground for many years," he said, shaking his head, "and we never had the kind of accidents they do now."

We talked for a few more minutes, and our new friend told us how to find the campground once we were in the state forest. As we climbed back in our car, the man turned to continue his walk up the steep road. As we rumbled slowly past him, he called to us, "Remember, there's only one thing Republicans hate more than Democrats—the truth!" Chuckling, he gave us a wave as we continued on our way up the mountain.

WEST VIRGINIA IS HANDS DOWN the most beautiful place on earth. Once Jesse and I crossed into Kanawha County and entered the state forest, the road became paved and wound gently through the trees. The forest canopy closed above the road, allowing just a little sunlight through to dapple the blacktop. The 9,300-acre Kanawha State Forest harbored more than a thousand flora species and scores of birds, including nineteen warbler species. A black-throated green warbler sang *zee zee zoo zoo zee* from the trees overhead as we cruised towards the campground.

To our delight, when we arrived at the "rustic" tent camping area, it was deserted. Vacant tent sites lined one side of Store Hollow Road, and beyond the sites ran a thin, trickling creek. A wooded mountain rose behind the creek, and another loomed on the other side of the road, forming the hollow. The road dead-ended at campsite 16, which we gleefully claimed; it was surrounded on three sides by the forested walls of the hollow, and the creek ran just next to it. The site included a picnic table, a trash can, and a fire pit. We normally avoided camping in designated "campgrounds"—we strongly preferred backpacking far from roads and picnic tables—but this site seemed like the best we could hope for in a state forest next to a large urban area. We hung a sign on the numbered post indicating that we were claiming the site, and we set up our freestanding two-person tent while Mr. Bones investigated the creek and surrounding undergrowth. When we had finished, we climbed in the car again and drove back to the state forest entrance to try to get another look at the mine we'd passed on the way in.

We wound back up the quiet road through the forest and stopped just outside the park boundary. A gated gravel road led up and into the woods to the left of the entrance; we snapped on Mr. Bones's leash and started hiking up it. As the road steadily climbed, Jesse and I scanned the canopy for birds. Mr. Bones's constant tugging on the leash made birding difficult; usually, we let him off his leash in the woods, but since we were on more of a road than a hiking trail, we were nervous we'd encounter a vehicle. When Mr. Bones gets a smell he likes, his beagle half takes over; with his nose to the ground and tail wagging, he zigzags along whatever scent trail he's found. When he's in beagle mode, we can call and call but he ignores us. So, to be safe, we kept him hooked to the leash.

We hadn't been walking more than a few minutes when we heard the call of a male cerulean warbler. We tilted back our heads, raised our binoculars, and searched the treetops, but we couldn't find him.

"Damn," said Jesse, lowering his binoculars, "I'd really like to see one of those guys today."

We pressed on, and the road switched back and continued to climb. My legs began to ache, and I regretted not bringing a bottle of water. Even though it was mid-afternoon, a few birds still sang in the forest. In addition to the cerulean, we heard more black-throated green warblers, Eastern wood-pewees, red-eyed vireos, yellow-throated vireos, and others. We passed a fresh pile of what I thought was coyote scat; Mr. Bones loved the way it smelled, and he wagged his tail faster and faster as he stood over the pile, sniffing deeply. At home, we sometimes heard coyotes running in the cow pastures behind our house. They howl and yap and sound like they're having a raucous party. Mr. Bones usually sits inside our screen door with his head cocked and his ears lifted, listening to the canine jamboree outside; perhaps something wild, buried deep in his genes, stirs as he listens. Mr. Bones lowered his head and prepared to roll in the fresh scat, but luckily Jesse pulled him away just in time, and we kept climbing.

Then, through a break in the trees, we glimpsed the barren edge of the strip mine on the opposite ridge. As we examined it through our binoculars, I felt my face flush with anger. So much life flourished along this road—thick, mature trees, birds singing and foraging, delicate wildflowers. Certainly there had once been just as much life on that ridge, too. I wondered how many animals had been killed outright; how many baby birds in their nests, too small to fly, had been buried alive under tons of dirt and rock? How many foxes and coyotes were displaced and forced to find new places to hunt? The part of the mine we could see looked like something big had come along and shaved off the side of the mountain—which, actually, was not far from the truth. We could see the different layers of earth; the layer toward the top of the wound was brownish-red, then below a layer of darker material, which might have been where the coal used to be, and then a layer of gray stone. Jesse and I continued walking all the way up the road, cursing the suit-and-tie executives of the surface mining industry who, we were certain, grew fat from the millions of dollars they made by destroying these ancient mountains and the people and animals who called them home.

We rounded another switchback, and the woods opened up to a clearing dominated by what we assumed was a natural gas well. We birded this "soft" edge habitat for a few minutes, but our stomachs were growling, so we decided we'd slowly make our way back to our car. We hadn't actually *seen* a cerulean, but we had all day tomorrow to continue searching. Just beyond the well, the wide gravel road narrowed to a thin gas-line path that led into the forest. The overgrown path headed back down the mountain in the general direction of our car, so we followed it. The path was steep and tangled with undergrowth; right away we heard another male cerulean singing. Again, we strained our necks searching, but we couldn't locate him high in the canopy. Perhaps my cerulean-searching skills were not as sharp as I'd thought. We tromped on, startling a roosting red-tailed hawk, and before long, through the trees, we could see the silver of our car at the bottom of the hill. Our gas-line path intersected with a small dirt road, which a few feet further met with the road we'd walked up.

The roads all converged close to where we'd parked our car, near the state forest's entrance. We were about to give up on birding and quickened our pace when we again heard a male cerulean singing softly overhead. I looked up and saw something fluttering in the high branches of a sugar maple. I raised my binoculars. "Redstart," I sighed. "Those things are everywhere."

"I've got a cerulean," Jesse whispered quickly. "I see his necklace." He explained how to find the bird, and as soon as I did, we both noticed a *third* bird this one a pale bluish-yellow, sort of like a washed-out looking watercolor painting. It foraged along a thin branch, hopping from twig to twig and running its bill along the undersides of leaves.

"That's a female cerulean," I whispered. Perhaps nearby the pair had built a nest of spider webs and grapevine bark on a lateral branch. The male sang softly again, like a song with the volume turned down. I realized we were hearing the "whisper song," and I nudged Jesse. We stood below, watching the pair forage, until our necks hurt. When Mr. Bones began to tug on his leash, Jesse and I quietly snuck back to our car, both of us grinning.

BEFORE SETTLING IN AT CAMP for the evening, Jesse and I got back in the car and headed toward Charleston to find a store. We agreed that our cerulean success deserved a celebratory bottle of wine; alcohol was of course prohibited in the state forest, but that didn't deter us. We exited the park, hoping to find a nearby store without having to drive all the way into the city, which was about eight miles north. The road led through the small town of Loudendale, which consisted mostly of a handful of houses and trailers along the main road. Bright, round peonies bloomed around driveways and mailboxes. A Confederate flag flapped from a garage, and an old hound dog snoozed on a wooden porch. Among the houses was a convenience store, and Jesse pulled into the parking lot. A clerk leaned against the outside wall, smoking; she took a long drag before stomping out the butt and following Jesse inside. He came out a few seconds later. Apparently, they had no wine, but sold single Bud Light bottles, if I'd rather. I didn't. We turned onto the steep road that led to Charleston.

The road wound and climbed, and soon we began to notice Charleston's sprawl. As we got closer to the city, the houses became larger and more luxurious. Most were brick and stone, with SUVs and basketball hoops in their blacktop driveways. Lawns were close-clipped and green, and the bright gardens neatly landscaped. It seemed that if Charleston grew any bigger, the city would push further and further in the direction of the Kanawha State Forest. The forest already seemed like an island, wedged between the city on its north and strip mines on its south, east, and west. We stopped at a gas station in the sprawl and picked up a cheap bottle of chilled chardonnay. It was still early, but we were looking forward to cooking our dinner of just-add-water sun-dried-tomato pasta and sitting around a campfire, so we headed back to the forest and site 16. When we arrived, we happily discovered that no one else had invaded Store Hollow.

We unpacked our camp stove and dinner, and Jesse poured us each a cup of wine. We drank from black plastic camp cups, which were worn from years of use—very discreet, we thought, in case a park ranger came through. As the sun sank lower and the temperature dropped, the birds tuned up for their evening songs. While Jesse stirred our dinner on the camp stove and I sipped chardonnay, we were serenaded by a wood thrush, a red-eyed vireo, and an Eastern woodpewee. An Acadian flycatcher called *pEET-sa* every few seconds from a pine tree along the creek. A Louisiana waterthrush investigated our tent, strutting around our campsite, bobbing his tail with each step. Mr. Bones lay next to the picnic table and watched him, but was too tired (or maybe too lazy) to get up and bother the bird. Chimney swifts chittered as they wheeled high overhead. Then, from the mountain slope beyond the creek, a cerulean warbler began to sing.

Jesse and I sat quietly amid all the birdsong. We each took a fork and began sharing mini-penne from the pot. Sipping sweet wine, eating pasta, relaxing in a wooded hollow with my husband and dog, listening to a singing cerulean warbler was perfect. Almost heaven.

I had just refilled my cup with chardonnay when a beige state-forest pickup turned onto Store Hollow Road. "Drink that whole cup," Jesse said softly.

"I just filled it," I answered. "It looks like we're drinking water or coffee, doesn't it?"

"Not if he gets out of the truck," Jesse answered, as he slowly lowered his cup and dumped its contents onto the ground. I reluctantly did the same and watched as the wine mixed with the sandy earth under the picnic table.

The truck came all the way down to our site, turned around, and drove back down the road without even a wave from the driver. "Figures," Jesse said, and as soon as the truck was out of sight, we refilled our cups, and Jesse began building a fire in the pit. The folks who had camped at this site the previous night had kindly left some firewood. Soon, orange flames were blazing.

The gates to the park closed at nine, and Jesse and I were delighted to have all of Store Hollow to ourselves. But just as a whippoorwill began calling in the growing darkness, another pickup truck turned onto the road and drove toward our campsite. "That's not the law again, is it?" I asked, squinting. The truck pulled into an empty campsite three or four down from us, and its two teenage passengers got out and slammed the doors. They began to unload a tent and other equipment from the bed of the truck.

"Oh well," said Jesse. Mr. Bones didn't like the other campers either, and growled deeply. We sipped our wine, poked at the fire, and tried to ignore the intruders.

Despite the fact that we were no longer alone in Store Hollow, I was in a great mood. Sitting in an Appalachian hardwood forest at dusk, watching and listening while the day faded to evening and then night, heightened my senses and made me feel truly alive. I inhaled deeply and let my head fill with the warm smell of the campfire. I jabbed at it with a carefully chosen stick and watched a balled-up page of newspaper collapse and smolder before erupting into orange flame. Simple, perfect. While I enjoyed sitting, watching, and listening, Jesse reveled in the small challenges of camping; he liked building campfires, especially when conditions weren't perfect—if the firewood was damp or wet, for example. He liked using his camp toys, especially his hatchet and buck knife. He always made sure our small tent was perfectly situated on its tarp, with its rain guard stretched tightly over the roof and walls. Jesse was almost always the one who unfurled and inflated the bedrolls and laid out our sleeping bags.

When Jesse and I crawled into those sleeping bags around ten (we'd planned to get an early start birding the next morning), our neighbors were still awake, talking loudly around their now-roaring campfire. At some point—probably an hour or so later—another vehicle drove down Store Hollow Road and stopped at their site. Car doors slammed. Loud greetings were exchanged. Mr. Bones, who slept inside the tent with us, growled again at the newcomers.

I eventually tried to fall asleep, but it was difficult because of the laughter and voices from the other campsite. I was glad that teenagers liked to hang out in places like state forests, but when I checked my watch at 3:30 a.m., they were still awake and talking. I briefly woke up again around 4:30 when the first birds of the morning started to sing, and by 5:30, Jesse was shuffling around our campsite, putting gear away and getting ready for our hike. I tried to stay in the tent and sleep longer, but it was futile.

By six, I was sitting at the picnic table, rubbing my eyes. The Acadian flycatcher was frantically calling again from the pine tree and two crows were taking turns raiding the other campsite. The teenagers were all sleeping inside the tent, and the crows marched around their fire pit, stealing little bits of food and cawing boisterously back and forth to each other. I made sure I slammed the car door a few times and talked a little more loudly than usual to Jesse, who smiled and shook his head at me as he smoothed his hair into a ponytail.

We loaded up a daypack with water, our camera, field guide, my notebook, and a few granola bars, and started up Store Hollow Trail, which began close to our campsite on the opposite side of the hollow from the creek and the other tent sites. Store Hollow Trail was a short, steep climb up out of the hollow, switching back a few times as it wound between red oaks and sugar maples. We let Mr. Bones off his leash and he had a pup celebration, sprinting up the trail, then back to us, leaping and twisting his body. He was definitely ready for a pup-venture in the woods. I may be accused of anthropomorphizing, but Mr. Bones seemed to be expressing pure joy as he galloped and skipped along in front of us.

The forested slope was dry—no gentle streams flowed, and no mud pooled in the trail. Almost immediately after starting up the trail we heard a cerulean, but we couldn't find him in the high canopy. We did, however, get a good look at a worm-eating warbler and a scarlet tanager; since worm-eaters stay close to the ground, they can sometimes be easily spotted, and the bright red tanager stood out amid the green. Ovenbirds chirped their dry *teacher teacher teacher* call and red-eyed vireos asked, *where are you? Can you hear?*

Soon, Store Hollow Trail met Pine Ridge Trail at the crest of the hill. Jesse and I turned right and hiked along the ridge. Thick, lichen-covered trees lined the trail, and sunlight broke through in patches, encouraging seedlings on the forest floor. I couldn't help myself—I hugged a few of those wide oaks. As we hiked along, we heard several more male ceruleans singing. We stopped near a rocky outcrop and sat down and searched until we found one of them, hopping and flitting around the thin branches that extended out over the edge of the ridge. He'd hop, then stop and sing, his dark beak opening wide, his head thrown back. Then he'd repeat the pattern of hop, stop, sing, sometimes mixing it up with flit, stop, sing. It occurred to me that this bird was fortunate that his territory was here, in the interior of the state forest, instead of beyond its borders. But even though this forest was pro-tected, it seemed safe to assume that there was coal within the mountain under us. Would there come a time when greed finally trumped conservation? Could the state of West Virginia sell this forest to a coal company?

We climbed around the outcrop for a few minutes, and I remembered some-thing that Dr. Wood had told me about Allegheny wood rats and their connection to cerulean warblers. Wood rats needed rocky outcrops in their habitat, and rocky outcrops often occurred along ridges. Cerulean warblers in this part of the county preferred to live on ridges. Both species, and scores of others, needed this same small piece of habitat. I imagined silent creatures hiding all around me, waiting for us to move on.

After a short walk along the ridge, the trail intersected with Dunlop Trail, which descended into Dunlop Hollow. We took Dunlop Trail to the left; soon, a small stream appeared next to us, and the woods darkened and became damp. Moss crept up the thick tree trunks, and the ground around the trail was covered in ferns and delicate wildflowers. This was exactly the kind of place where, as a child, I imagined fairies and unicorns lived. Bits of pollen suspended in the air, and the ferns around our feet were still wet with morning dew. The forest vibrated with life. Everywhere I looked, something was alive: the moss, the ferns, tiny blue wild-flowers, insects skittering in the narrow stream, hovering mosquitoes. The lazy *zur zur zur zeee* of a black-throated blue warbler, the *tuwee tuwee tuweeo* of a hooded warbler, and the ethereal chime of a wood thrush filled the hollow. I thought about the surface mine just outside the park entrance, and all the other mines within a few miles of here, and imagined this hollow choked with tons of dirt and rock and debris, the gentle stream filled in, the flowers and ferns buried. I wondered if the people in charge of local mountaintop removal operations had ever walked through a hollow like this one.

At the very bottom of Dunlop Hollow, the trail intersected a gravel road, and the tiny stream soon disappeared into larger Davis Creek. Hemlocks towered above the creek, blocking most of the sun. The understory here was less dense, and we were scolded by Carolina chickadees while a yellow-throated warbler sang from somewhere overhead. We continued along the gravel road, which led through meadows and eventually a picnic area with a baseball diamond. This proved to be a great spot to see birds. In addition to robins and other common birds, we identified Kentucky, yellow, and Tennessee warblers, lots of chipping sparrows, and—surprisingly—another cerulean, which Jesse actually identified by sight instead of by call. The bird foraged in a large sycamore at the edge of the meadow, but after a few minutes he took off and flew into the woods. Jesse and I took our cue from the cerulean and headed back to camp.

We loaded the rest of our gear into our car and left the same way we'd come in by the windy dirt road that passed the surface mine but at the bottom of the hill we turned left and headed east toward Hernshaw and Marmet, where we would merge onto Interstate 77 south. The road to Hernshaw—Route 94—passed close by a vast mountaintop removal site, but we couldn't see it from the road. Highway 94 intersected with the interstate near huge mounds of coal and a processing plant on the banks of the Kanawha River. Train cars lined up end to end near the plant, some filled with coal and some empty. Barges on the river also waited. A bulldozer crawled up one mountain of coal, and from a bridge over the Kanawha River we could just make out the very top of the golden M of a McDonald's.

As we drove south toward Blacksburg, we realized that the prime time for viewing ceruleans was almost past. Soon, the males would sing less frequently as nesting and raising chicks took top priority. Without the buzzy song, ceruleans would be almost impossible to locate high in the leafy canopy. I planned to lie low as well for the next few weeks and take care of my "nest" while Jesse headed to Georgia. Another portion of the cerulean's season had ended, but the next stage—babies!—was about to begin.

BIRD LIST, MAY 19-20
Kanawha State Forest

Red-tailed Hawk

Yellow-billed Cuckoo

Eastern Whip-poor-will

Chimney Swift

Ruby-throated Hummingbird

Red-bellied Woodpecker
Yellow-bellied Sapsucker
Pileated Woodpecker

Eastern Wood-pewee
Acadian Flycatcher
Eastern Phoebe

Yellow-throated Vireo
Blue-headed Vireo
Red-eyed Vireo

Blue Jay
American Crow

Carolina Chickadee
Tufted Titmouse

White-breasted Nuthatch

Blue-gray Gnatcatcher

Wood Thrush
American Robin

Gray Catbird

Ovenbird
Worm-eating Warbler
Louisiana Waterthrush
Black-and-white Warbler
Tennessee Warbler
Kentucky Warbler
Hooded Warbler
American Redstart
Cerulean Warbler
Northern Parula
Yellow Warbler
Black-throated Blue Warbler
Yellow-throated Warbler
Black-throated Green Warbler

Chipping Sparrow

Scarlet Tanager
Northern Cardinal

Brown-headed Cowbird

House Finch
American Goldfinch

PART TWO

Summer

ELEVEN

★

CUMBERLAND GAP

Lay down, boys, and take a little nap,
We're all going down to the Cumberland Gap.
Cumberland Gap, Cumberland Gap,
We're all going down to the Cumberland Gap.
  --Traditional

"WHEN YOU SAY 'FRIDAY,' do you mean the Friday two days from now?" I paced back and forth in my kitchen, phone pressed to my ear. Even though I had spent the month of June stuck in cerulean warbler-less Blacksburg, Jesse had just returned from three weeks in Georgia, and I felt guilty about immediately leaving him. For some reason, I assumed I'd be heading to Tennessee in a week or so, closer to the middle of July. But, as wildlife biologist Tiffany Beachy explained to me over the phone, if I wanted to see any active cerulean nests, I had to come sooner.

A Roanoke, Virginia, native, Tiffany was an alumna of Virginia Tech's Fisheries and Wildlife Department and the older sister of one of my undergraduate creative writing students. Currently, Tiffany was a graduate student at the University of Tennessee, where she worked on a variation of the same cerulean warbler project that was taking place at the Lewis Wetzel Wildlife Management Area in West Virginia and at a half-dozen other sites in Appalachia. The studies were collaborations by researchers from the Cerulean Warbler Technical Group; like Petra Wood at West Virginia University and Randy Dettmers at the US Fish and

Wildlife Service, Tiffany's professor, David A. Buehler, was a member. For the past two field seasons, the research teams had been surveying and banding ceruleans in their respective study sites. The logging treatments had been carried out last winter, so during this field season, in addition to banding and surveying as the researchers did before, they would also monitor and analyze how the different logging treatments affected the birds. The research could potentially be used to inform forest managers of the best management practices for balancing logging and bird conservation.

"We have one more nest with fledglings, but they could go any moment," Tiffany told me.

"Well," I sighed, "I don't think I'll be able to come that soon. My husband, Jesse, just got back from Georgia, and Friday's his birthday and Saturday's our wedding anniversary."

"I completely understand," she said. "Come down next week, then. We'll still be doing vegetation work."

I hung up the phone, sat down on the couch, and felt sorry for myself. I'd spent months researching, planning, traveling, writing, and thinking about ceruleans in their breeding habitat. I'd seen them defending territories, wooing mates, and even constructing a nest. But I'd never seen parents incubating eggs, and I'd certainly never seen a baby cerulean warbler. Now I'd have to wait another whole *year* before I'd have the chance again.

When Jesse called me from the veterinary school to tell me he'd be home for dinner, I told him that I'd missed out on baby ceruleans this season.

"Aren't you going to Tennessee?" he asked.

"The last babies are about to fledge, and I'm going to miss them," I whined.

"Why? Did the Tennessee people change their minds?"

"They want me to come now, but you just got back and your birthday's Friday and our anniversary's Saturday."

"So? Go see some babies."

THE NEXT DAY—THURSDAY, JULY 5—I swallowed my guilt, loaded up the Jeep again, and headed south. As I sped down Interstate 81, dodging eighteen-wheelers and suicidal minivans, I thought about the wagon trains two or three hundred years ago that traveled through this "Great Valley" to the Cumberland Gap, a natural break in the mountains where the present-day states of Virginia, Tennessee, and Kentucky meet. This congested highway was once little more than a wide dirt path, known by many names: the Great Road, the Wilderness Road, the Valley Pike, the Wagon Road, and others. The Cumberland Gap and this Great

Valley Road provided a migration route for buffalo and other animals, then gave Native Americans, and eventually that most invasive of species—white European settlers—a way to reach the fertile plains and prairies west of the Appalachians.

While there is apparently some controversy about its exact location, most sources claim the Great Road ran through the valley between the Blue Ridge Mountains on the east and the Allegheny Mountains to the west. The road began somewhere near Philadelphia or Lancaster, Pennsylvania, and headed southwest through Virginia's Shenandoah Valley, home to Civil War battlefields, wineries, and numerous chicken farms. After the towns of Staunton (pronounced STAN-ton) and Fincastle, Virginia, the exact historic route gets murkier. While some believe the road cut further west into the Alleghenies, others believe it continued southwest through Blacksburg, Radford, and the New River Valley to the town of Bristol ("The Birthplace of County Music" and home of the Bristol Speedway NASCAR track, "The World's Fastest Half-mile") before finally heading west through the valley to the Cumberland Gap. In a vehicle traveling, on average, seventy miles an hour, it takes approximately seven hours to get from southern Pennsylvania to Bristol, Virginia, on Interstate 81—I wonder how long it took those folks walking or riding horses.

Tiffany's cerulean warbler research sites were located just a few miles south of the Cumberland Gap in Tennessee's Cumberland Mountains; the site I'd be visiting was located within the 53,000-acre Royal Blue Wildlife Management Area near the small town of La Follette. Tiffany's other study site was in the nearby Sundquist Wildlife Management Area. Like the mountains where ceruleans breed in West Virginia, the Cumberlands hold coal deep within them. Both wildlife management areas in Tiffany's study had been previously mined and timbered. However, the Tennessee Wildlife Resources Agency took control of Royal Blue in 1992 and, since then, not much timbering has occurred. Prior to 1992, the Campbell Outdoor Recreation Association, a group of local hunters, fishermen, ATV riders, and other outdoor enthusiasts, used the area. And before that, Royal Blue's ridges and hollows were home to several mountain families.

While the Tennessee Wildlife Resources Agency manages the surface of Royal Blue, the Koppers Coal Reserve—which underlies most of the wildlife management area—is owned by the Tennessee Valley Authority. According to the TVA, they "acquired the rights to the Koppers Coal Reserve in 1962 as part of an effort to ensure reliable fuel supplies." The TVA estimates that the reserve holds 70 million tons of recoverable coal, and in 2003 they began "undertaking the development of a plan for managing [the] coal reserves on the Koppers property in response to an anticipated increase in demand for this coal." They announced that they would weigh five possible options for the Koppers Coal Reserve: no action (which would mean that the TVA would continue to consider mining lease requests "on an ad hoc basis"); managed surface and deep mining; deep mining only; no mining beyond the current leases; and the disposal of TVA's mineral rights at "fair market value" to either a coal company for the purposes of mining or to an entity that doesn't intend to mine (like me, once I win the lottery!). The TVA solicited public comments and announced that it would release a Draft Environmental Impact Statement in 2004, solicit more comments from the public, and then release a Final EIS in the spring of 2005. As of early 2008, no EIS had been issued.

The threat of potential surface mines on Royal Blue loomed over my trip to Tennessee and added a sense of urgency. According to the Cornell Laboratory of Ornithology's Cerulean Warbler Atlas Project, Royal Blue Wildlife Management Area held the world's largest documented breeding population of cerulean warblers, far surpassing its nearest rival. An article in the *Journal of Wildlife Management*, co-authored by Tiffany, shows that if surface mining was to occur, it "may displace 23% of the cerulean population on Royal Blue." Since the Cumberland Mountains probably harbor more than 20 percent of the total, range-wide cerulean population, loss of important habitat on Royal Blue could have a disproportionate effect on the global cerulean population—which has been declining at a rate of 3 percent a year without strip mining in its favorite breeding spot. It's depressing to think that our appetite for coal could doom this species.

I STOPPED AT THE TENNESSEE Welcome Center in Bristol to stretch my legs. I picked up a handful of brochures—most of which featured Dolly Parton—and got back in the Jeep after only a few minutes. Before I'd left home, I'd amassed all of my CDs that featured songs about Tennessee, and as I pulled back onto the interstate, I rocked out to "Don't Let the Smoky Mountain Smoke Get In Your Eyes." I wasn't technically going to the Smokies, but it was fun to sing anyway. Next up was "Dixieland Delight" by Alabama, then "Tennessee Jed" by the good old Grateful Dead; as the speed limit rose from 65 to 70, I turned up the volume and shouted along with Jerry. Finally, I played the most famous of Tennessee tunes, "Rocky Top." Traffic thinned out as I rolled past the exit for Davy Crockett's birthplace. I wished I had the "King of the Wild Frontier" song with me.

As I neared the metropolitan hub of Knoxville—at evening rush hour, of course—it started to drizzle. In my giddy sing-along drive through Tennessee, I hadn't noticed that clouds had crept across the sky. I called Tiffany to tell her I was almost there, and she informed me that they'd checked on the last clutch of cerulean babies earlier that day, but the nest was empty. *Empty.* No sign of babies or parents, no activity at all. They might have fledged, or they might have been pre-dated. Either way, I wouldn't get to see an active nest.

I merged onto Interstate 75 to head for La Follette, and the clouds opened. Thunder. Lightning. The windows fogged up and I couldn't see. The windshield wipers slapped back and forth as fast as they would go. My knuckles were white on the steering wheel; negotiating the bumper-to-bumper 65-mile-per-hour traffic took all my concentration. I sped along, hunched forward, trying to keep with the flow, my right foot jumping from gas pedal to brake to gas to brake. Tap, tap, on the brake. Gun it. Tap, tap, don't hydroplane. Keep the truck in front one car-length away.

Out of the corner of my eye, I saw a white flash that could have been a small dog running along the right side of the highway, heading in the opposite direction. I glanced in my rearview mirror, but my windows were too foggy for me to see anything. Was it a dog? I had to stop. Where? I couldn't pull over; there was barely a shoulder; there were no exits for miles; I couldn't see. The dog would get smashed, its neck and ribs broken by a bumper or a front tire, its soft white fur matted with blood and rain. My mouth twisted, and I couldn't stop the tears. There were no baby ceruleans. They were probably dead, too, their tiny wings broken by teeth or talons or the hard ground far below their nest. An angry psychopath killed my favorite student, killed everyone's favorite students, their bodies broken by bullets bought on eBay. *On eBay.* My throat closed up, and I couldn't breathe or see. I was an awful, unstable person. I should have stopped for that dog.

WHEN I ARRIVED IN THE small town of La Follette, about 40 miles northwest of Knoxville, it had stopped raining and I had regained my composure. During the field season, Tiffany and one of her two field crews rented a small yellow house in a residential neighborhood. I pulled into the house's steep driveway and checked myself in the rearview mirror. Did I look like I'd been crying? Yes, I did. My eyes were sunken, my cheeks pale. When two black puppies ran up to the Jeep, yipping frantically, I got out. They jumped and licked and nipped my hands. I shuffled down the steep hill toward the house and put on my happy face.

A young man and woman sat cross-legged on the wooden front porch, eating vegetarian dinners. They introduced themselves as Amy and her husband, Ethan. The crew had just gotten back from a long day in the field, and Tiffany was still in the shower, so I sat down on the porch, too. I learned that Ethan, a student, field technician, and cerulean aficionado, had spent the majority of the last two months camping up on Royal Blue, near one of the study plots. Just a day or two before I'd arrived, he'd come down from the mountain, shaved his beard, and cut his long hair. Everyone was still getting used to it. Amy, a ceramic artist with a studio in Knoxville, said Ethan had looked like a caveman.

Six people stayed in the small three-bedroom house; in addition to Tiffany, Ethan, and Amy, there was Brett, a field technician from Canada; Jenny, a marathon runner working on an edge-effect study for Tiffany; and Ana, a new graduate student from Mexico's Yucatán peninsula. And, of course, the two black puppies—the crew had found them alongside the road on the way to the study plots. Apparently, Royal Blue is known locally as the place to dump unwanted dogs and other pets. They'd found a dog last year, too, and one of the field technicians took him home. The pups weren't allowed inside the house, so they lived out in the yard. Amy didn't work in the field, so she kept a close watch on them.

The screen door of the house suddenly swung open and a tall, thin, young woman with wet hair stepped out. "Katie!" she said, with a huge smile and open arms. Even though we'd never met in person, Tiffany gave me a big hug, which was just what I'd needed. She absolutely radiated positive energy. We stood on the porch and got acquainted as she combed the tangles out of her long, light brown hair. After talking to her for only a few minutes, I was put completely at ease by her honest, uninhibited laugh. I admired her immediately.

After chatting about the drive, the book, and of course, the birds, I hauled my stuff inside. The tiny three-bedroom, one-bathroom house was filled with shoes, clothes, books, binoculars, and field equipment. I piled my packs and sleeping bag in a corner of the living room, where I'd sleep that night. I felt guilty again; I'd certainly take up almost the entire room. But then I remembered that I'd brought them a very small token of my appreciation, which I hoped would make up for my annoying presence in the middle of the floor. I pulled a small bag of shade-grown coffee out of my pack and handed it over. They seemed appreciative, and I felt slightly less bad about being in the way.

It was dinnertime, so Tiffany, Brett, and I drove to a local Japanese restaurant, where we met two more field technicians who were staying in another rental house across town—Rich, who was Tiffany's co-crew leader, and Liz, an undergraduate from Montana. Tiffany explained that her study involved two field teams, one for Royal Blue and one for Sundquist. The Royal Blue crew included Tiffany, Brett, Ana, and Ethan. The Sundquist crew was Rich, Liz, and Alex (whom I hadn't met yet). Jenny collected data for Tiffany's edge-effect project, and earlier in the spring, the team had worked with a bird-bander. "So, during the height of the bird season there were ten of us," Tiffany said, "but right now we're sort of one team. There were fewer territories on Sundquist, so they finished faster."

The friendly teenage waitress in the Japanese restaurant seemed sort of amused by us, and as she served our dinners (mine a delicious dish of broccoli, rice, and soy sauce), she asked where we were from. When she got five different answers, she laughed: "What're y'all doing in La *Follette*?!" She rolled her eyes and told us that the only thing to do in the evening was to head over to the Wal-Mart parking lot, where all the guys washed their pickup trucks.

On the way back to the house, we stopped at a grocery store to buy a few camping supplies; Tiffany had invited me to spend the following night with her at Ethan's camp near one of the study plots. She hadn't had a chance to camp out there at all this season, and my visit provided a perfect opportunity. While Tiffany and Brett went into the store, I stayed in the car and called Jesse in an attempt to make myself feel better for leaving him all alone on his birthday. It didn't work, and I ended up crying again when I told him about the dog alongside the highway. After ending the call, I dried my face on my T-shirt sleeves, closed my eyes, and tried to take deep breaths. I felt fragile and slightly out of control. I'd had two or three late-night panic attacks since the shootings at Virginia Tech—the kind where you can't see and your lungs won't inflate and nothing helps until it's run its course—and I *really* didn't want to have one in front of nice bird people I'd just met. Finally, the sliding grocery-store doors parted again, and Tiffany and Brett stepped through them.

Back at the house, Ethan had pumped up an air mattress for me, and I unrolled my sleeping bag on top of it. The mattress took up most of the living room floor; I was definitely in the way. As usual, I didn't sleep very well, mostly because I was anxious, and I began to feel very guilty again about being away from Jesse on his birthday and our anniversary. I wasn't accustomed to feeling this way; it seemed that my normal emotions were amplified by memories of the tragedy that had occurred almost three months earlier. While chasing ceruleans in West Virginia, I'd managed to push unpleasant thoughts from my mind, and while Jesse was away in Georgia, I immersed myself in cerulean research and writing. Now, for some reason, it felt like the emotions I'd been pushing aside had rushed back all at once.

As I tried to sleep, thunder rumbled outside and lightning flashed, illuminating the room in green light. The house's windows didn't have screens, so curious moths and hungry mosquitoes investigated my face. A few fireflies glowed in the room around me. Whenever I rolled over, the air mattress crinkled in the otherwise silent house. I concentrated on keeping still, and at some point, sleep came.

TWELVE

★

EMPTY NESTS

T HE HAZY SUNSHINE HAD ALMOST burned through the morning fog when "The Bird Wagon," a huge, black SUV with the University of Tennessee's seal on both front doors, turned off the highway and entered the Royal Blue Wildlife Management Area. As the guest of honor, I had been invited to sit in the front passenger seat. Ana, Ethan, Brett, and Jenny were crammed in the back, and Tiffany drove. Packs, water jugs, boots, binoculars, rain jackets, a stray box of tissues, and other necessary equipment filled the space behind the back seat. Music, too soft for me to recognize, whispered from the speaker next to my foot. Like so many valley routes in Appalachia, this flat, paved road ran parallel to railroad tracks. Green blankets of tangled kudzu—the invasive Japanese "vine that ate the South"—enveloped everything in sight. It was here, Ethan leaned forward to tell me, that they'd found the abandoned puppies.

We pushed deeper into Royal Blue; the kudzu disappeared and pavement soon turned to dirt. The road became steep, rocky, and deeply rutted as it snaked up the eastern side of Cross Mountain. Thick forest closed around us, and clusters of purple phlox bloomed alongside the road. Twisted grapevines drooping from tree limbs gave the impression of a jungle. As we ascended, the phlox gave way to abundant yellow-orange flowers called touch-me-nots, also known as jewelweed. Butterflies floated above the road like confetti. Tiffany did her best to steer around stagnant puddles that had formed in the deep ruts—if she had no other choice but to drive through them, she apologized out loud to the frogs and turtles that might have been hiding beneath their surfaces. Overhanging oak and maple branches slapped against the windshield as the Bird Wagon bumped slowly up the mountain. It was only 8:00 a.m., but the hot July sun already burned my arm as it rested on the open passenger window.

Tiffany's study area on Royal Blue consisted of four twenty-hectare (about fifty-acre) plots; each plot included a "treatment"—a logged area—and an unlogged buffer zone. Plot One, which had received the heaviest logging treatment, was nearly clear-cut; Plot Two was an unlogged control plot; Plot Three's treatment cut down about half of the trees; and in Plot Four, the lightest treatment, only a few selected trees had been removed. If the ceruleans seemed to prefer one type of treatment over another, that data could inform forest managers of the best ways to conserve the birds while potentially still harvesting some trees. Despite my skepticism, I admired the Cerulean Warbler Technical Group for attempting to build bridges between biologists and logging industry representatives. Petra Wood's statement from earlier this spring—"They don't want a spotted owl situation"—resonated.

When we reached a wide, cleared area along the road, we pulled over and dropped off Ethan and Jenny so they could conduct vegetation surveys in Plot Four, the light treatment. Tiffany explained that each plot included twenty random "vegetation points." In the area surrounding each point, the researchers measured the percentage of canopy cover, the diameter-at-breast-height of the trees, and several other complicated factors. They also placed a vegetation point directly below each nest they'd located. It certainly did not sound as interesting as watching birds, but it was, nevertheless, an important component of the research.

After dropping off Ethan and Jenny, Tiffany, Ana, Brett, and I took the Bird Wagon back the way we came but turned off onto a steep side road. We lurched and rattled over huge rocks and through more deep ruts before Tiffany pulled over again and shut off the engine. We climbed out, gathered our gear, and hitched on our packs. Ana and Brett set out in one direction to conduct vegetation surveys in Plot Two, and Tiffany and I went in the other direction to attempt to re-sight banded cerulean warblers in Plot Three.

The dirt road Tiffany and I walked on did not run along the ridgetop; the mountain rose steeply on our left and sloped downward on our right. I admitted to Tiffany that I was still deficient when it came to identifying tree species, so she called out their names as we strolled along—chestnut oak, basswood, buckeye, sugar maple, cucumber magnolia. She'd pull down a branch to show me a leaf's shape, and I did my best to commit it to memory.

"This plot," Tiffany explained as we walked, "Plot Three, is the intermediate treatment. It's called a 'shelterwood,' and they took, more or less, 50 percent of the trees." She paused to lift her binoculars to her eyes. "Redstart," she said, point-ing, "in that brush pile. Anyway, they took all the mid-story and understory, too. Basically, there are just some big trees left over and big gaps. Also, lots of pretty rocks with lichens and old decomposing logs. And now, new logs that will soon decompose." Sunlight beamed through openings in the canopy to the forest floor, which was brown with felled tree trunks and dry leaves. Cut branches and brush had been pushed into piles, presumably for wildlife habitat. I wiped a trickle of sweat from my cheek.

The woods were much quieter now in early July than they'd been in May. A small flock of cedar waxwings sang their high-pitched *see see see* song, but the ce-rulean warblers remained silent. When their hormones rage in the spring, males can be located as they frantically sing and viciously defend their chosen territories. And while the birds are incubating eggs, the researchers, once they find the nests, can just sit in one spot and observe what happens. After the babies leave the nests, though, everything changes. Territory boundaries blur as parents follow the ex-ploring fledglings and vice versa. There's no reason for males to sing anymore; the noise might attract the attention of predators. Therefore, tiny, well-camouflaged cerulean warblers become almost impossible to find. This is frustrating to re-searchers trying to monitor the birds' survival rates.

Tiffany pointed to more American redstarts, flitting around some tangled un-dergrowth and fanning their pale orange and black tails. An olive and yellow male hooded warbler, being closely followed by a begging fledgling, hopped to the top of a brush pile. "Awesome," Tiffany said, smiling at the birds. "Oh, there's a female scarlet tanager up there, too."

We continued to shuffle along the road, pausing every few steps to watch or listen to a bird. Once we'd left the redstarts and hooded warblers behind, Tif-fany took a portable CD player and small speakers out of her pack. She played a recorded male cerulean call to try to coax one of the now-silent birds out of hid-ing. It didn't work. She pulled out a worn field notebook and consulted a pencil-drawn map. "This is the edge of 'Rascal's' territory," she said, studying the map, "and 'Chris' and 'Rich' have territories nearby, too." Earlier in the season, Tiffany's research team mist-netted and banded ceruleans, much like Greg George's team had in West Virginia. Here, though, Tiffany gave each banded male a name; this made it easier for members of her research team to refer to the birds quickly while observing them in the field.

A bit further down the road, Tiffany tried the recording again. This time, a male cerulean answered from somewhere far down the ridge, but he didn't seem to venture any closer; if he did, he came quietly and left without calling again. "It was much easier at the beginning of the season," she sighed, stuffing the CD player

The road through Royal Blue.

back in her pack. Like my previous hosts, Tiffany seemed disappointed that the ceruleans weren't showing up for me. I didn't mind, though; walking around in the woods with a person who also loves birds is about as good as it gets.

We eventually stepped off the dusty road and began a steep ascent up the ridge to our left. Tiffany explained that we were hiking through an uncut buffer zone, next to the shelterwood treatment we'd just walked along. The buffer was markedly different from the logged plot—it was dense and green, cooler and more shaded, and we sat down among the roots of an ancient tree to catch our breath and watch for birds. Three ATVs rumbled along the dirt road below us and disappeared around a bend. According to the Tennessee Wildlife Federation, Royal Blue has the heaviest off-highway vehicle use in the state. Many local ATV riders are members of the Campbell Outdoor Recreation Association, the group that had controlled Royal Blue before the state took over in 1992. I'm somewhat conflicted about ATV use; the machines are loud, burn fossil fuel, and tear up the earth, but if they keep to already-cleared logging roads—as it appeared most in Royal Blue did—they don't seem so bad. Certainly, one reason to ride ATVs in this wildlife management area is its remote woodsy-ness; if ATV owners want to keep riding in a wild Royal Blue, then they have a stake in the forest's protection. Surface coal mines here would mean fewer places to ride. If I had to choose between a strip mine and a few ATVs,

I'd take the ATVs any day; however, if a forest were already protected from mining and logging, I'd probably choose to keep the ATVs out, too.

From our seats halfway up the slope, Tiffany pointed out a cerulean warbler nest in a sugar maple downhill from us, not far from the road. Through my binoculars, I could see that the nest was empty, sad, and very lonely, clinging to a lateral branch. The nest was built in a similar location to the one I'd seen the female constructing in Lewis Wetzel—anchored to a little nub on a branch, several yards from the trunk of the tree. Not much vegetation grew between the nest and the forest floor, though a few leaves overhung the top of the nest. In this case, however, they didn't provide adequate cover from an aerial predator.

"Ethan and Brett were both coming up to the nest at the same time from different locations," Tiffany told me, "and happened to look up at the nest and see this red-bellied woodpecker go and take a chick and leave. And the parents were freaking out. The female went down to the road and took a bath, as if she was washing her hands of it. And then a few minutes later, the red-bellied returned and took another chick."

I shook my head in disbelief. I don't think I would have been able to watch that—I understand the balance of nature, and I love woodpeckers as much as I love all birds. I'd recently watched a Cooper's hawk devour a mourning dove beneath one of my birdfeeders, and I'd rehabilitated hundreds of predatory birds. But this was different; this was a *cerulean warbler* nest! Those babies were important individuals of an imperiled species. I'd be compelled to throw a rock or shout to deter the woodpecker. I told Tiffany this, and she laughed: "You'd interfere?"

"Yes," I said. "I feed those red-bellies suet all winter. They should leave my baby ceruleans alone."

We watched the empty nest for a few more minutes, and it reminded me that Jesse was all alone on his birthday. That night, he and the dog would sleep in our bed without me, and I'd be in my sleeping bag without them. The helpless baby ceruleans were eaten. By a *woodpecker*. I pictured a red-bellied at my feeder, hammering the suet cake with its long, sharp beak, tilting back its head and swallowing the chunks. Then I pictured it hammering a baby cerulean warbler. My mouth twisted like it does when I'm trying not to cry, but the empty nest was too much. Tears squeaked out the corners of my eyes. "I'm sorry," I said, wiping my cheeks with my fingertips.

"Aw," Tiffany said. "Make sure you call Jesse today and wish him happy birthday."

I took a few deep breaths and composed myself, and Tiffany told me another depressing story; Ana had been observing a nest in Plot Two, the single-tree selection light treatment plot, and watched a male cerulean fly to his nest, perch on the lip, look inside, and fly away. "A little while later," Tiffany continued, "a sharp-shinned hawk went directly to the nest, as if he knew where it was already, and looked in like he was expecting more. So we're assuming that he probably predated it earlier and was coming back for seconds." Somehow, a hawk eating the babies didn't seem as tragic as a red-bellied woodpecker, but I still wished it hadn't happened.

After a few swigs of water, we left our shady spot and continued climbing the ridge. We passed through patches of wildflowers, all of whose names Tiffany knew: bloodroot, hog peanut, jack-in-the-pulpit, green dragon, black cohosh. She explained how to identify each different kind, carefully touching their leaves as she pointed out distinguishing features. Meadow rue was my favorite; its small leaves, which resembled tiny paws, felt as soft as delicate velvet. Tiffany also named the abundant ferns—Christmas, New York, and maidenhair—and showed me the difference between Virginia creeper (which has five shiny leaves, and was all over the place) and poison ivy (which has three shiny leaves, and was also all over the place). We climbed through a waist-high patch of stinging nettle that made me itchy through my nylon pants. Small welts rose on my forearms.

When we finally arrived at the top of the ridge, we headed for a nearby rocky outcrop to eat our lunches. I hadn't realized how much time had passed, but it was already after eleven o'clock. We climbed onto the pile of rocks, and I let my pack slip from my shoulders. The outcrop provided a panoramic view of the forest below us, and as I turned slowly in a circle with the hot sun on my face, I felt like the king of the mountain.

"This outcrop used to be shaded," Tiffany said, frowning.

I glanced around and noticed several huge, wide stumps nearby, surrounded by sawdust. Even though the trees had been felled as part of the effort to find out more about the cerulean warbler, it made me profoundly sad to see the massive stumps and flecks of wood shavings. I felt implicated in the trees' deaths; my mouth started twitching, but thankfully I held back the tears and sat down next to Tiffany.

"This rock," she said, pulling a sandwich and some carrot sticks out of her pack, "is actually a battleground for three different cerulean territories. We can stand right below this rock, and the birds will counter-sing all day long and have fights and stuff. But no one guy can claim ownership to the very top of the rock."

I pulled out a granola bar, and Tiffany scolded me for not bringing something more substantial for lunch.

I unscrewed the cap of my water bottle and asked Tiffany what she thought of the theory that claimed ceruleans preferred to breed in forests with gaps in the canopy. Between bites, she said, "I think the most important thing for ceruleans is probably structural diversity. If you have a really steep ridge, like out here, you're going to have trees staggered above the ones below them on the slope. If that gets at what a gap would do, then that's great for a cerulean." She paused to crunch a carrot. "In Canada," she continued, at the northernmost edge of the cerulean's range, where other members of the Cerulean Warbler Technical Group are carrying out valuable research, "even though it's flat or gently rolling, they have some huge hickories that stick up above the rest of the tree canopy. Cerulean males like to hang out and sing in these super-emergent trees."

"I would like to be called 'super-emergent,'" I said, swallowing a chunk of granola.

Tiffany laughed. "Ceruleans probably sing from these super-emergent trees because their song is so weak," she said.

"Don't offend them!" I said in mock horror. "That's why they weren't answering your recording this morning."

"I didn't say that, guys!" she called into the forest, laughing and tucking a loose strand of hair behind her ear. "It's just not as loud as some of the others. It'll go further distances from the super-emergent trees. Please take a carrot." She pushed the baggie toward me, and I obliged. An Eastern wood-pewee called from somewhere nearby.

I asked her how many cerulean territories she had on each study plot.

"Well," she said, "both of my sites are very different. The density of ceruleans here in Royal Blue is much, much higher than in Sundquist. And we're going to be analyzing possible reasons for that. There's a lot more fragmentation in Sundquist, but we don't know if that's what's causing it. Out here in Royal Blue, there are usually more than twenty cerulean territories per plot. In this particular plot, we have thirty territories this year. In fifty acres. I think this is the highest density of any of the other sites."

"In the world," I nodded, and scanned the forest around me.

"But in Sundquist," she continued, "which is only seven or eight miles southwest of here, as the crow flies, there's a whole different story. There, there are maybe thirty territories total, across all four plots."

One of the most glaring differences between the Sundquist and Royal Blue Wildlife Management Areas are the ways they've been used by the coal and timber industries. The state took control of the surface of Royal Blue in 1992, and the Tennessee Valley Authority has owned the rights to the minerals beneath its surface since 1962. The state didn't gain control of Sundquist until 2003, and it continues to be surface-mined and logged. It seemed obvious to me why there weren't as many ceruleans on Sundquist: more strip mining, more logging, and more forest fragmentation. I know scientists can't make claims like that without thorough, time-consuming, meticulous experiments and analysis. But I'm not a scientist, and the answer seemed as clear to me as the July sky over our heads.

WHEN TIFFANY AND I FINISHED eating, we hoisted on our packs, climbed off the rocks, and began scrambling down the opposite side of the ridge to meet up with Ana and Brett back at the truck. On our way down the steep slope, Tiffany took me to see another failed cerulean nest, this one located in the buffer zone. We stood under the nest tree, tilted our heads, and looked straight up at the bottom of the tiny cup nest. It, too, was on a lateral branch, near a nub, without much vegetation between it and the ground where we stood beneath. The nest had come apart a bit and appeared lopsided and saggy on the branch.

Tiffany estimated that more than half of all the nests they'd located in Royal Blue had failed to fledge a chick. And even if a nest did manage to fledge chicks, there's no guarantee that the fledglings would survive. The fledgling stage is a critical and dangerous time in the life of all young birds, when they're very susceptible to predation and injury. If more than half of the nests in the densest cerulean warbler breeding area in the world had failed to produce fledglings this season, what did that mean for the species as a whole?

After losing the thin trail once or twice, Tiffany and I skidded down through thick undergrowth to the hard-packed dirt road below. When we finally made it back to the Bird Wagon, Ana and Brett had already arrived and were leaning up against the SUV's dusty tailgate eating their lunches. We piled in and rumbled along the rough road again, heading back to the other study plot to check on Ethan and Jenny's progress. During the drive, we pulled over to let a man on an ATV speed past us. A few minutes later, we caught up to him again, pulled over on the side of the road. Tiffany, who is easily the friendliest person I've ever met, stopped the truck to talk to him.

The man wore a camouflage baseball hat over his bright white hair, which we saw when he lifted the hat's brim to wipe sweat from his brow. His heavy boots and thin gloves were accented with camouflage, too, and his round stomach spilled over the top of his tight blue jeans. In a deep, drawling voice, he asked if we'd seen any rattlesnakes, and then he went on to describe several encounters he'd had with the reptiles while digging ginseng in Royal Blue. He told us he'd made a lot of money—several thousand dollars—from ginsenging. Like Chinese ginseng, the root of the American ginseng herb, which grows wild in Appalachian forests, is traditionally reported to have healing properties. He gave us a final warning about copperheads, which he considered less honest than rattlesnakes, and we drove on.

We reached the bend and parking area along the road near Plot Four, where we'd dropped off Ethan and Jenny early that morning. Along the edge of the parking area, a female box turtle—who hid under a stack of logs—had scraped a nest in a rut made by a logging truck. Even though Brett, Ana, and Tiffany made a square boundary around the turtle nest with fallen twigs, the scrape looked like little more than a slight disturbance in the dirt to me. I crouched down next to the pile of logs to get a closer look at the mama turtle. She was about the size of a cantaloupe and had tucked herself neatly into a narrow space between logs. I envied her ability to blend in and disappear. She peeked out from beneath her shell with a deep brown eye, set just behind her hooked, parrot-like mouth. Like everything else here, her brown and black shell, legs, claws, and face were coated in dry dust. I resisted the urge to pet her and backed away slowly, carefully avoiding the spot where they'd told me her nest was located.

As we stood over the nest talking about turtles, our friend on the ATV caught up to us again. We waved him to a stop and showed him the turtle nest, mostly in the hopes that he wouldn't run it over. He cut the ATV's engine and dismounted, pulling off his camouflaged gloves and again lifting his cap to wipe sweat from his lined forehead. The end of his nose was porous and sunburned, and he looked down at us with piercing blue eyes. His name was Jim, and when he found out we were researching birds, his interest was piqued.

"I've got a bird at the house," he began slowly, "now you tell me what it is. It looks about like a sparrow, but it's got red on its neck."

"House finch," said Tiffany, smiling.

"That what it is?" he asked. "I never did see one growing up. I don't know where the things come from, but I see them now."

We all glanced at each other and laughed. "They came from out west," we said.

Jim told us about a wren that had made a home in a bird-box he'd hung on his barn, and then about a mockingbird that had nested in one of his wife's spider plants on their porch. As I stood on the dusty road, listening to the curiosity and pride this man felt because of the birds around his home, it occurred to me that Jim was the second elderly man on an ATV who I'd met this summer who loved backyard birds. He was also the second elderly man on an ATV to warn me about rattlesnakes.

In addition to his affection for birds, Jim's love for the Royal Blue Wildlife Management Area was obvious. He asked us where we were from, and upon hearing that none of us were local, he told us a bit about the area, starting with a local legend about a man who had lived here on Cross Mountain and distilled illegal liquor. He couldn't remember the name of the moonshiner, but another man—Silcox—reported him to the police. So one day, when Silcox was riding his mule down the mountain, the moonshiner hid up on some rocks above the road and shot and killed Silcox. "I figure that murderer died in jail," Jim said, nodding.

"I wonder if any of his liquor is still up here," I laughed.

"Could be. I think he had a son somewhere around here. You can still see their old shed, a log shed. You find a lot of that in the mountains."

Ana sat down on a log, and I wiped another trickle of sweat from my temple and took a step backward into the shade.

Jim opened his arms and gestured to the forest around us. "All this ground through here's nice woods. Kinda rough. Not many places like it, you know. Not anymore. I hope they don't ever build in here or sell any of it off." He shook his head and sighed. "The money-making people want to do that, of course. Over on North Lake, they want to build a motel. I don't see much advantage to it, but they say it can draw people in. I don't hardly see it."

"Not having people here seems like the nice thing about this area," I said.

"That's right," Jim agreed, nodding. "Exactly right."

He continued to tell us about the superb hunting on Royal Blue; it sounded like he hunted every animal that had a season, but he especially bragged about the area's turkey and ruffed grouse. "No place like it for turkey in the whole country," he insisted. "I sure hope they don't cut any more of these oaks. Without the oaks, you don't have the turkeys."

The more Jim talked, the more I liked him. Here, I thought, was a perfect example of an environmentalist, an ecologist, and a conservationist who would probably never call himself any of those things. There must be thousands of folks like him. Here was an ally—a tree-hugging, ginseng-digging, camo-wearing, anti-development activist on an Arctic Cat ATV. I smiled at him and to myself; there was hope for us yet.

When Jim began to talk about his views on birds of prey, however, my smile faded and I shifted uncomfortably.

"I don't particularly like hawks," he said, his voice darkening. "Those big hawks, those big old red-tailed hawks, they make quick work of stuff, especially little turkeys."

I glanced sideways at Tiffany. Before I could tell Jim that some of my best friends were red-tailed hawks, he continued.

"And the owls, too. If people lived up here, you wouldn't have as many owls as you do now. People had to kill the hawks and the owls that would kill their chickens."

I wanted to tell him that this was bullshit, of course, and there was no good reason to kill hawks and owls. I reevaluated our friend Jim: for all his old-time mountain-man talk, he was driving an expensive ATV. Modern-day hunting is not cheap, either, and I doubt he needed to hunt to keep from starving. So what if a hawk or owl eats a turkey now and then? That's nature. I'm no stranger to hunting—I grew up in rural Pennsylvania, the white-tailed deer capital of the world, and my father-in-law has more rifles than anyone I know. I generally support people who hunt for food; I have been a vegetarian for more than fifteen years, and this perplexes some of my fellow vegetarian friends. But I've thought about it extensively, and I've reached the conclusion that it's ultimately more beneficial for the environment (and for humans) if people get out in the woods and shoot some white-tailed deer instead of chowing down on antibiotic-filled burgers from factory-farmed cows. "Game" animals need habitat, and in a healthy ecosystem, that habitat can support hundreds of non-game animals, too. Cerulean warblers love mature oak trees and so do wild turkeys—and so, therefore, do the turkey hunters. Unfortunately, a few hunters still hold onto the belief that predators like hawks and owls should be killed because they "compete" with humans for food; this is antiquated, shortsighted, and ridiculous. I still liked Jim, but his heroic status dropped a few notches.

After telling us heart-wrenching stories about stray dogs and cats that he'd seen in Royal Blue, Jim sighed and pulled his gloves back on. "Well, ladies, I think I'll ride up the other end." He looked at the clear blue sky and smiled. "I ride fifty miles, some days." He walked a few steps to his ATV, bent down and picked up a piece of trash. "Stuff like that everywhere," he grumbled. "Nice to meet y'all."

After Jim sped away on his ATV—coming dangerously close to the box turtle nest, which was why we'd flagged him down in the first place—we hiked up into Plot Four. The research team still had to finish conducting vegetation surveys, so I sat cross-legged on the ground in the cool, green forest, amid Virginia creeper and poison ivy. I picked up a fallen sugar maple leaf and suddenly felt sad again, and guilty for enjoying myself out in the Tennessee wilderness. Here I was, stomping around the woods with my wonderful hosts, searching for birds and talking to interesting locals, while Jesse was probably having a hectic day in the veterinary teaching hospital's cardiac ward. He would come home to an empty house on his birthday.

While Ana, Brett, and Tiffany finished up the day's vegetation work, Ethan and Jenny came down the mountain from another direction. Ethan presented me with a turkey feather he'd found, which I immediately stuck in my ponytail. We all hiked down to the Bird Wagon, raised the tailgate, and loaded most of the gear. Ethan, Jenny, Brett, and Ana piled in and rumbled away, leaving Tiffany and me in the woods.

The two of us trudged back up the slope to Ethan's campsite, where he'd lived for the majority of the field season. After dropping our packs near the tent and peeling off our heavy boots, Tiffany announced that she was going to go "talk to God" on the mountain. I hadn't realized that she was a religious person, and at first I wondered if "talking to God" was a euphemism for smoking marijuana or going to the bathroom, but it wasn't. After she'd set off enthusiastically into the forest, I crawled into Ethan's tent, unrolled my camp pad and sleeping bag, lay down on it, and cried. I called Jesse on my cell phone, wished him happy birthday, and cried some more. He tried to assure me that he didn't mind that I wasn't home, and that trips like this were good for me. But it didn't matter what he said.

When I started to lose the signal, I closed my phone and collapsed back on my sleeping bag. It wasn't just missing Jesse's birthday and our anniversary; memories of the shootings at Virginia Tech kept filling my head. I'd never dealt with a tragedy like this before, and I wasn't sure how I was supposed to feel. It made sense that I'd mourned in the days and weeks afterward, but the shootings had happened almost three months earlier. Was it *normal* for me to still be upset like this? Would memories from that day always creep up and shake me unexpectedly? Would a part of me be sad for the rest of my life? A dog running on the side of the road had reminded me of April 16. And an empty cerulean warbler nest. And now, being alone in the woods. I wept myself to sleep.

When I woke up an hour or so later I felt better, even though my face was stiff from crying and my contact lenses were glued to my eyeballs. I climbed out of the tent and sat on a folding canvas camp chair. A blue-headed vireo sang from the canopy. A white-breasted nuthatch sounded its nasal *yank yank yank*. Some pretty purplish-pink flowers (I think sweet pea) bloomed nearby.

After another hour passed with no sign of Tiffany, I began to get a little nervous. I heard the hum of distant ATV engines and wondered what I would do if a group of them stopped to investigate the campsite. In reality, just about every ATV owner I'd ever known was a good-old-boy who liked to have fun in the woods—probably not the kind of folks I should be afraid of. But unexpected things can happen at any moment. What if a rapist or murderer decided to venture into Royal Blue on his ATV? No one would hear me scream. If I had to run away, where would I go? A sudden panic gripped me, and I felt like I was being watched. I scanned the still, silent trees. The setting sun, now lower in the sky, cast everything in long shadows. *Stupid girl,* I thought. *You're a stupid girl, alone out here.* I didn't want to be afraid— I was in the woods, in my safe place, my sanctuary. I took a few more deep breaths and let my head fill with the smell of leaves and dry forest.

Once I'd calmed down, I remembered that I was a writer, and I retrieved my notebook from my pack and forced myself to make notes about my day. As soon as I started, a huge deer fly began buzzing around my head. I swatted it and forced myself to keep writing. The fly landed on the top of my head, and I swatted. I scrawled a few lines, and it landed on my arm. Swat, scrawl, swat, scrawl. I hated that fly, but it did distract me from my fear.

Finally, Tiffany came back, smiling, refreshed, and exuberantly happy, which made me feel happy, too. I introduced her to my pet deer fly. We were hungry, so she offered to make dinner if I would build a fire. Usually when I went camping or backpacking, my role was to "supervise" while Jesse took care of things. It's not just because I'm lazy, but because Jesse enjoys it; we're not really camping if Jesse doesn't bleed or singe his eyelashes.

Tiffany poured a can of black beans, one of corn, and one of tomatoes in a pot. With her pocketknife she diced some fresh garlic and added it, too, and cooked it all over her small camp stove. I scrounged around for firewood, trying my best to plunge my hands into the poison ivy that surrounded the campsite.

After half a book of matches and two sheets of notebook paper, I had a blazing fire. Tiffany and I talked about men and how, to them, building a fire was some kind of penis-comparison or pissing contest. We forked beans into our mouths and laughed. As I got up to add more wood, it occurred to me that I hadn't camped without Jesse in seven or eight years. And I hadn't been to a girls-only campout since high school. I didn't always enjoy spending time with other women—perhaps I engaged in pissing contests of my own—but I'd gladly follow Tiffany Beachy into the woods any day.

We talked until 11:00 p.m. and then went to bed, I in Ethan's tent and Tiffany outside under the stars. I fell asleep to the sound of a creature scritching nearby—perhaps a small rodent—and I only woke up once or twice during the night when my sleeping bag became wrapped too tightly around me. I expected creepy dreams, but they didn't come.

In the morning, I opened my eyes to the song of a wood thrush. Then other wood thrushes started to sing, too—I could hear four different wood thrushes singing from each of their separate territories. If I woke up to that song every morning, I'd never have a bad day. How can a person be angry or stressed when a wood thrush is singing? I remembered Longfellow: *And where the shadows deepest fell, the wood thrush rang his silver bell.* I lay awake in my sleeping bag, letting the wood thrushes' silver songs trickle over me. A pewee started singing, too. And then my friend, the blue-headed vireo. I stretched, unzipped my sleeping bag, and got ready to meet the dawn.

THIRTEEN

★

FLEDGING

Little birdie, little birdie, come sing to me your song.
Got a short time to stay here and a long time to be gone.
–Traditional

I SENT A "HAPPY ANNIVERSARY" TEXT message to Jesse, then stepped out onto the dirt road and slammed shut the Bird Wagon's passenger-side door. The bright morning sun glinted off the truck's side mirror, and small bees buzzed frantically around delicate yellow flowers that grew alongside the road. On meeting up with the field crew after our night of camping, Tiffany commandeered the truck and drove us here to Plot One, which had received the heaviest logging treatment of any of the study plots. The rest of the crew stayed in Plot Four to finish vegetation surveys. Tiffany wanted to show me the startling differences between Plot One and the light-treatment plot that we'd camped near.

I followed Tiffany into the dense forest of Plot One's buffer zone, where we soon picked up a thin trail. The morning sun was already high in the sky, and I realized that I smelled like sweat, dirt, and campfire. I still wore the same faded, gray T-shirt that I'd had on all day yesterday and then slept in. My lightweight nylon pants were dappled with dirt; my socks and boots had been trying to rub a blister onto the side of my right big toe since I got to Tennessee.

As we left the road further behind us, the forest cooled and darkened. After a few minutes of walking through the lush greenery, Tiffany stopped and turned to face me. "I want to warn you before we enter the plot," she said. "It's kind of sad. It's like, savannah conditions. A few big oaks and hickories and stuff are kind of dotted across, but with no mid-story or understory to speak of."

I swallowed and nodded, certain that I'd cry again. As we stood there in the shaded greenness of the forest, we heard chipping and scolding in the canopy above us. We both tilted our heads and raised our binoculars. Tiffany identified the birds immediately as cerulean warblers, but all I could see were shadows flitting about in the high green leaves. She said she saw at least one fledgling, and she pulled her field notebook out of her pack while I continued to search the canopy; unfortunately, I never got a good look at the birds, and, frowning, I lowered my binoculars.

When the birds moved deeper into the dense buffer zone, I followed Tiffany along the trail toward brightness ahead. We stepped through the trees into a hot, dry, ugly place. I looked around, squinting in the sunlight. It appeared as if a tornado had touched down here, wreaked havoc, and then spun away. Several tall trees were left standing; Tiffany told me that for the purposes of her study, "modified shelterwood" meant that ten to twenty square feet of residual basal area per acre was left by the loggers. Tiffany explained "basal area" this way: "If you're in a forest and you cut down every single tree, it's the surface area that the stumps would take up if you squished them all together." So, in this fifty-acre plot, the bases of the remaining trees covered a total of ten to twenty square feet per acre.

Despite the few standing trees, the plot was indeed sad—there were at least a dozen brown, jumbled brush piles heaped with thin saplings (just starting their lives!) and numerous wide stumps where mature oaks and maples had stood for generations. I spotted a male Eastern towhee perching on one of the brush piles, but he quickly dove into it as we approached. Walking across the plot proved difficult, and I immediately began to sweat; not only was the slope quite steep, but all the stumps and tangled, downed branches made finding footing awkward. A sense of harshness and loss hung over Plot One. There were no ferns or lush wildflower beds here.

We hiked out to the middle of the plot on a thin trail that ran parallel to the ridge top. From this vantage point, we could see for miles and miles and miles— there were mountains just across the valley; then larger mountains beyond those; and even faint, hazy mountains beyond those. We agreed that the view was nice, but we'd rather have the trees. Tiffany pointed to the far left side of the visible horizon. "That's Zeb Mountain," she said.

"Zeb Mountain. Why does that name sound familiar?" I wondered aloud.

"Well," said Tiffany, "it's the largest strip mine in the state."

I looked to where she'd pointed, and I saw it—the familiar brown, flat edge of a once-green ridge. And then I remembered why I'd heard of Zeb Mountain; in addition to being Tennessee's largest strip mine, it was also home to the state's first mountaintop removal operation, though here they called it "cross-ridge mining."

In the summer of 2003, the Knoxville Office of Surface Mining and the Tennessee Department of Environment and Conservation issued a permit for a 2,100-acre surface mine on Zeb Mountain. There was an immediate outcry from concerned residents who lived in the valley communities around the proposed mine site. A local organization, Save Our Cumberland Mountains, encouraged citizens to write letters to the governor, urging him not to allow "the devastation that has happened in West Virginia [to] happen in Tennessee." Despite the uproar, the coal company forged ahead, permit in hand, and began mining.

Feeling like the issue was out of their control, some citizens resorted to civil disobedience; Zeb Mountain was the site of at least two nonviolent direct actions by citizens opposing the mining. In August 2003, three men known as "The Rocky Top Trio," an affinity group of Earth First!, blocked the entrance to the mine by locking themselves to two barrels filled with rocks and cement and then sitting in the road. The barrels had "DON'T CHOP ROCKY TOP" painted on them and a banner stretched above the road read, "STOP MOUNTAINTOP REMOVAL!" Two years later, at 3:30 a.m. on August 15, 2005, citizens affiliated with the group Mountain Justice blocked the entrance again, this time with a tireless station wagon, a thirty-foot tall wooden tripod with a human in a hammock swinging from its apex, and a half-dozen or so protesters cemented to equipment and barrels. Seven hours later, the blockade had been dismantled and nine protestors arrested.

I've never been brave enough to participate in a public act of civil disobedience. I'm generally a rule-follower, and I avoid confrontations if I can. I don't like to make other people nervous. However, I respect passionate individuals who engage in nonviolent protest to make their voices heard, and I admire nature writers such as Edward Abbey and good old H. D. Thoreau for inspiring would-be activists. Thoreau famously spent a night in jail for refusing to pay taxes. Abbey contributed to the formation of Earth First! and spoke at the group's kickoff event near the Glen Canyon Dam. Would I ever be the kind of "brave cowboy" that Abbey lionized in *The Monkey Wrench Gang* and other works? Doubtful.

As we stared at Zeb Mountain through our binoculars, we heard some bird activity across the plot, off to our right and down the slope a bit. We swung our gazes towards the sound. In a small grove of trees—a basswood, a buckeye, and a sugar maple—we saw a male cerulean warbler fluttering around with another bird and chittering loudly. The two birds scolded and spun around each other as they dropped toward the ground. I couldn't tell the other bird's species. After the fracas, the male cerulean flew up and into the crown of another nearby tree. Tiffany and I sat down on the ground (taking care not to impale ourselves on sharp, broken sticks) to watch what might unfold.

I raised my binoculars and scanned the trees' branches for the boisterous cerulean warbler. I was momentarily fooled by an indigo bunting, apparently an innocent bystander. I also caught sight of a black-throated green warbler flitting about, foraging for food. A ruby-throated hummingbird buzzed around the tree branches, too, and a downy woodpecker clung to a nearby snag. My first thought was, why are all these birds here? But then it occurred to me that they were probably just easier to see because there were fewer trees. If Tiffany and I could see them, then the birds were certainly more vulnerable to predators. The scenario put me in mind of shipwrecked passengers, all trying to cling to the same inner tube to keep from drowning.

After only a few seconds, Tiffany announced that she'd re-sighted the male cerulean and discovered that he had a fledgling nearby, tucked behind a few of the basswood's large flat leaves, near some twisted grapevines. *A baby!* I grinned. A baby cerulean warbler, *alive*, not dead, not eaten—this was what I'd been waiting for!

Tiffany described to me where he was perched.

I looked. I couldn't find him.

She gave a more detailed description, and I still couldn't find him. I began to grow desperate, my grin fading.

Tiffany began a play-by-play: "Aw, look, the fledgling is begging and the male is feeding it! Now the male's chasing away the hummingbird. The fledgling's just sitting there, calm as can be. Don't you see them yet? They're *right there*, the fledgling's near the trunk, sort of hidden behind some leaves."

I felt like an idiot. My heart was pounding, but I still couldn't find this baby bird. My head started to hurt from frustration and from squinting through my binoculars into the bright sun. Sweat trickled down the side of my neck. I began to more fully appreciate the difficulties researchers faced trying to study these birds in the field; I'm not a terrible birder, but I would never have spotted that fledgling. On a blank page in her field notebook, Tiffany drew me a diagram of the tree and the bird's location. That helped, and after an eternity of searching, I finally found the baby.

He (I say "he," but I don't know for sure) was an adorable little critter, closely resembling a fuzzy ping-pong ball. His tail hadn't grown in yet, which made his body look perfectly round and soft. The feathers of his fluffy white chest were puffed out, and he carefully preened them. I wanted to reach out and grab him, snuggle him next to my face, and give him a kiss on top of his baby head.

A cerulean warbler fledgling.

We cooed and watched the bird for a while, and then Tiffany hiked down a bit closer to the grove of trees to try to see if the male cerulean was banded. If the male wasn't sporting a band, then this baby probably fledged from a nest the researchers had not found. I felt the sun burning my face, so I retreated a few feet higher up the ridge to the tree line and plopped down in the shade.

As I watched Tiffany taking notes down the hill from me, I worried about our baby bird. How could a little ball of fluff possibly hope to survive in this cruel world of hungry woodpeckers, massive strip mines, and full-sun coffee plantations? In only a month, our fledgling would have to begin his long migratory journey. His tiny wings would need to be strong enough to carry him above the southeastern United States, across the wide Gulf of Mexico, and down the Central American coastline before finally arriving at the Andean wintering grounds, some three thousand miles from here. It's amazing that *any* birds survive.

I looked out at the horizon again, and my gaze stopped on the brown edge of the mine on Zeb Mountain. An eerie feeling of déjà vu washed over me. For the second time this season, I could see a cerulean warbler and a mountaintop removal mine at the same time. My mouth contorted, and my eyes stung. Crap, I thought. I can't cry in front of poor Tiffany again. But since she seemed occupied watching the birds, I let a few tears fall. What if the TVA someday decided to issue permits for new surface mines here, on Royal Blue, to get the coal that rested below my haunches?

I made a promise to the baby cerulean warbler in the basswood tree: wherever I am, whatever I'm doing, if a coal company tried to blast off Royal Blue's ancient mountaintops, I'd come back here and do whatever I could to stop them. I don't think folks like our new friend Jim on the ATV would stand for surface mining here, either—I think he'd be civilly disobedient with me. Each acre of Appalachia destroyed by a mountaintop removal mine is an acre of Appalachia that will remain unsuitable for cerulean warblers (and most other living things) for a very long time—perhaps a hundred years, perhaps forever. How will this species recover without suitable habitat?

I took a few deep breaths and regained my composure before Tiffany turned and hiked back up to me.

"Could you see his little supercilium?" she asked, crouching down next to me. She readjusted the folded blue bandana that kept hair and sweat out of her eyes.

I shook my head.

"Up close, you can see two crown stripes—little eye stripes."

"Aw," I said. "Very cute."

"They were hanging out high in the tree, not in the scrubby stuff," she said, reading through her field notes and making some final additions. "He probably left the nest between one and three days ago."

It was hot, I definitely stank of sweat and campfire, and we'd been on the plot for almost two hours, so we retreated into the green shade of the buffer zone. Tiffany wanted to show me an old mine shaft nearby, so I followed her back into the thick woods.

"Sometimes people see the elk up here on this plot," she said over her shoulder.

I'd forgotten about Royal Blue's elk herd, and at their mention, I felt something like fear. I'd lived in Appalachia my entire life, and therefore my experience with wild megafauna was limited primarily to white-tailed deer. I'd seen an occasional black bear and coyote, but an *elk* is another thing altogether. A few years ago, Jesse spent a summer working in western Maine, and while I visited him, we camped along the banks of the Rapid River near the Lake Umbagog National Wildlife Refuge. In the middle of the night, several moose strolled through our campsite; their casual splashing and heavy footfalls woke Jesse and me. Finally, Mr. Bones woke up, too, and growled, causing a minor moose stampede uncomfortably close to our fragile tent. I tend to lump moose and elk in the same category—horse-sized ungulates that were only mildly afraid of humans, often equipped with prehistoric antlers wider than I was tall. Deer should be fragile, bounding, Bambi-like creatures, not looming, cloven-hoofed monsters.

I know it's silly to be afraid of elk, and they certainly have a rightful place in the Appalachian Mountains. The story of the extirpation of eastern elk is a familiar one: as European settlers overran North America and began to push westward, they killed all the elk. They also killed all the woodland bison, wolves, cougars, passenger pigeons, Carolina parakeets, and dozens of other species. Some of the species, such as the elk and bison, had western counterparts that survived. Unfortunately, many other species, such as the Carolina parakeet, only lived in the east and therefore disappeared from the earth, save for a few lifeless museum specimens with glass eyes.

In the 1990s, the Tennessee Wildlife Resources Agency (TWRA), whose mission is, in part, "to restore extirpated wildlife when and where it is biologically and sociologically feasible," explored options for reintroducing elk to the state. They partnered with several hunting, conservation, and recreation groups, and in December 2000 they obtained fifty elk from Alberta, Canada's Elk Island National Park. Elk Island, "a fenced refuge for the protection and preservation of 3,000 head of hoofed mammals...was the first federally controlled area in Canada to be enclosed to protect a native mammal, the elk." The TWRA released these Canadian elk in Royal Blue. Over the following two years, they released 86 additional elk, for a total of 136 elk in Royal Blue. They also released thirty-one elk in nearby Sundquist Wildlife Management Area. The TWRA has designated a 670,000-acre "elk restoration zone" across five eastern Tennessee counties; if the elk wander out of the zone, they're recaptured and returned or killed. By 2007, the Tennessee elk population had grown to about two hundred animals, but the TWRA hopes to eventually increase their numbers to between 1,400 and 2,000. And, of course, the TWRA eventually plans to issue hunting permits for bull elk. One of the project's four goals is to "develop a self-sustaining elk herd capable of providing hunting and wildlife viewing opportunities."

I like the idea of restoring native wildlife; believe me, I do. But why hunt these elk? The concept seemed odd to me: state and private agencies work for decades to restore an elk population, only to kill a few of the beasts as soon as they can. The elk were released in the "elk zone" because the area "contains few farm crops and few people and has habitat suitable for supporting an elk herd." Sounds great— why not release some wolves, too? And some cougars? Then self-sustaining native predators can cull the self-sustaining elk herd.

Interestingly, even though the TWRA says that the elk zone contains suitable habitat, it also admits, "Habitat improvements are continuing on the WMA's to provide elk with the requirements they need to thrive. Food plots, clearings, timber operations, waterholes, and the like are being developed." Forgive my cynicism: but isn't releasing captive-bred animals into a highly managed habitat, only to eventually shoot them, a bit unfair? If the vague possibility of shooting a bull elk in Tennessee helps preserve public lands for other wildlife and for recreation, then I guess I'm for it. Perhaps that vague possibility will be enough for would-be elk hunters to oppose surface mines on Royal Blue. But what if the elk ultimately damage public land, which belongs to all members of "the public," not just elk hunters? What if the elk render it useless to other species or to humans? Then I'd be concerned—especially if ideal cerulean warbler habitat in the absolute epicenter of the bird's breeding range is cleared for elk food plots.

As we tromped through the woods, I asked Tiffany what she thought of the elk restoration project.

"Well," she began slowly, "their goal is to get the herd up to about two thousand. And I know there probably used to be that many up here, but they're really going to have to do a lot of habitat alteration for them. Elk will browse in the forest, but they also like open areas for grazing."

Open field areas near forest edges could make ceruleans (and other interior forest nesters) more susceptible to predators. In addition to hawks and woodpeckers that might eat the baby birds outright, cleared areas attract parasitic brown-headed cowbirds.

"The first time I went up to one of the elk plots last spring," Tiffany told me, "I saw two cowbirds flying across it."

"Did you have cowbird babies fledge from any cerulean nests this season?" I asked, cringing.

"We did have one cerulean nest this year with a cowbird chick in it, but I don't believe that it was successful. The parents were very smart about not feeding it much. The male, whose name is Moe, would come with his little pink band and perch on the lip of the nest and look in and be like, 'What's *that* ugly thing,' and fly away without feeding it. They would feed it every once in a while, but not regularly, and it seemed to be taking a long time to develop. The cowbird was the only head we ever saw in that nest, and it never really got to the point where it was about to fledge. We think the ceruleans were smart and just didn't feed that cowbird and probably let it starve to death or get predated or something."

I ducked a low-hanging branch and smiled to myself. I hated to take pleasure in the death of a baby cowbird, but I admit I did.

AS THE SUN ROSE HIGHER in the sky, even the deep green of the forest's shade couldn't keep me cool. My back felt sweaty under my daypack. Tiffany and I left Plot One and the dirt road that ran along the ridge further and further behind us. We'd been gradually progressing down the slope when the ground dropped off sharply at an almost vertical angle.

Tiffany explained that this cut in the side of the mountain was a remnant of an old highwall mine. She half-slid and half-leapt down the embankment and turned to see if I needed help. I squatted and sort of skidded along on my feet, my butt, and the palms of my hands. I got quite dirty—dirti*er*—but made it safely to the ground below. We continued walking along a flat area below the highwall on what seemed like an old road or trail. We skidded down another vertical embankment and kept going.

"Don't worry, we're almost there," Tiffany said, smiling over her shoulder at me. I watched her golden-brown ponytail and hoped she was right. I was already thinking ahead to how I would make it back up those vertical highwall cliffs.

As we descended, the woods became a darker green and more deeply shaded, and the forest floor was carpeted with ferns and Virginia creeper. A blue-headed vireo sang from the canopy. We soon came upon a rusted contraption inside a concrete base affixed to the side of the mountain, which dropped steeply from where we stood. The machine measured about eight feet across and consisted of two large, rusted outer wheels or gears with two smaller wheels in between them. One of the outer gears had teeth. Tiffany thought it might be a crank or a winch of some sort, perhaps once used to pull mine cars and miners up the steep mountain, or maybe to send down loaded coal cars. It was strange to see the abandoned mining equipment rusting in the forest. It looked archaic and dangerous, and it made me think of ghosts. I scanned the lush, quiet forest and tried to imagine it teeming with grimy miners and conveyer belts, or tremoring with muffled explosions and the grind of heavy machinery.

In Tennessee—unlike in West Virginia, Pennsylvania, and Kentucky—the coal mining industry does not seem to carry heavy cultural weight. The "coal is our heritage and we need it" refrain, sung throughout the halls of West Virginia government, seemed, thankfully, much quieter in Tennessee. According to the *Tennessee Encyclopedia of History and Culture*, coal wasn't mined extensively in Tennessee until after the Civil War, when "investors" from the north spread into central and southern Appalachia, gobbling up timber and mineral rights. By the 1880s, Tennessee ranked thirteenth among coal-producing states in the value of the coal it produced. Mining peaked in 1973, because of new strip-mining methods, but has declined in the state since then.

In 2005, the National Mining Association (NMA) ranked Tennessee twenty-first in the nation in coal production, churning out 3,217,000 short tons of bituminous coal, slightly less than Mississippi and just a bit more than Oklahoma. Until viewing the NMA's chart, I hadn't realized that those states—and others, like Louisiana, Washington, and Maryland—mined any coal at all, let alone more than Tennessee. West Virginia, by comparison, produced 153,650,000 short tons of coal, ranking second in the nation behind Wyoming, and neighboring Kentucky produced 119,734,000, for a third-place ranking. Pennsylvania ranked fourth, and Texas held down the fifth spot. Hopefully, Tennesseans will heed the warning of groups like Save Our Cumberland Mountains and will not allow their majestic ridges and valleys to be destroyed by mountaintop removal mining.

Tiffany and I left the rusted machine behind and continued along the trail. Soon we arrived at our destination: the mouth of an abandoned underground mine shaft. I let my daypack slip from my shoulders and climbed up the mound of stones around the shaft's opening. The thin, flaky stones slid under my boots as I scrambled closer and leaned cautiously forward. From its mouth, the shaft led gradually downward into darkness; I could only see a few feet into the mine. Cool air came out of the shaft, like a deep breath from the earth itself.

Tiffany climbed up next to me and peered inside. "Let's go in," she suggested, "just a little ways."

I shook my head. It felt a bit too much like an After School Special to me—two hikers decide to explore an abandoned mine and are never heard from again, until their bones are found decades later.

"Are you sure?" she asked. I was. She told me Ethan and Rich had explored the mine a bit, and they had found support beams and other mining remnants down there, but she hadn't ventured very far into the mine herself.

I stared into the cool darkness in front of me and imagined what it must have been like to go into that hole, deep into the earth. I don't think that I could do it. I thought of my great-great-grandfather William, going down into a mine like that every day. I thought of my great-grandfather Ignatius; how deep underground had he been when, due to a partial collapse of a mineshaft, he'd lost his eye? Did his fellow miners carry him out, bleeding and screaming? I thought of my grandfather Touffy, an uneducated, non-English speaking Syrian boy, just twelve years old when he went to work as a breaker at a Pennsylvania coal mine. I imagined him standing near a machine not unlike the one abandoned in the forest, his young hands sifting through anthracite coal, shale, and waste material, separating the good from the slag. What dirty, dangerous jobs. I'm thankful my family found ways out of the industry.

I have respect—and something akin to sympathy—for folks who still mine coal, and I don't blame them for the rise of large-scale surface mining. I may be naïve, but I refuse to believe that the people who work on modern-day mountaintop removal operations *enjoy* destroying old-growth forests, ancient ridges, bubbling streams, and the lives of local residents. It's a job that pays well, so they do it. Orders come down from an air-conditioned office somewhere out of state, and the orders must be followed. But on the other hand, it's *just* a job. There are other—cleaner, safer, more sustainable—jobs.

Shards of coal were scattered amid the flaky gray stones around the mouth of the shaft. I stuffed a few pieces into the cargo pockets of my pants and turned away from the mine. Tiffany and I decided to try a more direct route back to the Bird Wagon—straight up the mountain instead of on meandering switchback trails—so we scrambled up the embankment and began the steep climb. As I pulled myself over a pile of rocks, I remembered home, and Jesse, and realized that if I drove fast, I could make it back to Virginia in time for a late anniversary dinner. I followed close behind Tiffany, lumps of coal cold against my leg.

FOURTEEN

★

LONG JOURNEYS

Mr. Bones and I sat on the back porch in the sun, watching gold-finches cling to the drooping heads of sunflowers that, to the birds' delight, had sprouted in the mulch beneath the feeders. A cicada buzzed in the afternoon heat, and I inched my plastic porch chair back into the shade. Mr. Bones panted as he watched a song sparrow scratch around beneath the feeders.

Jesse was somewhere in the bowels of the veterinary school's teaching hospital, working on his orthopedic surgery rotation. After my Tennessee adventure, Jesse and I had taken a quick trip north to see our parents and had now returned to Virginia. Like the early days of March, early August hummed with anticipation, albeit differently from the promises of spring. In the spring, the birds gear up for the breeding season while the humans (or at least I) begin looking forward to the return of leaves, flowers, and the long hot days of summer. In August, though, the migratory songbirds ready themselves for their trips south for the winter; where "south" is varies by species. For cerulean warblers, it means the Andes Mountains in northern South America. For some species, "south" means Texas, Florida, or even Virginia. For others, like the Arctic tern, fall migration takes them all the way from northern Canada to Antarctica—nearly pole to pole.

August heralds summer's end for me, too; school-related emails begin to appear in my inbox, and my thoughts turn from my own writing and traveling to preparing syllabi, responding to students hoping to add my courses, and planning assignments. For me, like the migratory birds, August means gearing up for a change of pace. By now, most ceruleans were probably either on their way south or about to begin their three thousand mile trips. I hoped the birds I'd helped to band in Lewis Wetzel made it safely to their wintering grounds, and I hoped that the wee baby cerulean I'd seen in Royal Blue was big enough and strong enough for his first journey. He had seemed so small and fragile; how could such a little thing possibly make the trip?

Migration is the least-known part of the cerulean's life cycle; while scientists can make some claims about the route ceruleans take, no one can say for certain how most of the birds get from North America to South America and vice versa. During the spring migration, many researchers believe that ceruleans depart from their winter homes in the Andes in March and then fly above Panama, Costa Rica, Nicaragua, and Honduras before stopping in Belize, Guatemala, or Chiapas, Mexico, though the exact route may vary. From there, they take off across the Gulf of Mexico, flying nonstop until they reach the Gulf Coast of the United States, probably in Louisiana, Mississippi, Alabama, or even the west coast of Florida. While it's difficult to measure, most biologists think it takes songbirds about fifteen hours to cross the Gulf of Mexico from Central America. According to Paul Hamel's species account in *The Birds of North America*, the cerulean's fall migration patterns need more study. He writes, "Fall routes [are] presumably the reverse of spring," but acknowledges that there is little data on the subject. He notes that the cerulean's fall migration could begin as early as July and extend until October; in Ohio, migration peaks from August to early September, with "coastal Alabama records" from July 18 until September 16. In Panama, ceruleans have been recorded passing through en route to South America from late August to early October.

Most biologists agree that migration is the most dangerous time for songbirds. Melinda Welton, a biologist who has studied the spring migration of cerulean warblers in Central America, suggests that up to 89 percent of annual mortality could occur during migration. Studying this perilous time in the birds' lives is difficult for many reasons. First, the timing: most ceruleans pass through Central America in early April, peaking between April 3 and April 10. "The work is very labor intensive," Welton explained to me, "and we only get about two weeks to do it."

The areas of Central America where biologists assume the birds briefly stop on their way north are remote, rugged, and extremely difficult to reach. From 2004 to 2007, Welton conducted several studies in four Central American countries, beginning with Belize in 2004. To reach the first study site in the Maya Mountains, Welton and her local guides had to endure a three-day hike through a forested area that had recently been devastated by a hurricane. "We had to negotiate these massive tree piles," she said, and since the Maya Mountains have very little surface water, they had to carry all their water with them. Soon after reaching the study site on the third day, they spotted a male cerulean warbler, which was especially rewarding after a difficult trek. Welton observed sixteen ceruleans in the vicinity of the study site—making them the most common migrant—but she had to cut fieldwork short because they ran out of food; their last meal before leaving camp consisted of river snails.

The Belize study site was chosen, at least in part, because of research conducted by Ted Parker, one of the first biologists to study cerulean migration. Parker suggested that after leaving South America, ceruleans crossed the Caribbean Sea (bypassing Panama, Costa Rica, and Nicaragua) before landing in Belize, where the birds would spend a few weeks preparing for their trans-Gulf flight. Tragically, in 1993 Parker was killed in a small-plane crash; he was just forty years old. In 2005, the research area was expanded to include study sites in Guatemala and Honduras, where Welton's team tallied a total of twenty-nine migrating cerulean warblers. More study sites were added in 2006, and the team observed forty-eight ceruleans. In 2007, Tiffany Beachy joined Welton's crew to help develop a "habitat model" that could be used to predict areas favorable to passing-through ceruleans. Tiffany began searching for ceruleans in Chiapas, Mexico, a region Welton hadn't studied yet.

Some of the results of the four-year study revealed that ceruleans were most likely to be found in primary forest in tall, mid-story trees. Some were found in second-growth trees as well, but in lesser numbers. Unfortunately for migrating ceruleans, much of the primary forest in Central America has met the same fate as primary forest in North and South America—the trees are razed for cattle pasture and other forms of agriculture and development. This forces ceruleans to retreat to shrinking patches of suitable habitat, often to remote parts of countries where widespread development hasn't yet reached.

In addition to timing and the remoteness of the study areas, another difficulty is that during migration ceruleans tend to join mixed-species flocks. According to Welton, migrating ceruleans were often found in flocks that included lesser greenlets (a tropical member of the vireo family), American redstarts, Magnolia warblers, Tennessee warblers, and black-and-white warblers. Tiffany described to me the process of locating ceruleans in these mixed groups: "Whenever we'd find a flock, we'd identify every species, including residents. The lesser greenlets were pretty vocal, and they were resident, so whenever we'd hear one singing, we'd stop what we were doing and look for it and see if it was hanging out in flock. They almost always were. So we'd look through the flock to see if there was a cerulean." Sometimes they would play a recorded male cerulean song to try to lure one of the birds into view. "If one did sing in response," she explained, "it was brief and really quiet. Sometimes they just come down and check it out. We'd usually just get a quick glimpse. The cerulean would show up, make an appearance, and disappear." Despite these challenges, in 2007 the team observed a total of 133 migrating ceruleans across the four countries—Mexico, Belize, Honduras, and Guatemala.

While 133 is a significantly higher tally than 2004's total of 16, it still begs the question: where are the rest of the migrating ceruleans? If the US Fish and Wildlife Service is correct, and the total cerulean population hovers around 400,000, where do all the birds go during migration? It doesn't seem likely that teams of experienced biologists somehow missed hundreds of thousands of cerulean warblers funneling through Central America. One hypothesis is that some birds do not need to stop there; some individuals may have sufficient energy stores to fly all the way from the Northern Andes to the Gulf Coast of North America. A few records of migrating cerulean warblers in Cuba also exist, though this route is considered atypical. Hopefully, emerging research tools, such as measuring stable isotopes in cerulean blood or feathers, and the continued refinement of more traditional research tools, such as radio telemetry, will help answer some of the difficult questions about the cerulean's migration route.

I sighed, and Mr. Bones stood up, scratched his ear with a back paw, and then settled back on the grass. I watched the goldfinches flit from sunflower to honeysuckle bush and back to sunflower; soon, their bright yellow plumage would fade to the drab olive they wear all winter. I wiped my forehead with my T-shirt sleeve. It was odd to think about winter when the weather was still sweltering, the leaves still green, and the birds still in their breeding plumage. But we all knew changes were coming.

Mr. Bones and I went inside to escape the heat. For a distraction, I turned on the television. A cable news channel reported about a hurricane swirling in the Caribbean; its name was Dean, the first Atlantic hurricane of the season. Meteorologists expected Dean to strengthen and become a Category 5 before making landfall, probably on Mexico's Yucatan Peninsula. I watched the spiraling satellite images and felt a pang of fear. Mid-August was the beginning of the cerulean's peak migration time. Surely some of the tiny blue birds had already been caught up in the high winds and heavy rains. I imagined them trying to beat their fragile wings against the massive storm, then growing tired and desperate, and finally dropping into the sea to their deaths.

I turned off the television and sat on my couch in silence. I looked up at the Audubon print hanging above my fish tank. What a leap of faith it was to fly across the vast Gulf of Mexico. The fledgling cerulean warbler that we'd watched in the basswood tree in Tennessee had never made the journey before, but something told him he had to do it. Maybe the earth's magnetism, or photoperiod, or temperature, or prey patterns, or some combination of those factors directs them. Whatever guides the birds, I can only imagine what it's like to take off over open water with just my wings to carry me—one mistake, one storm, one faltering could mean death by drowning.

I hoped my journey back to the classroom would be smoother than the ceruleans' journeys back south; I hoped I wouldn't meet my own hurricane somewhere between here and where I was headed. But the seasons will keep changing no matter what happens to us. Fall will eventually arrive and turn to winter. Challenges will loom and fade. Spring will come again and—hopefully—some cerulean warblers will make it back to Appalachia and the cycle will repeat.

PART THREE

Fall

FIFTEEN

★

THE ONLY RISK
IS WANTING TO STAY

I SQUINTED IN THE BRIGHT OCTOBER sunshine and followed the distracted crowd of biologists across the runway of the Palo Negro airport in northeastern Colombia. I made my way through the small terminal and out the other side to where I heard our chartered bus would be waiting for us. More birding occurred on the stroll across the landscaped area near the parked bus; in addition to white-winged swallows and buff-breasted martins, I added the ruddy ground dove and bi-colored wren to my life list. A red and black vermillion flycatcher, a bird I'd only seen once before, in Arizona, perched on a branch and bobbed its tail.

Our bus, a large, modern Chevy, idled nearby. Painted orange and white, it had *COOTRANSMAGDALENA* printed on its side and across the grill and *Somos Colombia* in script above the windshield. In addition to several depictions of the Virgin Mary, the bus had sort of a Bart Simpson theme; on a side window, an outline of the cartoon mooned us as we approached with our luggage—which we stowed in a compartment below, not strapped to the top like on the *chivas* I'd heard about. Inside, the bus had spacious, comfortable seats; I settled in beside a window near the front of the bus, and cerulean warbler godfather Paul Hamel took the seat next to me, smiling and loosening his tie.

Before the Cerulean Warbler Summit, I'd only communicated with Dr. Hamel via email, and he was even more charming in real life. Despite the fact that he was one of the—if not *the*—pioneers of cerulean warbler research, he seemed humble and kind. His steel-gray hair and professional suit and tie were offset by his goatee and the small gold hoop he wore in his left ear. During the summit, he'd acted as sort of the bilingual master of ceremonies. He smiled a lot and seemed to genuinely care about the *people* involved with cerulean warblers. I also reunited with the lovely Tiffany Beachy, who had just finished her master of science degree; we shared a hotel room, and she introduced me to many cerulean folks I'd yet to meet. Randy Dettmers, nest-finding expert extraordinaire, had helped plan the summit and led several sessions; unfortunately, the West Virginia contingent—Petra Wood and Greg George—were unable to attend. The second part of the summit— a visit to the 545-acre Cerulean Warbler Reserve near the town of San Vicente de Chucurí—began here, in Bucaramanga, the capital of the Department (or state) of Santander. About two dozen of us made the trip from Bogotá. Bucaramanga is only about 180 miles northeast of Bogotá, but it takes about ten hours to get there by bus. We flew.

During the summit, one of the South American biologists described this mountainous region of Santander as "a paradise for birds." Once the ceruleans arrive here in the fall, they disperse to the middle elevations of the Andes in Colombia, Venezuela, Ecuador, and Peru, where they spend the winter months in mixed-species flocks. Ceruleans aren't the only Neotropical migrants that travel to this region; they are joined by the American redstart, Swainson's thrush, gray catbird, scarlet tanager, rose-breasted grosbeak, and a wide variety of others familiar to bird lovers in the United States. In South America, "our" migratory songbirds share the habitat with tropical residents bearing marvelous names, such as the deep-blue flowerpiercer, the white-vented euphonia, the ocellated tapaculo, the sooty-capped puffbird, and hundreds of others. Literally, *hundreds* of others. In fact, Colombia hosts a wider variety of birds than any other country on the planet: an incredible 1,870 species. By comparison, the continental United States has approximately 654 bird species.

Colombia is able to harbor such a vast number of birds because of its size and varied habitats. Nearly twice as big as Texas, Colombia is the only South American country with shores on both the Pacific Ocean and the Caribbean Sea, separated by the Isthmus of Panama. Colombia boasts a total of 1,993 miles of coastline—twice as much as California. The country is roughly bisected northeast to southwest by three parallel Andean mountain ranges, or *cordilleras*. While Colombia's Andes aren't as high as the peaks in Peru or Chile, its tallest summit measures 18,946 feet, more than 400 feet higher than any mountain in the contiguous United States. The westernmost range, not far inland from the Pacific, is the Cordillera Occidental; the Cauca River runs through the valley between the Cordillera Occidental and the Cordillera Central. The Magdalena River—the country's most important waterway, which begins in south-central Colombia and flows more than nine hundred miles north until it reaches the Caribbean Sea near the city of Barranquilla—cuts through the deep valley that separates the central range from the eastern range, the Cordillera Oriental. Bogotá, Colombia's capital city of more than eight million people, sits 8,000 feet above sea level near the geographic center of the country, on the Cordillera Oriental. To the east of the Cordillera Oriental are the *llanos,* or arid lowland plains, and to the southeast, the tropical jungles of the Amazon. These vastly different habitats—two coasts, high mountains, rainforests, and plains—make Colombia one of the most biodiverse countries on the planet.

Unfortunately, Colombia's unparalleled biodiversity faces an array of complicated threats. As lands are cleared for agriculture and development, forests are fragmented. Coffee, which is grown on the slopes of all three of Colombia's mountain ranges, holds an extremely important place in the country's economy. Small family farms grow and harvest much of Colombia's coffee. I learned during the summit that these farmers, called *cafeteros,* do not want to be known as "the destroyers of birds," but as the global demand for their product increases, they face a difficult choice: cut down the trees and grow coffee quickly in the full sun, or leave the shade trees and grow coffee more slowly. Of course, growing coffee more slowly means selling fewer beans, which in turn means less money for the *cafeteros* and their families. The cerulean warbler finds itself in the middle of this conundrum.

Colombia's coffee-growing regions overlap with the cerulean's wintering range; like coffee, ceruleans can be found on all three of Colombia's *cordilleras.* Ceruleans and coffee also occur at approximately the same elevation—3,000 to 6,000 feet. While many researchers believe that unfragmented primary forest provides the ideal habitat for wintering ceruleans, the birds definitely do forage in the trees of shade-grown coffee farms. Ceruleans—along with American redstarts, Blackburnian warblers, Tennessee warblers, and others—glean spiders, caterpillars, and small insects from the leaves and flowers of bucaré, inga, laurel, and other trees that commonly shade coffee shrubs. While coffee farms may not provide the *ideal* wintering habitat, purchasing Colombian shade-grown or "bird friendly" coffee will help conserve the cerulean warbler and other Neotropical migratory songbirds.

I LET OUT A DEEP breath as our bus rumbled to life; this was my first time traveling in the Andes, and I'd been steeling myself for a harrowing bus ride. Surprisingly, though, the road was wide and well paved, complete with a double yellow line. On our way out of town and away from Palo Negro airport, we passed many small shops and roadside bars, most adorned with yellow billboards advertising Aguila, *La Cerveza de Colombia*. As the landscape became more rural, the road steepened and wound up a mountainside. The bus driver didn't seem to know the rule about slowing down before he reached the apex of a turn; we whipped around curve after curve, and I felt certain the bus would go careening over a ledge at any moment—or hit another vehicle head on, since the ones barreling down the steep highway seemed even more out of control than ours. As Paul Hamel pointed out cacao shrubs and citrus trees along the road, I felt my stomach begin to gurgle uncomfortably. I popped another Dramamine and tried to focus on the horizon.

When I (and I think several others) were almost ready to vomit, the bus pulled off the road into the dusty parking lot of La Renta, a brick open-air restaurant painted orange and lime green. A young waitress in a tank top and jean shorts remained calm as the gringos took over nearly every table in the place with cameras, backpacks, and most importantly, binoculars. A few nearby tables of Colombians smiled curiously at us. Camila, the Colombian biologist who'd bravely organized the logistics of the trip, arranged for us to be served a breakfast of eggs, doughy potato dumplings, and fresh tangerines. All the coffee was served *con leche*; the waitress seemed surprised when I asked for mine black.

The front of the restaurant was open to the parking lot; a few flies buzzed around us, and a cat curled between our legs beneath the table. Livestock trucks, yellow pod-shaped taxis, and small pickups sped along in front of the restaurant; across the street, a small shop sold what appeared to be recently slaughtered and skinned creatures. I couldn't exactly tell what they were, but I suspected young goats or perhaps piglets. A cow with a hump and floppy ears stood in a pen next to the shop; perhaps in a few days she'd be suspended from the ceiling, too. A woman behind the counter wrapped red chunks in sheets of wax paper, and a man in knee-high rubber boots and a cowboy hat slumped on a stool, waiting. A brown and white pit bull–like dog with a docked tail lounged on the dusty grass nearby.

Suddenly, someone spotted a yellow-headed caracara in a tall tree across the road. The birders dropped their tangerine peels, sprung from the plastic chairs, and spilled across the busy highway, clutching their binoculars and pointing. Several were almost run down by speeding cattle trucks. The Colombians at nearby tables continued to smile at us and our bizarre behavior. Once the caracara excitement waned, we piled back on the bus; just beyond La Renta, we turned off the highway onto a gravel road and headed towards San Vicente de Chucurí, our destination, about fifty miles away.

As soon as we left the main road, many of my expectations about traveling in the Andes finally manifested themselves. The bus slowed to a rumbling crawl as we lurched around hairpin switchbacks and through deep ruts. Although the road was technically "two lanes," we barely squeaked past other crawling vehicles. In one case we squeezed by another bus, this one quite a bit more rickety; a little girl in a window seat waved and grinned at us as we passed inches from each other. We did actually pull over occasionally for other vehicles to pass; I grew thankful for those times. Often, though, the road had no shoulder—six inches from the berm, the mountain dropped off steeply. Rusted barbed wire strung between weathered fence posts sometimes served as a boundary between winding road and deep ravine. While a bit terrifying, the landscape was ruggedly beautiful, emerald green, and obviously agricultural.

We approached a patch of thick vegetation, and someone a few rows back called out, "Coffee on the right!"

"No," said Paul Hamel, swiveling, "that's cacao."

Cacao grew on shrubs that resembled rhododendrons. Contrary to what I'd once thought, chocolate comes from cacao and cocaine comes from coca (also an important industry, but illegal, of course). In addition to coffee and cacao, cattle are integral to Colombia's economy. We'd passed several small groups of cows, most of which had humped shoulders and long, floppy ears. While much of the land looked like pasture, thick patches of trees remained on some of the steep mountain slopes. A fast-moving river twisted through a valley below us. I thought it may have been the Magdalena, but it wasn't; the Magdalena, I was told, was a hell of a lot bigger. This stream was a tributary, possibly the Rio Chucurí.

"Speaking of cacao..." Dr. Hamel said, bending to rummage in his pack. "Ah." He sat up with a can of chocolate-covered coffee beans and handed them to me. "You start," he said, smiling, "then pass them around."

As I crunched one of the candies, our bus creaked and chugged around another tight switchback. I looked out the window, and far below us I could see a dusty portion of the road we'd just driven up. Then the driver suddenly lurched to a stop and beeped the horn. I pressed my temple against the window to try to see what we'd stopped for. A few seconds later, a gray burro with long stalks of sugar cane lashed to its back trotted past my window; there were so many stalks of cut sugarcane that it looked as if the burro was carrying the raw materials for a beaver dam. The bus growled to life and continued crawling. We passed two other laden burros, and then a thin man with a machete; he, too, waved at us and flashed a toothy grin. The scene brought to mind the commercial images of Juan Valdez and his mule.

In addition to Juan and coffee, I (like other people from the United States) often associated Colombia with kidnapping and cocaine cartels—stereotypes fueled by Hollywood and a news media obsessed with catastrophes. Before traveling to Colombia, I gave myself a crash course in the country's history, which I learned is often confusing and complicated, from Colombia's indigenous beginnings, to Spanish colonization, to Simón Bolívar, and onward to modern times. Even though all of my experiences in the country so far had been wonderful—not scary and not the least bit threatening—its violent recent past was never far from my mind. I also learned that the Department of Santander, and specifically the towns of San Vicente de Chucurí and nearby Barrancabermeja, have a somewhat turbulent history.

As I understood it, Colombia's political turmoil of the last fifty years began with a series of related events: a class struggle between wealthy and peasant coffee farmers in the 1940s and the assassination of a popular politician in 1948, which led to a bloody backlash that spread across Colombia. This period of widespread murder, rape, and torture lasted about ten years, took at least 200,000 lives, and is known, appropriately, as *La Violencia*. By the mid-1960s, the various opposing political and ideological forces involved in *La Violencia* (Communists, Conservatives, Liberals, paramilitaries, narcotics traffickers, guerrillas, Catholic priests, leftist intellectuals, peasants) began to organize. In 1964, two prominent rebel armies emerged. The largest, the *Fuerzas Armadas Revolucionarias de Colombia* (Revolutionary Armed Forces of Colombia, or FARC), mobilized as a Marxist-Leninist offshoot of Colombia's Communist Party. The FARC, classified by the United States, the European Union, and just about everyone else as a terrorist organization, is notorious for kidnapping and ransoming politicians, tourists, wealthy Colombians, and random passersby. As of early 2008, the FARC's membership was estimated at 9,000 (down from 17,000 in 2002), but the group still held as many as 700 people captive throughout Colombia, some for more than eight years.

The second-largest rebel group, the *Ejército de Liberación Nacional* (National Liberation Army, or ELN) also emerged in 1964; one of its first appearances was a march through the streets of San Vicente de Chucurí, the small mountain town where we were headed. Despite the fact that its members, too, participate in kidnapping and ransoming, the ELN is sometimes seen as more ideological than the FARC; it draws inspiration from the Cuban Revolution, Che Guevara, and Catholic liberation theology. As of 2008, the ELN reportedly had about 3,000 members. The center of its activities was historically northeastern Colombia, including the Department of Santander. In addition to a guerrilla presence, the region has also had to deal with right-wing, paramilitary death squads, such as the *Autodefensas Unidas de Colombia*, or AUC, whose mission is to eliminate the left-wing guerrilla groups and their sympathizers. The towns of Barrancabermeja and San Vicente de Chucurí were subject to competing guerrilla and paramilitary presences until very recently—as recently as 2002.

I watched the steep green mountains, lush pastures, and tangled vegetation outside the bus's window; it was difficult to imagine violence and terrorism in such an idyllic locale. Colombia's many factions seemed to be engaged in never-ending struggles—and, as in so many other complicated, international struggles, the United States found a way to intervene. While I believe (perhaps naïvely) that my government usually has the best of intentions, it seems that we sometimes make matters worse, or we find that our actions have unintended consequences. In 1999, the US and Colombian governments initiated "Plan Colombia," still ongoing in 2008. The plan, a multifaceted strategy to combat the illegal narcotics trade, includes the training of the Colombian military by the US military, the aerial herbicidal spraying of suspected coca farms, and $5 billion in military and economic aid to Colombia. Despite these expensive efforts, in 2008 the Associated Press reported that Colombia was still "the source of 90% of the cocaine in the United States and most of the heroin consumed east of the Mississippi River." While it has apparently failed to significantly reduce the production of cocaine, one of the results of Plan Colombia was growth in the memberships of the country's military and police forces, and a corresponding decline in the membership of guerrilla groups. Because of these shifts, Colombia is no longer known as "the kidnap capital of the world"; in fact, the Colombian government announced that kidnappings in the country were down 80 percent since 2002, and they launched a new tourism campaign with a bold slogan—"Colombia is Passion: The Only Risk is Wanting to Stay."

Despite the Colombian government's insistence on the country's safety, I was nervous about traveling there. Of course, I realized that the Cerulean Warbler Technical Group wouldn't hold its annual meeting in Bogotá and San Vicente de Chucurí if those places weren't at least somewhat safe, and I figured that the US State Department's warnings about traveling in Colombia probably fell into the "better safe than sorry" category. Deadly acts of random violence could occur at any time, in any place, and I couldn't live my life in a bubble. At least, that's what I tried to convince myself of as I chewed my fingernails in the Miami airport a few days earlier, waiting for my flight to Bogotá. But, up to this point, my Colombian adventure had been nothing but positive. Bogotá seemed similar to many other large cities I'd visited: street vendors sold candy, magazines, and cigarettes; taxis and buses sped up and down the congested avenues; citizens in suits and heels hurried along crowded sidewalks. The Colombian biologists, environmental educators, and coffee federation representatives had been friendly, generous hosts. So far, my only regret was that I didn't speak much Spanish, despite having several semesters of it in college. I often found myself saying, "Lo siento, mi Español no es bueno."

Colombia's political situation can, at times, make studying cerulean warblers difficult. Wintering ceruleans inhabit the country's forested mountains; in addition to overlapping with coffee-growing regions, the cerulean's range also overlaps with areas formerly inhabited by guerrilla and paramilitary groups. When the Colombian military forced these groups to abandon their camps and retreat, the guerrillas left deadly surprises behind: landmines. Soldiers and police are the intended targets, but children and civilians are maimed and killed by the mines as well. As of 2006, Colombia ranked third in the world for landmine fatalities and injuries, behind Cambodia and Afghanistan. The Departments of Santander and Antioquia to its west consistently fall near the top of the within-country list of landmine incidences; these two departments are also cerulean warbler strongholds. Biologists studying the birds in these remote areas literally risk life and limb.

In addition to the threat posed by guerrilla landmines, cerulean researchers in the tropics face other challenges. In the Appalachians during the breeding season, male ceruleans—filled with testosterone and quick to defend their territories—sing and counter-sing all morning. Once the birds pair up and begin to build nests, researchers can flag, map, and monitor the locations. In the wintering grounds, however, biologists have no such luck; the birds occasionally sing and respond to playback, but not with the fervor of springtime. For the most part, non-breeding ceruleans stay quiet, and there are no nests for biologists to observe.

Because of these factors and others, much of the research on cerulean warblers (and Neotropical migrants in general) has been conducted on the breeding grounds. One summit presentation stated that from 1996 to 2006, 75 percent of migratory songbird studies focused on the breeding season; thus, the answers to some important questions about how ceruleans spend the winter months remain unclear. For example, researchers admit that they do not yet know the exact location of the nucleus of the cerulean's wintering range. Do the majority of ceruleans spend the season in Colombia? Or Venezuela? Could Peru or Ecuador potentially hold the core wintering area? How many ceruleans over-winter in Bolivia? Despite the many challenges, biologists in North and South America continue to work together to unravel the mystery of how—and where—cerulean warblers spend their non-breeding months.

SIXTEEN

★

SAN VICENTE DE CHUCURÍ

*A*s steep mountains passed by outside the window, I noticed the bus seemed to be slowing down. We rumbled past a few modest homes that sat close to the road; chickens scratched the ground around their side doors, and dusty motorcycles leaned against stucco walls. Flowers bloomed in yards in every shade of orange, peach, and salmon.

"San Vicente," Dr. Hamel said, smiling as he straightened his tie and suit jacket.

I glanced at my watch; it had taken us almost three hours to drive fifty miles. Our bus, which seemed too big for the steep, narrow streets, bumped into the busy, brightly colored town. Stucco and brick buildings—painted pink, tan, orange, and lime green—lined the streets. Almost all of the shops had open fronts: restaurants, bars with yellow Aguila signs, grocery stores, clothing boutiques, cell phone vendors. The bus pulled up to the Hotel Faraones, located just a few steps from San Vicente's *parque principal*, the town square. I stepped off the bus and onto Calle 10, one of the town's main streets. At a bar and restaurant on the corner near our hotel, people sitting at tables stopped eating to watch as we unloaded our luggage from beneath the bus. We were very conspicuous; people in nearby stores came to the edge of the sidewalk to stare at us. I smiled uncertainly as I waited for Tiffany to collect her pack. It was warmer and more humid here than in Bogotá; I wiped sweat from my temple and glanced around.

San Vicente de Chucurí bustled with life on this Friday afternoon. Motorcycles zipped along the streets, and yellow pod-taxis waited along the town square.

Mud-caked compact pickup trucks seemed to be the vehicle of choice. There was also an abundance of short, colorful buses and small livestock trucks, which had high sides of metal or wooden slats and tarps for roofs. Men leaning in doorways wore jeans, T-shirts, and knee-high rubber boots, which I'd begun to notice were a trend here in Santander, and probably necessary for working outdoors in agriculture.

A dark-haired boy, perhaps five years old, ventured out of a clothing shop and onto the sidewalk near me. I smiled at him, and he looked up at me curiously while chewing on a fingernail. "*¿Gringa?*" he asked.

"*Sí,*" I nodded. "*Buenas tardes.*"

The boy spun and ran back into the store.

I smiled and followed Tiffany into the doorway of our hotel and up a staircase to the second floor. At the top of the stairs was the check-in desk and reception area, complete with a few couches and a television tuned to a soccer game. Two huge, permanently open arched windows looked out over the street below. While Camila arranged the room assignments with the woman behind the desk, I rested my elbows on the window's ledge and leaned out. To the left was the town square, and to the right more stores lined the street; after a block or two, the buildings seemed to transition to residences. The horizon beyond the town was made of green mountains, and beyond those, gray mountains. Directly across the street was another brick hotel with similar second-floor open windows; two dark-haired women leaned on the ledge, watching the remaining gringos recover their luggage from beneath the bus. None of the buildings I'd seen so far looked taller than three stories, and most seemed to have one or two. Below the hotel across the street was a *Restaurante y Asadero* advertising *pollo asado,* or roast chicken. Nearby, a brightly painted clothing boutique, a convenience store, and a veterinarian's office welcomed customers.

Tiffany and I were assigned a room on the hotel's third floor. Our group needed to assemble in a few minutes for lunch at a nearby restaurant, so we unlocked our door, dropped our packs on our single beds, and quickly used the bathroom. Our room was small but neat; the two beds and the nightstand between them were the only pieces of furniture, save for a small television mounted on the wall opposite the beds. An oscillating fan hung above Tiffany's bed, and a window that opened to the second-floor reception area was above mine. When it was my turn to use our room's pink bathroom, I noticed the single knob to control the water in the sink. Tiffany, who had, in the past, spent months traveling in this part of the world, explained to me that outside of major urban areas, a lack of hot water was typical. "And try not to flush any paper down the toilet," she warned. "Most sewers in Latin American towns can't handle it."

After splashing cold water on my face and changing out of my T-shirt into a lighter linen blouse, Tiffany and I met up with the rest of our group and walked half a block to a second-floor restaurant. Two long tables were set for us; folks from our group began to sit down at one of the tables. Our Colombian hosts—some of whom had been at the summit in Bogotá, as well as some new faces—settled in chairs at the other table. Tiffany and I and a few biologists from the United States decided to mix things up and sit with our hosts.

We all introduced ourselves and learned that many of our tablemates worked for Fundación ProAves Colombia, a nonprofit organization and one of the sponsors of the summit. Formed in 1998, ProAves's mission is "to protect birds and their habitats in Colombia through research, conservation action and community outreach." Through partnerships, outreach, and passionate staff and volunteers, ProAves has become one of the most effective conservation organizations in all of Latin America. One of their primary goals is to protect key bird habitat by developing a system of reserves, such as the 545-acre *La Reserva Natural de las Aves Reinita Cielo Azul*, the Cerulean Warbler Reserve, which I'd be visiting the following day. ProAves managed eleven reserves across Colombia, totaling more than 37,000 acres and protecting more than 10 percent of the world's bird species; in 2006, they formed EcoTurs Colombia to boost ecotourism in these areas.

In addition to protecting important bird habitat, ProAves worked diligently to involve local communities in conservation. One of their educational outreach programs, *Amigos de las Aves* (Friends of the Birds), has enrolled more than three thousand children throughout Colombia. These groups of children participate in conservation campaigns while learning about the importance of protecting birds and their habitats. Schools can also become *Escuelas Amigas de las Aves* by incorporating bird-friendly lessons into their curriculums. One of the most impressive ProAves outreach tools is the *Loro Bus*, or Parrot Bus, a brightly painted mobile classroom. Since 2005 the *Loro Bus* has toured most of Colombia, spreading ProAves's message of bird conservation to even the most remote regions of the country. During demonstrations, a ProAves staff member dresses in a yellow-eared parrot costume, to the delight of the children. ProAves also formed *Las Mujeres para la Conservación*, a group of women from rural areas who make jewelry and other handcrafts to sell at ProAves's reserves. *Las Mujeres* had a table displaying their wares at the summit in Bogotá; I'd purchased a beaded cerulean warbler bracelet for myself and several necklaces as gifts.

I learned that our visit coincided with the kickoff of ProAves's Fifth Annual Migratory Birds Festival, and that after lunch there would be a parade through the streets of San Vicente, followed by a ceremony near the town square. Tiffany, who spoke Spanish fluently, translated the ProAves staff's words for us while I chewed

on the most delicious slice of papaya I'd ever tasted. A parade? I had no idea what
to expect.

I WAS DEFINITELY NOT PREPARED for the marching band. After hurriedly finishing our lunches, our group filed down the stairs to the town square. The heat
from the sultry late-afternoon sun made me sweat, and I was surprised to see
hundreds of *Chucureños* crowding the square, many sipping water and clutching
digital cameras, waiting for the parade; a few stray dogs wound between the spec-
tators, and I noticed that several vendors with food carts had appeared along the
sidewalk. Mothers in tight jeans chatted with each other as they balanced infants
on their hips, white-haired grandfathers smiled while talking into cell phones, and
young men with tattooed shoulders sported white tank tops and gold chains. Our
group of more than twenty gringos drew the attention of many in the crowd. Almost as soon as we arrived on the square, we heard the cadence of snare drums as
the parade turned down the street.

My jaw literally dropped. Leading the parade were four young teenagers in
blue pants, white shirts, and yellow visors; each visor had either a cut-out cerulean warbler or golden-winged warbler attached to its front. I noticed that each
bird was slightly different—they'd obviously been hand painted by the children.
Tears stung my eyes, but I blinked them away. Each of the four leaders held onto
a corner of a banner that announced, *"Aves Migratorias ¡Viajeras Extremas!"* and
featured an outline of North and South America as well as pictures of a cerulean
warbler, a golden-winged warbler, a Canada warbler, and an olive-sided flycatcher.
Behind the banner marched a procession of students in their school uniforms; the
girls wore black and white plaid, knee-length jumper dresses over short-sleeved
white blouses, white mid-calf socks, and black Mary Janes. The boys, looking definitely more comfortable, wore white button-down shirts and black trousers. The
students, mostly girls, each twirled a long baton adorned with red, yellow, and blue
tassels on one end—the colors of Colombia's flag. The rows of twirlers stepped to
the rhythm beat by the band marching behind them. Everyone in our group (including me, I'm sure) wore the same facial expression, characterized by wide eyes
and huge grins, and punctuated by laughter and applause. The band's cymbals,
trumpeters, and chime players led the rows of snare and bass drums. Several of the
students beating drums added flourishes and spins with their drumsticks.

Behind the band, five more students held up another banner, this one with *"Con-
servamos Los Recursos Naturales"* printed on it, along with artistic renditions of people watching birds, farming, and riding in buses, all near a river and a forest. The
banner was beautiful, but behind the banner followed one of the most spectacular

Boys dressed as warblers, and girls dressed as fairies.

things I have ever seen: dozens of elementary school children wearing cerulean and golden-winged warbler costumes. I am usually embarrassed for children who are forced to dress in silly outfits and parade around (Ralphie wearing the bunny suit in *A Christmas Story* comes to mind), but these bird-children were too darn *cute* for me to feel sympathy for them. The costumes consisted of bodysuits that covered the children from their necks down to their knees. The bodysuits were painted to resemble the features of the two warbler species; the cerulean suits even included black "necklaces" across the chests. Each child wore a hood of either blue or yellow, complete with pointed black visors—"beaks." The children's shoes were covered by cutout bird feet that attached around the ankles, and their arms and hands were hidden inside "wings" that the children flapped when they drew close to our group along the sidewalk. After the flapping episode, I did begin to feel a bit sorry for the children, many of whose "beaks" had either slipped down their faces or had been propped on top of their heads. But I didn't let my sympathy stop me from *ooh*ing and *ahh*ing and snapping about a million photographs.

After the warbler children, I thought the parade would end; there couldn't possibly be more youngsters in the small town of San Vicente de Chucurí. Of course, I was wrong. Next came a group of children dressed as fairies. At least, the girls were dressed as fairies, brandishing glittery magic wands and wearing conical hats with streamers; the boys in the group wore black headbands and camouflage. In the center of the group, a boy in an elaborate military uniform and a girl dressed as a fairy walked arm in arm, each wearing a crown. Behind this group of children were even more children, mostly boys, it seemed, carrying tall sticks with painted wooden cutouts of rainforest creatures attached to them—birds, frogs, trees, snails, flowers, butterflies. If I had to guess, I'd say these boys were dressed as Juan Valdez; most had red or black bandanas tied around their necks, untucked button-down shirts, and a variety of wide-brimmed hats. Some even had eyeliner mustaches and wore cloth satchels across their chests. Next came another group of children, all wearing cerulean or golden-winged warbler visors, and finally, bringing up the rear, was a ProAves pickup truck followed by the brightly painted Loro Bus.

The pickup truck's hood was covered with a banner announcing the Migratory Bird Festival, and the truck's driver—wearing a ProAves cap—had a cerulean warbler puppet on his left hand. Kids in warbler visors filled the truck's bed and surrounded the ProAves mascot, the yellow-eared parrot. The costumed parrot flapped his wings at the crowd as the kids in the back of the truck excitedly waved and called, "Hello! Hello!" to our group.

"¡*Hola!*" we called back, all of us laughing.

More visor-wearing children hung out the open windows of the green, yellow, blue, and red Loro Bus, and they waved and buzzed kazoos. We cheered and clapped and realized the parade had ended when a muddy cattle truck rattled past behind the Loro Bus.

The parade wrapped around San Vicente's *parque principal*, and word spread through our group that we needed to head over to the other side, where the ceremony would be held. We wound our way through the crowded square, under the spreading boughs of thick, ancient trees, around vendors selling chocolate and jewelry, before eventually reaching the square's opposite corner. We settled on the edge of the sidewalk; across the street was a raised permanent brick stage, and between the stage and us the marching band finished their final song. Once they marched past, the rest of the parade sort of disintegrated as parents swooped in for pictures of their adorned children. A teacher tried in vain to encourage the kids dressed as warblers to flap their wings once more, but I could see the perspiration running down the children's faces as a few of them pushed back their hoods. When parents handed their sweating children plastic packets of water, the neat parade rows broke down even further, and a mob of parents and kids milled around on the street in front of us.

I had been wildly snapping pictures the entire time, but I felt a little awkward about it; would these parents welcome strange gringos photographing their children? My uneasiness dissipated, however, when it suddenly seemed that every child in San Vicente pulled away from the parents and surrounded us, their curiosity finally becoming too great to ignore. At first, gangs of children clustered in front of us, whispering to each other and giggling. We kept taking pictures, so the kids began posing—they threw their arms around each other and grinned, several of them flashing peace signs and giving us thumbs-up. After posing for a picture they'd rush over, hoping to see the image on the back of a digital camera. Eventually they swarmed in even closer, putting their arms around us, asking us to pose for pictures with them, tugging on our sleeves to get our attention. I sat down on the edge of the sidewalk and immediately children sat next to me, in front of me, and squeezed in on all sides, as near as they could get.

"Hello," a few of them ventured, shyly.

"Hello," I answered, which caused them to giggle.

A girl dressed as a fairy squirmed next to me and tapped me on the arm. I leaned closer to her and she whispered, "What is your name?" Then she spun to her friend next to her and they both collapsed into each other, giggling.

"*Mi nombre es Katie,*" I said, trying to pronounce the words carefully. "*¿Cómo te llamas?*"

This caused the girls to straighten up a bit, and every child within hearing distance rattled off their full names to me, many of which seemed to contain four or five names.

"*Mucho gusto,*" I replied to each, causing more laughter all around. My *amiga* tried to form other questions in English, but each time, she'd begin to giggle uncontrollably before she'd finish the question. My mouth began to hurt from smiling so much.

While the girls continued to giggle, I glanced around and noticed that many members of our group were surrounded by their own gaggles of happy children. Chris Eberly, a biologist who worked for the nonprofit organization Partners in Flight, crouched at the center of a swarm of kids; Chris had taken his Swarovski binoculars out of his pack and handed them over to a group of fairies and Juan Valdez impersonators. One of the boys looked through the sights, tilted his head skyward, and called out, "*Chollo,*" the Spanish name for black vulture. Than Boves, the University of Tennessee graduate student who would take over Tiffany's cerulean project, was surrounded by a similar group of binocular-hounds, as was American Bird Conservancy biologist Brian Smith.

At some point during all of this, the ceremony onstage had begun. Ten or eleven well-dressed people sat on chairs, among them Paul Hamel and Emilce Suarez Pimiento, San Vicente de Chucurí's mayor. The hot sun managed to flood the stage in spite of its curved roof; one of the men held an umbrella over the mayor's head to shade her. A man approached the microphone and spoke in Spanish. The crowd quieted, and we all rose to our feet while Colombia's national anthem blared through the speakers along the stage. Afterward, we remained standing for a second song, and then a third; the second song, apparently, was the anthem of the Department of Santander, and the third, San Vicente's song. When the music stopped, I sat back down on the curb, and the children resumed their happy swarming and chattering. The ceremony onstage continued, and while most of the *Chucureño* adults in the crowd listened, I was too overwhelmed by the entire scene to pay close attention; and since it was in Spanish, I didn't understand most of what was said, but I got the impression that regional officials were offering us a warm welcome to Santander and the town of San Vicente.

To the left of the stage, I noticed two stern young men in full camouflage; I knew that summit participants—many who worked as biologists for the United States government—had been guaranteed protection by the Colombian military during our stay in Santander. I scanned the edges of the crowd and noticed more frowning men in camouflage along the buildings on the right side of the square. Each soldier carried a large machine gun; an Israeli-designed Galil assault rifle, I learned later. The young soldiers didn't seem to be having as much fun as the rest of us, and I realized that a crowd milling and mobbing around the gringos made protecting us much more difficult. I looked at the children in cerulean warbler visors and found myself wondering whom the military was protecting us from. I

Under the protection of the Colombian military.

knew I was being naïve, but this town had given us a wonderful welcome, and I felt a bit embarrassed that we were being guarded—grateful, if the soldiers were indeed necessary—but awkward nonetheless. When I watched one of the soldiers take a call on his cell phone, I felt a bit more at ease; maybe they were there for our embassy's peace of mind, after all.

Through the speakers, I heard a few words of English and realized Paul Hamel was at the podium. He presented a plaque to San Vicente's mayor on behalf of the Cerulean Warbler Technical Group and the Golden-winged Warbler Working Group; she accepted it to boisterous applause and stepped up to the microphone. After a few statements and a question, Dr. Hamel returned to the podium and informed us in English that the mayor had invited us all to walk over and look for birds together in San Vicente's fourteen-acre ecological park, *Parque Ecologico Miraflores*. The edge of the park was only about two blocks from the square; of course, we accepted, and all of us—the gringos, the children, their parents, townspeople, the mayor, the soldiers—we all followed each other away from the square and down a side street toward the park in the lengthening afternoon shadows.

I followed the children down a concrete stairway along the stucco backside of a building; the stairway overlooked a patch of thick shrubs, palm trees, and taller thin trees. I noticed avocados hanging pendulously from one of the tree's branches

as the calling of unknown birds reached my ears. Biologists from our group quickly lined the stairs and began to shout out species names: tropical kingbird, yellow
warbler, blue-gray tanager. The local kids helped, leaning against the metal railing
and pointing into the trees. One of the straw-hatted boys who'd stuck by my side
through much of the ceremony tugged my sleeve and pointed up at the wall of the
building behind us. I spun and looked in the direction he'd pointed, and I spotted a small bird foraging in a vine that resembled Virginia creeper; the bird had
a bright yellow belly, a black head, and a prominent white eye-stripe. I called out
its location to everyone standing near me, and the bird was quickly identified as
a bananaquit; even though the *Birds of Northern South America* calls the species
"fearless and ubiquitous," I was thrilled to log another life-bird, pointed out to me
by a young *Chucureño*.

We continued down the stairs, then turned away from the town and crossed a
wooden suspension bridge above a roaring creek. The *Parque Ecologico Miraflores*
began on the other side of the bridge; I followed the gang of children into the park,
which was heavily shaded by the canopies of many tall trees. Even though we were
only a few hundred yards from the center of town, the park felt isolated. The ground
was covered with grass and ferns, and stone paths curved between some of the larger tree trunks. Several soldiers sat on a concrete bench nearby, looking a bit bored.
One smoked a cigarette and watched as we searched the canopy for birds. When a
familiar racket in the trees overhead caught my attention, I politely snatched my
binoculars back from a child. I knew that scream because I heard one just like it every day inside my home in Virginia; it was the unmistakable nasal squawk of a conure, either an *Aratinga* or *Pyrrhura* species. The bird who lived in my house, named
Asha, was a blue-crowned conure, also known as a blue-crowned parakeet. I didn't
think their native range included this part of Colombia, but my heart pounded in
my chest at the possibility. Someone else in our group spotted the large green birds
first, clinging to the trunk of a tall tree; they were orange-chinned parakeets. After
several minutes of fracas, they retreated deeper into the park.

I sighed and lowered my binoculars; it was growing dark, so I decided to
take my cue from the parakeets and explore *Miraflores* a bit. Tom Will, a biologist and member of the Golden-winged Warbler Working Group, joined me, and
we strolled along the wide stone path toward the park's basketball court, where
some of our group seemed to be gathering. The path was lined with dense ferns
and shrubs taller than I was; gray, mossy boulders, short palms, and towering
trees contributed to the darkness. The park echoed with birdcalls, and large bats
emerged from the trees to hunt for insects.

Tom and I reached the basketball court, where a lone soldier, machine gun slung
loosely over his shoulder, watched a group of biologists share their binoculars with

children. Beyond the basketball court's fence appeared to be a dense forest; perhaps this was the park's boundary. The soldier nodded curtly to us as we approached; we smiled, and a conversation began. Tom spoke fluent Spanish and I did not, so perhaps it's more accurate to say that *they* had a conversation while I listened. This soldier seemed a few years older than the others I'd seen in the town. He was about my height and several scars lined his dark face. When he reached up to wipe sweat from his brow, I attempted to join the conversation: "*Estoy caliente,*" I said, "Er—*hace calor,*" and fanned myself with my hand. One of those "I'm hot" phrases referred to temperature, but the other referred to something else entirely. I wasn't sure which was which, but I hoped that fanning myself would illustrate "temperature."

"*Sí,*" the soldier nodded.

I pointed to his various cargo pockets, which I assumed were filled with ammunition. "You must be hot carrying all that stuff," I added in English.

To my surprise, the soldier grabbed his assault rifle, slipped it off his shoulder, and handed it to me. I somehow remained composed as I took the weapon from him; it was heavier than I'd imagined, and for a brief, crazy moment I considered asking Tom to take my picture holding the gun. Instead, after a few seconds I passed the rifle back to the soldier, who quickly re-shouldered it.

"That gun is heavy," I said, smiling and curling my arm as if making a muscle, then pointing to my bicep. I figured he would understand this as the universal sign for strength.

The soldier laughed, then, smiling, asked me something in Spanish. I looked to Tom for a translation. "He wants to know what you think of Colombia," Tom obliged, also smiling.

"I love Colombia," I said quickly, gesturing at the forest around us. "*¡Que linda! Muy bonita.*"

The soldier smiled again, then asked me something else. I looked at Tom, but instead of translating, he said something back to the soldier. The soldier glanced at me, then back at Tom, and finally shrugged and nodded.

As the two of them continued to converse in Spanish, my pulse thudded in my ears. He'd just willingly handed me his assault rifle; that had to be against the rules, didn't it? Maybe he'd interpreted my "you're strong" gesture as flirting; maybe that *was* flirting. Yikes.

The soldier turned and began to walk away and gestured for us to come with him. "He wants to show us the swimming pool," Tom said, as we began to follow. "They're really proud of this park," he continued. "He told me that a few years ago, it wasn't safe to walk here because there were so many guerrillas in the area."

I looked around at the park's dense foliage; it would be easy to hide here, that was certain. "What did he ask me back there?" I ventured.

"He wanted to know if you'd meet up with him in the morning, so he could take you for a walk and show you more beautiful places. He said he'd bring his gun to keep you safe. I explained to him that you weren't interested because we had a full day planned for tomorrow at the Cerulean Reserve."

"Oh!" I said, glancing at Tom. "Thank you."

AROUND 10:00 P.M., I CLIMBED the stairs to our hotel room, utterly exhausted from the long day. After our walk in *Parque Ecologico Miraflores*, we'd been served a delicious dinner, complete with fresh fruit juice and a few cold bottles of Aguila. Then we'd been treated as guests of honor at a local music festival on the town square. Several bands performed for us as we sat in the rows of chairs lined up in front of San Vicente's outdoor stage; young Colombians dragged the gringos out of their seats and onto the street, where they tried to teach us hip-wiggling salsas as well as more traditional dance steps. I'm sure I embarrassed myself, but I didn't care; I was too tired to care, and I'd been having too much fun. My legs ached and my face still hurt from grinning; I don't think I'd ever strained my smile-muscles before. My usual cynicism and insecurities had, at least for the moment, faded into the warm Andean night.

As I crawled under the thin sheet of my narrow bed—with the sounds of *vallenato* music floating through my open window and visions of children dressed as cerulean warblers marching through my head—it occurred to me that this country's tourism promoters were correct: wanting to stay in Colombia truly *is* a risk.

SEVENTEEN

★

THE SKY-BLUE LITTLE QUEEN

W E MET NEAR THE HISTORIC San Vincente Ferrer church on the town square. It was about 5:00 a.m., and the sun hadn't risen yet. A misty rain fell. Along with Tiffany and biologists Kamal Islam and David Buehler, I huddled under the fronds of a palm tree and waited for the truck that would take us to *La Reserva Natural de las Aves Reinita Cielo Azul*, the Cerulean Warbler Reserve. Several taxis idled next to the curb, and a few men stood near their parked motorcycles, which I had pieced together were sometimes used as taxis for one passenger; the night before at the music festival, I'd been offered a ride or two, which I'd respectfully declined. As I shivered in the pre-dawn drizzle, I promised myself that I would see a cerulean today; I *had* to see a cerulean. My trip to Colombia had been a great adventure, but if I didn't see at least one cerulean warbler, it would be incomplete. Yesterday at dusk, during our walk through the *Parque Ecologico Miraflores*, several members of our group saw a cerulean foraging in one of the park's tall canopy trees. I'd missed it; I wasn't in the immediate area, and by the time I'd rushed over, the bird had disappeared. I couldn't let that happen today.

In the center of the town square, large bird boxes on metal poles were filled with sleeping pigeons, their round faces and thin bills visible inside the boxes' arched doors. The pigeons in San Vicente seemed larger and more colorful than the ones at home. While we huddled and waited, all the birds in *parque principal* suddenly woke up, as if the sun had imperceptibly crested the Andes beyond the rooftops of the town; the pigeons shot from their angular houses and fluttered to the pavement of the street in front of us, bobbing and cooing as they foraged for remnants from last night's festivities. A plaintive mewing began in one of the square's sprawling, ancient trees, and all at once smaller birds appeared from between its leaves, dispersing into the brightening sky. I recognized them from the day before as blue-gray tanagers—common, smallish birds with bright blue wings and slate-blue bellies. The only tanager I was accustomed to seeing at home was the scarlet tanager, and even then I would usually only be able to make out a flash of red high in the canopy of a leafy deciduous forest; these blue-gray tanagers seemed to be *city* birds, or at least neighborhood birds, sharing the same urban habitat as the ubiquitous pigeons.

Two small pickup trucks turned onto the square and pulled up to the curb, scattering the pigeons, and we all squeezed in. I sat in the middle in the back seat. San Vicente de Chucurí was quiet at this early hour; an occasional small dog trotted up a sidewalk in the morning mist, and a few men in knee-high rubber boots moved slowly between brick buildings. Once outside the town, dark green foliage quickly surrounded the road and the mist thickened. The reserve was three miles from San Vicente, and as we ascended, the road grew steeper and more winding. The pavement gave way to dirt as we switch-backed and lurched up the mountain. Little birds flitted in the dense shrubs around us; we weren't able to identify them, although we thought we heard a chestnut-sided warbler sounding his *pleased-pleased-pleased-to-MEET-you* call. I recognized the rhododendron-like cacao bushes; last night I'd learned that cacao was San Vicente's most important economic product, and the town prided itself on being "The Cacao Capital of Colombia." Coffee was also an important cash crop, along with oranges, lemons, tangerines, bananas, and avocados.

We turned off one dirt road and onto another, and finally rounded a bend and passed through an open metal gate. In front of us, a large green and yellow sign welcomed us to *La Reserva Natural de las Aves Reinita Cielo Azul*. It displayed the reserve's logo, an adorable stick-figure cerulean warbler, complete with upturned tail and dark necklace. The perma-grin that I'd been wearing since yesterday afternoon faltered just a bit when I noticed a half-dozen camouflaged soldiers with assault rifles surrounding the entrance to the reserve. These guards seemed a bit younger and sterner than the guards in San Vicente the day before; I couldn't picture them handing me their machine guns as an act of flirtation. The reserve's driveway continued up the hill toward stucco buildings, and another road turned off to the right. As I looked around the misty intersection, I noticed that there seemed to be an outpost of soldiers here; they had set up camp in front of a barn near the reserve's entrance. I wasn't sure if the soldiers typically camped here, or if they were here to protect the gringos. Every Colombian I'd met had been warm and welcoming, and the military protection felt almost like an insult; I suspected I was being naïve again, but automatic weapons (even if they're being used to protect me) made me nervous. I tried not to allow myself to be troubled by the soldiers—or troubled by the reasons we might need protection—and as we rumbled through the reserve's entrance, I focused instead on the two sorrel burros that grazed peacefully in the fenced-in pasture around the open-sided barn; higher on the mountainside, above the barn (but before a forest's wooded edge), white cattle with humped shoulders and floppy ears browsed on waist-high grass.

The driveway curved through the misty Garden of Eden, or at least an approximation of how I'd always pictured the biblical paradise: shrubs and bushes of flowers with brilliant orange, yellow, red, purple, magenta, and white petals; mandarin, papaya, and other fruit trees; and everywhere tucked among the plants, nectar and platform feeders for the birds. We pulled up in front of the reserve's stucco headquarters; one building held private sleeping quarters and another, sleeping facilities for a group. Another building housed kitchen, dining, and common areas. The reserve's resident hound dog, Tony, stood in the parking lot to greet us, slowly wagging his thick tail and barking deeply. Once he realized we weren't a threat, he plopped down on the ground and enjoyed an ear scratch from me. Tony—with his white paws, mostly black fur, chubby body, and obvious beagle ancestry—could have been Mr. Bones's long-lost Colombian cousin.

The reserve's stucco lodge sported a large painting of ProAves's logo, a yellow-eared parrot with its wings spread in flight. The lodge's porches looked out over the gardens, though the majority of the Cerulean Warbler Reserve was further up the mountain, behind the lodge. The 500-acre forest was reportedly one of the last remaining stands of natural oak forest in this part of Colombia; much of the original *bosque* in this region had been cleared or fragmented for pastureland or for growing crops. In addition to the intact forest, forty-five acres of shade-grown coffee were part of the reserve. Both the oak forest and the coffee farm's shade trees provided winter homes for cerulean warblers and other Neotropical migrants, such as Canada warblers, mourning warblers, and summer tanagers. Of course, scores of tropical resident birds also lived in the reserve; three critically endangered species—the gorgeted wood-quail, the Colombian mountain grackle, and the chestnut-bellied hummingbird—could also be found here. Despite the reserve's wide variety of avian species, the cerulean warbler was its star; in fact, *La Reserva Natural de las Aves Reinita Cielo Azul* was the first South American reserve for a bird that breeds in North America. Created through a partnership between ProAves and the American Bird Conservancy, and made possible through the donations of private citizens (particularly a generous naturalist from the United Kingdom), the Cerulean Warbler Reserve opened its gates in 2005.

Because there were too many visitors to explore the reserve together, we separated into groups; my group would walk through the coffee farm in the morning and then the 500-acre Colombian oak forest after lunch. As we milled around the reserve's buildings, readying ourselves for our excursions, we suddenly noticed the birds: they were everywhere, dozens of them, all around us. Binoculars were hurriedly yanked from packs and glued to eyes; everyone started calling out directions, descriptions, and possible identifications. I did my best to balance binoculars, notebook, camera, and the unwieldy *Birds of Northern South America*. I eventually gave up on guide, camera, and notebook, and tried to zero in on the avifauna flitting and flapping though my binoculars' sights.

The life-birds came almost too quickly for me to enjoy them: tropical mockingbird, yellow-backed oriole, a slew of hummingbirds, lemon-rumped tanager, crimson-backed tanager, and scrub tanager. My senses were overloaded; I felt intoxicated by tanagers. I lowered my focus to watch a cute rufous-collared sparrow (a species that had already been dubbed a "trash bird" by some in our group) kick around on the ground beneath a platform feeder. And then—in a thick shrub with waxy leaves, right next to the feeder—I saw something that made me gasp. A small hop, a tremble of a branch, and a tiny warbler the color of a washed-out watercolor painting peeked from between the leaves. Could it be?!

I doubted myself, and I blamed the sighting on my almost rabid desire to see a cerulean warbler in Colombia; certainly the bird was a redstart or a parula or some tropical resident. Certainly not a cerulean. I held my breath and pressed my lips together to keep my mouth clamped shut. I would not blurt out this mistake. I had to be wrong. My emotions were playing tricks with my eyes. My pride would never recover if I squealed, "*Cerulean! Cerulean!*" in front of these folks. But a split-second later, one of the biologists barked, "Cerulean female—in the shrub near the feeder!" Everyone swiveled toward the feeder. The bird cocked her head, gave us a sideways glance, and then vanished. Members of the ProAves staff standing nearby were barraged with questions: Do ceruleans ever eat bananas or nectar from the feeders? Where else can they see ceruleans? The discussion faded into a mixture of Spanish and English, and I lifted my binoculars and tried to find the female cerulean again. I couldn't. She'd disappeared into the shrub or the mist that surrounded us all.

As I lowered my binoculars and finally exhaled, the magnitude of this bird's journey became real to me. Only five short months earlier, that particular female cerulean warbler—*that* bird, the one in the shrub—had probably been wooed by a male cerulean somewhere in the central Appalachian Mountains of eastern North America—a whisper-singing, caterpillar-bringing, electric-blue suitor. She'd selected a nest site on a lateral branch of a deciduous tree, maybe a sugar maple, maybe a chestnut oak, perhaps a sycamore, and then she alone carefully wove a nest, a bark-flake and spider-web surrogate womb. She'd spent a dozen days in danger, hunkering discreetly over the three or four eggs she'd laid, listening to calling blue jays at dawn and screech owls at night. Then, once the babies pecked themselves out of their shells, the female cerulean warbler spent another dozen days guarding, feeding, and keeping her featherless chicks warm. If the babies survived to make their leaps of faith from a nest more than thirty feet high in the tree, she kept track of them as they bobbled and fluttered through the dangerous forest mid-story. Bound by evolutionary necessity, she followed her fledglings as they learned how to cope—if they didn't perish during their education.

And then, as soon as her fledglings began to find aphids and leafhoppers on their own, she prepared her nine-gram body and her sixty-six-millimeter wings to make a two-thousand-mile flight across the Gulf of Mexico during hurricane season to the Andes Mountains of northern South America. Once there, what does she do? She tries to find food, safe shelter, and a place to rest and regain her strength before starting the whole cycle again. She settles down in Colombia's Santander Department, on a western-facing slope three thousand feet above the Río Chucurí in the inviting shade trees of the Cerulean Warbler Reserve. She doesn't plan to stay forever, but she does stick around long enough to pop out of a shrub and give a group of gringo birders a thrill. Even without anthropomorphizing, her story is *amazing*.

I pulled out my notebook to jot down a description of the bird's location, and in my excitement I found myself beginning to write "*cielo*" instead of "cerulean." Literally translated, the Colombian phrase for cerulean warbler—*reinita cielo azul*—means "sky-blue little queen." Before, I hadn't thought much about the phrase, but after glimpsing the bird in the shrub I decided it fit; she was royalty indeed, at least to her admirers in her reserve.

AFTER THE CERULEAN SIGHTING, everyone was itchy to see more birds. Our coffee-farm group followed Misael, our ProAves guide, back down the reserve's driveway to the intersection with the other gravel road, near the small group of armed soldiers and the reserve's welcome sign. We posed for pictures by the sign, exchanged "*Buenos días*" greetings and curt nods with the young soldiers, and began hiking up the dirt road that led into the forty-five-acre coffee farm. Our group consisted of four gringos—Tiffany, Kamal Islam, David Buehler, and myself—and four Colombians. In addition to Misael, we were joined by three representatives from the *Federación Nacional de Cafeteros de Colombia*, who would explain to us the way shade-grown coffee farms worked. Since they spoke primarily Spanish and we spoke primarily English, Tiffany would again play the role of translator, as she had for much of the trip. The coffee federation folks seemed fascinated by our obsession with stopping every ten feet to look at birds. One of the reps, Cesár, had a special interest in insects and spiders, and his partner, Tatiana, loved trees; they pointed out various species as we passed them: oaks, bamboo, ficus, cedro, bucaré. Cesár wore a bright yellow polo shirt with the coffee federation's logo—an outline of Juan Valdez and his burro with the Andes in the background—on the chest.

As we walked up the gravel road, I felt a little awkward. My Spanish was terrible, and my knowledge of tropical bird species was poor. All of our group members (except me) had birded in the tropics before; they knew names of whole bird families that I'd never heard of. And, of course, they were all experts. Dr. Buehler had been studying ceruleans as well as golden-winged warblers, ruffed grouse, bald eagles, and other bird species for decades, and he directed a cadre of master's and doctoral students at the University of Tennessee, including Tiffany. Dr. Islam's important work on ceruleans in southern Indiana included projects on territoriality, kleptoparasitism, and habitat selection; he researched a variety of other bird species as well, from tragopans to buntings. Tiffany, too, had already amassed impressive credentials; she'd co-authored at least two scientific papers and had others on the way, and she'd worked on field studies in Mexico, Central America, the Galápagos, and soon Venezuela. I was—by *far*—the weakest link. My binoculars were inadequate, as were my sneakers. And I wore jeans and a T-shirt, not zip-off field pants. I eyed Tiffany's boots and nylon pants with envy. Drs. Islam and Buehler also wore hiking boots and lightweight trousers. Because of my obsession with *not* having to check luggage, I'd crammed a week's worth of clothing into my trusty daypack and canvas tote bag. I tried to bring clothes that would be appropriate for both conferencing and going out to dinner in Bogotá, and clothes that I could wear on a walk through the bird reserve. Now I wished I'd checked a bag and brought more clothing; perhaps one day I will learn.

The road gently ascended, and we hadn't made it far when we spotted bird activity in a large nearby tree; it resembled one of our big deciduous oaks, but I suspected this species never lost its leaves. A few tiny birds fluttered and spun in the upper branches; Tiffany identified one of them as a cerulean warbler—a young male, she thought. Perhaps fresh from his first migration. He was exploring this reserve for the first time, too. His flight across the Gulf of Mexico was probably quite a bit more tiring than mine, though. We soon lost sight of the cerulean, so we continued to slowly hike up the gravel road, stopping frequently to watch great kiskadees, boat-billed flycatchers, and black-billed thrushes. An American kestrel perched high on a snag, and we were surprised by a red-crowned woodpecker that swooped across the road.

We crested a hill and saw fields planted with coffee lining both sides of the road. The slope rose to our left and descended to our right. Beyond the coffee plot to the right was a spectacular view; the morning mist had almost burned off, but wispy clouds still hung in the deep valley below. The ridge far across from us was green and jagged, and a few small homes dotted the mountainside. The plot's shoulder-high coffee shrubs grew in straight, organized rows; the plants' leaves were large and shiny, resembling the shape of poinsettia leaves. Oval fruits the size of grapes lined their woody branches; some of the beans were green, some a deep purplish-red, some almost brown, and many others an in-between tannish-orange color. It pleased me immensely to know that my potential coffee beans grew here, as part of the bird reserve, where they had a spectacular view of the valley below and the green mountains beyond. I hoped that drinking coffee made from these beans would bring this view back to me at home.

I knew that the coffee farm before me was not exactly typical. At the summit in Bogotá, Dr. Gabriel Cadena, director of Colombia's National Coffee Research Center, welcomed the participants and assured us that these "magnificent birds can unite us to work together for their survival," and that we could count on the *Federación* and on the coffee-growing families of Colombia. But by planting coffee shrubs in the shade of taller trees, the farmers were taking an economic risk. Because coffee grown in the shade takes longer to mature, the farmers cannot produce as many beans as quickly as they could if they grew the shrubs in the full sun. There also needs to be a better market for shade-grown coffee, Dr. Cadena continued, and more of the farms that grow shade-coffee need to be certified as such. Rainforest Friendly, Bird Friendly, organic, Fair Trade, and other certifications connect the coffee consumers with the coffee producers; consumers must increase the demand for certified coffees, which will therefore help the farmers who are working to preserve the biodiversity of their country. In addition to birds, shade-grown coffee helps protect the soil, the forest, and the water. The diminished need for pesticides also allows the coffee farmers and their families to live healthier lives.

One theory about why cerulean warblers sometimes forage in shade-grown coffee plantations is linked to a theory about their breeding habitat. Several biologists have suggested that, in the breeding season, ceruleans seemed to prefer forests with a heterogeneous canopy structure—some short trees, some tall trees, and some towering super-emergent trees. This apparent preference led to the development of the selective logging and canopy-gap studies in West Virginia, Tennessee, and elsewhere in Appalachia. Since coffee is grown in the mountains, it's possible that ceruleans spend time in the shade trees because, along with the steep slope, they provide a heterogeneous canopy structure that the birds prefer. While this theory hasn't been tested yet, to a non-scientist like me, it makes sense.

Banana trees border rows of coffee plants.

All of the coffee in the Cerulean Warbler Reserve is shade grown. We walked
between fields of shrubs in various stages of development; one plot was filled with
rows of knee-high plants, while in another the coffee shrubs were head and shoulder height. Dense rows or clusters of medium-height, small-leafed trees with thin
trunks, such as tropical species of ficus and laurel, separated the different plots. As I
looked out across the coffee plants, my sense of what "shade grown" meant changed a
bit; the amount and type of shade varied from plot to plot. In some, several medium-
height thin-trunked trees were scattered among the coffee plants; other plots lacked
the small trees, but made up for it with one or two huge, ancient-looking trees filled
with birds. In one of these large trees—a mature tropical ficus—we observed birds
of a dozen different species. In addition to some of the species we'd already identified earlier on our walk, we spotted a bay-headed tanager, a golden-faced tyrannulet,
and the vulnerable turquoise dacnis-tanager, a Colombian endemic. Two roadside
hawks circled above the coffee shrubs beyond the enormous tree; their calls sounded
like a cross between a pewee and a red-tailed hawk.

More common than these thick, sprawling trees, though, were banana trees.
While taller than the coffee shrubs, the banana trees were short and thin-trunked,
and their crowns were made of wide, spreading fronds. Bunches of clustered,
green bananas hung from where the fronds separated. Banana trees bordered some

of the coffee plots, while other plots contained straight rows of banana trees in between the rows of coffee. From an economic perspective, planting bananas made sense; they allowed farmers to harvest more than one type of crop from the same plot. However, if I were a cerulean warbler or a beryl-spangled tanager, I'd probably rather hang out in a many-branched, fully leafed ficus, bucaré, or laurel. While the banana trees did technically provide shade, they didn't seem as attractive to birds, most of which flocked to the larger trees.

But banana trees (or *bananos*, as Tatiana called them) were not the only fruit trees planted above and around the coffee shrubs. Cesár plucked a small, oval fruit off a tree along the road and handed it to me. The fruit, a guava, was light green and about the size of a chicken egg. He bit into his, and I did the same. Inside the tough, green exterior, the fruit was pink and not overly juicy or sweet; I knew the flavor but couldn't quite place it—it almost reminded me of cinnamon. I took another bite and got a mouthful of seeds, which I tried to discreetly pluck from my teeth for the next several hours. In addition to coffee, another plot contained waist-high plants filled with greenish-orange *lulo* fruit. In Bogotá a few days earlier, I'd thoroughly enjoyed a tall glass of fresh-squeezed lulo juice. I couldn't believe that I'd never heard of such a delicious fruit before. My local grocery store in Virginia certainly didn't carry lulos! We also passed an avocado tree, its branches heavy with the dark green fruit. When I'm at a restaurant in the United States and I order guacamole, I don't usually think about where the avocados that made up the dip were grown. But from now on, I will; they might have been grown in Colombia, on a small tree among coffee shrubs.

We rounded a bend and came upon a house along the road. The one-story structure had a corrugated metal roof and a covered porch along the front. I noticed that the house had four identical doors; perhaps it was an apartment house. A calico cat curled up on the roof above the porch, and a brown sheep tethered near the side of the house grazed peacefully. A large cage on the porch contained what appeared to be small green parrots. Several domestic turkeys strutted around the grass near the house, too; a splendid male Tom was in full display while two drab females—who completely ignored his efforts—pecked around in the grass. Across the street from the house, on the upslope, a thin man wearing safety glasses swung a weed-whacker (called a *machete mechanica*) between rows of coffee. He stopped when we drew near, turned off the weed-whacker, and exchanged a few pleasant words with Misael. Just beyond the house was another plot of coffee, thickly planted with banana trees. A few of the trees seemed like they should bow under the weight of the huge bunches of green bananas hanging pendulously from their crowns. Tatiana pointed out *platanos* trees amid the slightly sturdier-looking banana trees. We'd eaten fried plantains at several meals so far, but Tatiana told me that plantains could not be eaten raw; neither my Spanish nor her English were good enough for me to understand the reason. Around another bend in the road, we passed another house, this one made of cinderblocks, rusted sheet metal, and rough wooden beams. Another sheep grazed in front of the house, and a black cow eyed us lazily from a nearby pen. Chickens scratched around the grass, and a black dog emerged from somewhere within and barked at us. The road curved behind and above the house, and I noticed a little boy in a red T-shirt playing in the yard. Laundry flapped on a line near the several mandarin orange trees.

Up and around another bend in the steep road, we took a small side trail into a patch of forest. Cesár explained that this was native rainforest, one of the last remaining tracks amid the coffee and fruit plots. We walked into the thick, lush trees, and I was struck by how much it reminded me of an Appalachian forest. The air felt heavy with moisture, and there was moss and mud and vines—not the grapevines I was accustomed to, but the kinds of vines Tarzan might swing on. The forest's understory consisted of ferns and plants with large, flat leaves; while the vegetative species in this rainforest were certainly different from my forests at home, the *feeling* here was similar and was perhaps shared by thick forests everywhere. The forest felt thoroughly alive—pulsing, trembling, breathing.

Cesár stood along the trail, examining something on the muddy bank; he motioned for me to come look. A huge black spider had excavated a hole in the soft soil, where it would wait for prey to become entangled in its nearby web. Cesár smiled under his navy *Cafeteros de Colombia* cap and snapped a few close-up pictures of the spider. In turn, I took a short digital video of Cesár; when he realized what I was doing, he smiled even wider, pointed to the Juan Valdez logo on his chest, and said in English, "Best coffee in the world."

Our spider-watching was disturbed by loud rattling sounds overhead as a flock of large, noisy birds zipped through the trees and stopped to forage somewhere behind us. I tried to focus my binoculars on them, but they kept hopping and foraging. I saw flashes of yellow tail feathers and long, pointed bills. Someone identified them as russet-backed oropendolas; Cesár said they sometimes ate bananas off the trees. When the raucous flock of oropendolas swooped deeper into the forest, we became aware of other large birds moving slowly in the canopy. We craned our heads and raised our binoculars. I could see something greenish and a few moving leaves, but Tiffany helped me readjust and I caught sight of a bird far above us: light-green body, longish tail, curved, reddish bill—a crimson-rumped toucanet.

While admiring the stealthy toucanets, I heard a muffled noise that sounded like my cell phone ringing. I slipped my daypack off one shoulder, swung it around, and began digging for my phone; I found it, answered, and heard my husband's voice. I was shocked; I didn't get a cell signal in San Vicente, so I hadn't bothered to charge my phone. I'd forgotten I'd had it with me. As soon as I finished squeal-ing about the toucanets, the phone beeped at me: the battery was about to die. Jes-se managed to briefly wish me "Happy Birthday" before the phone cut. I'd been so immersed in birds and coffee that I'd almost forgotten about my birthday. Tiffany, however, did not forget, and as we emerged from the forest onto the gravel road, she nodded to the rest of the group and they broke into song. I never know what to do when people sing "Happy Birthday," so I stood on the gravel of the road—be-tween plots of coffee shrubs and banana trees on a misty slope of the Andes—and grinned. After the familiar English version, they sang me the Colombian version in Spanish, which includes, at its end, counting up from *uno* while clapping (hap-pily, the counting and clapping didn't continue all the way to my age, but ended somewhere around *veinte*). I was very flattered. Spending my birthday in a rainfor-est goes near the top of my best-things-ever list.

AFTER OUR WALK IN THE rainforest, we began our descent back down the road. Although several hours had passed—it was almost time for lunch, Misael told us—it felt like only a few minutes. On the way back down we saw a young boy, an older man, and a dog walking between rows of banana trees alongside the road. The boy, maybe ten years old, carried a long pole with a knife at the end. They nod-ded and smiled at us and their dog—a thin, brown creature that resembled a small Lab—barked menacingly and raised his hackles. Since our walk down the hill was slowed by frequent stops to look at birds, several minutes later the same boy walked back past us, bent under the weight of the bunch of bananas balanced on his back. Near a small shed along the road, the boy carefully let the bananas slide off his back and onto a blanket spread out on the ground. He turned and jogged back up the hill. On Saturday mornings in the US, many boys his age would still be in bed, or huddled around a television watching cartoons, or perhaps on their way to a Little League game. I ate a banana almost every day with my lunch, and now I knew who harvested them.

We continued down the hill, back through the coffee plantation, back to the Cerulean Reserve sign near the soldiers. At the reserve's headquarters, we hung around and shared stories with the folks who'd hiked in the oak forest while we went through the coffee. We compared bird lists; the other group had spotted both ceruleans and golden-winged warblers during their hike, but our turquoise dacnis-tanager seemed to be the most impressive sighting. The ProAves staff generously served us lunch, and they even provided me and one of the biologists with cheese sandwiches, since we were both *vegetarianas*. After lunch—and after another round of "Happy Birthday," sung to me while I blushed and grinned—our little group (minus the coffee federation representatives, who headed back to town) set off for our walk in the oak forest.

We followed Misael down a path that wound around the barn where the soldiers were encamped; I noticed a pile of guns and olive green packs. Some—clearly the "on duty" ones—wore full camouflage and stood near the perimeter, assault rifles hanging on their shoulders, but others wore olive T-shirts and lounged in small groups, talking quietly and enjoying a campfire. I sort of wanted to go over and talk with them and ask if there were always soldiers stationed near the reserve, or if they were here solely for our protection. But I also wanted to walk in the oak forest, and it was already mid-afternoon; plus, the soldiers looked *very* young—a lot like my freshmen students at Virginia Tech. The number of machine guns intimidated me, so I just smiled as we walked past.

Beyond the barn, the wide trail began to climb through the pasture on the side of the mountain. The white cows lifted their lop-eared heads as we walked past. The afternoon had grown humid, and the hike was steep; before long I began to perspire. Dr. Buehler wiped sweat from his brow, too, and joked about how being from Wisconsin put him at a disadvantage hiking in the tropics. Thankfully, our group stopped often to watch ruddy-breasted seedeaters, yellow-faced grassquits, and lesser goldfinches as they foraged in the tall grass. The trail through the pasture was muddy in places and marred by an occasional pile of cow flop; a barbed-wire fence separated us from the grazing livestock, and every so often Misael would have to unlatch and swing open a metal gate for us to pass through. As I walked, I brushed my fingers along the tops of the high grass, but then suddenly I wondered what kinds of ticks lived in the tropics; I lowered my hands to my sides.

We drew closer to the fortress-like edge of the forest, thick with tall, straight, many-leafed trees as well as palms. When we finally reached the tree line, the path became cobblestone and wide, and the air cooler, wet, and dense. We followed the trail into the dark greenness of the forest. Mosquitoes hung lazily in the still air, and I remembered that I had 98 percent DEET bug spray in my daypack. I dug it out, coated my blue bandana with it, and tied the bandana around my head.

The stone path, I learned, was more than 150 years old and was known as *Camino de Lengerke*. According to ProAves's literature, the path was "a vital trading route between the Magdalena River and the interior. The meter-wide trail gently winds up the Yariguíes Mountain from the subtropical coffee plantations into the oak forest reserve." I looked at the smooth stones beneath my sneakers and wondered about the feet that had beaten this path before mine. This *camino* had been here before the start of *La Violencia*, before the ELN and the FARC, before the United States made cocaine illegal. Who used the path in the mid-1800s? Coffee and cacao traders, certainly. Eventually, perhaps guerrillas and the illegal paramilitaries who

At the edge of the forest.

opposed them. This area had been a guerrilla stronghold until very recently, and judging from the military protection, perhaps the Colombian and United States governments still worried about illegal activity in the region. As we pushed deeper into the forest, the ferns, vines, epiphytes, and tree trunks thickened. It was easy to see why guerrillas chose to hide here; I felt as if I could step off the trail and disappear. This thought made me a bit nervous, and I remembered some of the online posts I'd read that warned about hiking in Colombia. Our group consisted of just five people, and as far as I knew, none of us were armed, and none of us were particularly intimidating. The most dangerous thing in my possession was my two-ounce squirt bottle of 98 percent DEET.

My thoughts of spraying DEET in the eyes of an armed rebel fighter were cut short by bird activity overhead. I felt something buzz past my ear, and then I heard chittering from above. It was a hummingbird—no, a pair of hummingbirds. But the light and the position of the birds made it difficult for us to identify the species. We kept disagreeing about what distinguishing features we were seeing, and we flipped through the thick *Birds of Northern South America*. Could they be white-bellied woodstars? What about tyrian metaltails? Blue-tailed emeralds? After a frustrating half-hour, we gave up. In Virginia, our only common hummingbird is the ruby-throated; Colombia has more than a hundred varieties.

We kept walking along the gently ascending stone path, birding as we progressed. Then it began to drizzle. We debated whether or not to put on our raingear. Fortunately, we all had jackets in our packs; everyone, that is, except for Misael, who wore jeans, a white ProAves T-shirt, and an American Bird Conservancy cap. He also wore enviable rubber boots—rubber boots that became more and more enviable as the rain increased and my sneakers quickly became soaked. We stepped off the trail into the forest to pull on our jackets and allow the trees to slow the rain a bit. Misael insisted that the storm would pass in a few minutes, but half an hour later, it was still coming down, *hard*. While we stood there in the forest, we watched a beautiful red, black, and white bird—a masked trogon—taking a bath in a nearby tree. He flicked his wings and ruffled his feathers.

When it became clear that the rain had no intention of stopping, we decided to head back to the reserve's headquarters to catch the vehicle that would take us down the mountain to San Vicente. We cautiously made our way out of the trees and onto the trail. The drops fell with surprising force, as if the sky was trying to punish the ground. The 150-year-old cobblestone path that I'd admired so much had become a slick creek bed—water actually flowed down the stone trail, in the same direction we were headed. Footing was treacherously slippery. It didn't take long before Tiffany went down, flat on her back. She insisted she was all right, though, and after she struggled to her feet, we pressed on. My sneakers soon became useless wet weights, and my jeans sagged under the heaviness of the water. I hoped my fellow birders didn't notice that my soaked jeans were in real danger of falling down; they kept slipping below my hipbones, and I had to repeatedly hitch them up.

Once we got out of the forest, the rain slowed and then abruptly stopped, but the water rushing down the trail did not. I tried very hard not to fall down on piles of wet, disintegrating cow poop. I licked my lips and tasted something bitter; the DEET from my bandana must have been running down my face. Even though my feet, jeans, and entire body were soaking wet, when the clouds began to clear, I paused to gasp at a rainbow that had formed above us, arcing from the edge of the forest to the pasture. The sun soon began to set, too, and we were awarded a spectacular view. Yellow and white wildflowers that twisted up wooden fence posts glistened with raindrops, and white wispy clouds floated up and out of the valleys. I could see a group of houses in a valley far, far below me; green mountains rose beyond the houses, and deep blue mountains soared beyond those. The light was perfect; the dissipating clouds and even the water running through my sneakers made me feel fresh and renewed. The ethereal blue sky looked close enough to taste. I wanted to hop the barbed wire fence, sprint through the pasture, flop down on my back in the wet grass, and wait for the stars to fill the heavens.

Instead, of course, I snapped a few pictures and followed Misael down the trail. As the sun set further and the pasture began to grow darker, my romantic notions of spending the night alone on a mountainside in Colombia evaporated like the rain clouds. I started to worry, because we were running quite late; we were supposed to catch our ride to San Vicente at 5:00, but that time had already passed. I became antsy and tried to hurry the group along. My feet were cold, and I was quite certain I'd ingested all the DEET from my bandana. When we stopped to watch tanagers foraging in a fruit tree, Dr. Islam, perhaps sensing my growing anxiety, smiled at me from under his khaki cap and said, "Katie, you're a real field biologist now," which made me smile, too, despite everything.

By the time we reached the bottom of the pasture, it was pitch black. More campfires burned near the soldiers' barn, and two trucks waited for us at the reserve's entrance. Their engines were running, and they were surrounded by soldiers and two police officers on a motorcycle. The group who had walked through the coffee farms in the afternoon already sat in the vehicles; Brian Smith of the American Bird Conservancy helped haul me into the covered bed of the small pickup, and the others crammed into the cab. I elected to ride in the back because of how wet and mud-caked my jeans and sneakers had become. As the truck started to pull away, I waved goodbye to the cluster of young soldiers; they waved back, their assault rifles red in the brake lights' glare.

BIRD LIST, OCTOBER 25
Cerulean Warbler Reserve and
San Vicente de Chucurí, Santander, Colombia

Black Vulture
Turkey Vulture

Roadside Hawk

American Kestrel

Rock Pigeon
Ruddy Ground-Dove

Orange-chinned Parakeet

Smooth-billed Ani

Andean Emerald
Indigo-capped Hummingbird

Masked Trogon

Crimson-rumped Toucanet

Red-crowned Woodpecker

Strong-billed Woodcreeper

Golden-faced Tyrannulet
Yellow-bellied Elaenia

Boat-billed Flycatcher
Ornate Flycatcher
Tropical Kingbird

Southern Rough-winged Swallow
Barn Swallow

Bicolor Wren

Great Thrush
Pale-breasted Thrush
Black-billed Thrush

Tropical Mockingbird

Cerulean Warbler
Blackburnian Warbler
Yellow Warbler
Chestnut-sided Warbler
Canada Warbler

Bananaquit

Crimson-backed Tanager
Blue-gray Tanager
Palm Tanager
Bay-headed Tanager
Turquoise Dacnis-Tanager
Lemon-rumped Tanager
Scrub Tanager
Beryl-spangled Tanager
Blue-necked Tanager

Blue-black Grassquit
Yellow-breasted Seedeater
Ruddy-breasted Seedeater
Yellow-faced Grassquit
Rufous-collared Sparrow

Summer Tanager

Giant Cowbird
Yellow-backed Oriole
Russet-backed Oropendola

Lesser Goldfinch

EIGHTEEN

*

FULL CIRCLE

*W*HEN I CLIMBED INTO A TAXI at 2:00 a.m., San Vicente's beer festival was still ongoing. Most of the square had been closed to traffic; a large, yellow Aguila tent filled one of the streets, and a stage had been erected at another end of the square. A live band, playing salsa, cumbia, and vallenato tunes, entertained the crowd of *Chucureños* (and the handful of gringos) who had gathered on the streets. I sipped Aguila from a huge plastic cup and wore a yellow cardboard hat; I shook hands, practiced my terrible Spanish, posed for pictures, and had "Happy Birthday" sung to me by several groups of slightly intoxicated Colombians. I had only two regrets: that I could not stay in San Vicente de Chucurí longer, and that the yellow Aguila hat wouldn't fit in my luggage.

Because of our flight times, US Geological Survey biologist Deanna Dawson and I were the only two leaving by taxi; most of the others in the group would leave a bit later in the morning. The afternoon rainstorm had washed out some local roads, and the driver was nervous that we wouldn't make it to Bucaramanga in time for our 7:30 a.m. flight to Bogotá; the supposed two-hour drive on the mostly dirt road could take twice that long.

We left the lights of San Vicente behind and plunged into the rural, Andean darkness. This was the part of the trip that had worried me the most. According to the stories I'd read, this was how tourists found trouble in Colombia: guerrillas would set up roadblocks and take small groups of people captive, and the tourists wouldn't be heard from again for three or six or eight years.

Somehow, though, the switch-backing, single-lane dirt road, towering vegetation, and occasional small house with a porch light burning all comforted me. I
rested the back of my head against the soft taxi seat and looked out the window.
Bright stars filled the cloudless sky above the dark, jagged peaks of the Andes
Mountains. The Rio Chucurí flowed somewhere below us, and the mighty Magdalena somewhere below that. And all around us, I knew the trees were filled with
birds. I took a deep breath and closed my eyes.

TWENTY-SIX HOURS LATER, I WALKED into my home in Virginia. No parade
awaited me; no rare birds clung to the sugar maple branches around the driveway.
After my three-hour taxi ride from San Vicente, I flew from Bucaramanga to Bogotá, Bogotá to Miami, and Miami to Charlotte, North Carolina. After staggering
around Charlotte's poorly lit long-term parking lot, I eventually found my Jeep.
Another three-hour drive later, I arrived in Blacksburg.

I dropped my bags on the floor and stumbled through the quiet darkness to the
bedroom. The small reading light on my nightstand was lit, but Jesse slept soundly
under the covers. Mr. Bones, snuggled up against my pillow, lifted his head and
blinked at me. A second later, he realized who I was and that he hadn't seen me in
a while; he thumped his tail, uncurled, stretched his legs stiffly, and stood up to
properly greet me with kisses and wiggling.

"Hey," Jesse said, rolling over. He sat up to hug me, then collapsed back onto
his pillow. "Sorry I couldn't wait up. Glad you're home safe."

I kicked off my shoes and decided that my still-soaked jeans and sneakers—
stuffed into plastic bags in my daypack—could wait until tomorrow. Thankfully,
no Colombian or United States security official had thoroughly searched my bags;
I hadn't been looking forward to explaining (or unfurling) my balled-up, muddy,
soaking-wet pants.

As I crawled into my warm bed and inhaled the familiar smell of my pillow,
I wondered: could this—comfort, relief, exhaustion—be what cerulean warblers
feel when they arrive back in Appalachia after months in the tropics? Or is the reverse true—that the Andes feel more like home than the breeding grounds? Could
it be both? Perhaps the birds "feel" nothing and simply respond instinctively to
subtle changes in photoperiod or temperature, and don't privilege one landscape
over another but use both to their evolutionary advantage. The rationalist in me
believes this is the answer, of course; but the romantic in me—the part of me that
anthropomorphizes—imagines a more satisfying, touchy-feely conclusion to an
ultimately unanswerable question. I thought of lines from Wendell Berry's poem
"The Peace of Wild Things": "When despair for the world grows in me / ... / I

come into the peace of wild things / who do not tax their lives with forethought / of grief..." For the sake of the cerulean warbler, I hoped these sentiments were true; I hoped their lives were not "taxed with forethought of grief" about full-sun coffee farms, powerful hurricanes, mountaintop removal mines. So much grief would be crippling.

The fate of the cerulean warbler remains uncertain; every year, more and more of the tiny, bright blue birds—sky-blue little queens—disappear from the forest canopies. Every year, more critical habitat is transformed, some irreparably. If the species is to survive, it will be because of the cooperative efforts of biologists, farmers, miners, and academics; foresters, politicians, naturalists, and coffee drinkers; ornithologists, artists, statisticians, and birders. Luckily, cerulean warblers have many admirers who are working hard to save them, but the species is a long way from saved.

I reached up and clicked off the light. Mr. Bones stretched out against me, sighed, and before long was quietly snoring. Jesse seemed to have fallen back to sleep, too, and a moment later I would join them. But first, I remembered the female cerulean's face as she peeked out at me from the shrub. I hoped to meet her again someday.

★

HELP SAVE THE
CERULEAN WARBLER

*W*HILE FINDING AND OBSERVING cerulean warblers in the wild can be frustrating, it is relatively easy to contribute to conservation efforts. Below is a list of ways that concerned citizens can make a difference.

Purchase shade-grown coffee. Coffee grown in the shade of other trees can benefit everyone involved. Most coffee experts agree that shade-grown coffee is richer and more flavorful than coffee grown in the full sun. Since the coffee beans take longer to develop in the shade, their flavors have more time to mature. The forest canopy that shelters the coffee shrubs can also provide a winter home for not just ceruleans, but a wide variety of migratory and resident warblers, orioles, swallows, thrushes, hummingbirds, and other birds. Coffee grown in the shade does not require the amount of pesticide and herbicide used on full-sun farms; this helps protect the local coffee farmers and their communities from exposure to dangerous chemicals. Shade-grown coffee is a win-win-win-win situation: the birds, the ecosystem, the local communities, and the coffee drinkers all benefit from this simple consumer choice. Buying shade-grown coffee is one of the easiest ways to contribute to Neotropical migratory songbird conservation.

Contribute to organizations that support cerulean warbler conservation. Although cerulean warbler research is often partially funded through grants from federal and state governments, private organizations also provide funding to ongoing research projects, to purchase and protect habitat, and to educate the public. By making a donation to one (or more) of these private organizations, you help support important conservation initiatives. Nonprofit organizations that directly support cerulean warblers include the National Fish and Wildlife Foundation, the National Council for Air and Stream Improvement, the Nature Conservancy, the American Bird Conservancy, Fundación ProAves Colombia, the American Birding Association, the Cornell Laboratory of Ornithology, Partners in Flight, the Smithsonian Migratory Bird Center, Birdlife International, and the National Audubon Society. This list is not exhaustive, but it is a good place to start.

Support the efforts of the Appalachian Regional Reforestation Initiative. This group, part of the Office of Surface Mining, has ambitious plans to plant native trees on mined land in the seven Appalachian coal states. Using their five-step method (described in chapter 3), they hope to restore hardwood forests—filled with oaks, maples, black walnuts, and even American chestnuts—to compacted, barren strip-mine sites throughout Appalachia. Although it's true that a "new" hardwood forest could take a hundred years to mature on an ARRI-reclaimed mine site, it's also true that it would take a hardwood forest much longer than that to take root and mature on its own on an un-reclaimed site. Reforesting former strip-mine sites in Appalachia helps undo some of the damage caused by extracting coal. If you live near a strip mine and would like ARRI's assistance with potentially reforesting it, visit http://arri.osmre.gov/.

Speak out against mountaintop removal coal mining. This type of large-scale surface mining destroys Appalachian peaks every day. In addition to contributing to floods, contaminated drinking water, degraded streams and rivers, the loss of jobs, and global climate change, mountaintop removal eliminates breeding habitat for the cerulean warbler and thousands of other species in the world's oldest mountain range.

Robert F. Kennedy Jr. calls mountaintop removal "the worst example of what human beings can do to their environment when they behave irresponsibly." Virtually every argument in favor of this mining practice can be refuted. The best way to learn more about mountaintop removal is to visit an active site. Larry Gibson, "the Keeper of the Mountains," offers tours of what remains of his property on Kayford Mountain in West Virginia. His website is www.mountainkeeper.org. Several nonprofit organizations focus on mountaintop removal; in West Virginia, these organizations include the Ohio Valley Environmental Coalition (www.ohvec.org), Coal River Mountain Watch (www.crmw.net), and the West Virginia

Highlands Conservancy (www.wvhighlands.org). Another nonprofit organization, South Wings (www.southwings.org), will fly citizens over areas affected by mountaintop removal.

Conserve energy. You've heard it many times before: fossil fuels are going to run out someday, perhaps not in our lifetimes, but in the foreseeable future. Alternatives will become more widely available if we demand them. There are countless ways to reduce the amount of energy we use in our day-to-day lives—drive fuel-efficient vehicles, turn the thermostat down a few degrees in the winter and up a few degrees in the summer, make sure your home's windows are properly sealed, use compact fluorescent or LED light bulbs, recycle whatever you can. In addition to slowing global climate change by reducing the amount of carbon dioxide we put into the atmosphere, we will also burn fewer fossil fuels, thereby reducing the need for expanded mining and drilling.

Learn the names of things. In writing and researching this book, I discovered that I didn't know much. I didn't even know the names of all of the tree species that grew in my yard. I'd been a hiker and a backpacker my entire life, but I didn't know wild geranium from meadow rue. I didn't know that the viney stuff all over the telephone poles in my neighborhood was Virginia creeper. Learning to name the other species that live and grow around me has made me appreciate them much more, and it has been a humbling experience. Pick up a field guide from your local bookstore or library to help you identify the species that share your world.

Let nature help you heal. I am a wallower, a brooder. When left to my own devices, I think and think and relive (or reimagine) horrible events. Following the senseless tragedy at my university, I curled up in my pajamas and stared at my television and computer screen for weeks. Getting outside to look for these little blue birds helped me re-center, refocus, and remember myself. The sensations of the outdoors—the sun on my skin, the smell of mud, the clear notes of a wood thrush, a glimpse of a hooded warbler before it dives under a brush pile—reminded me that life is beautiful and I shouldn't waste it slugging around in misery, obsessing over events that I cannot change. Mourn, yes; grieve, of course; lie awake at night, perhaps inevitable. But think and think and *think* until you are afraid to leave the house—well, then it's time to go birding. I am not a psychologist, but I can tell you that being outdoors searching for a bird helped me heal.

Get out there. I challenge you to find a cerulean warbler in the wild. If you've made it this far, you know many of the cerulean's habits, what they look like, what they sound like, and some of the forests where they can be observed during both the breeding and non-breeding seasons. Grab a pair of binoculars, and head for the Appalachian Mountains—or the Andes Mountains! While I can't guarantee that you'll spot a cerulean, I promise you'll have fun trying.

BIBLIOGRAPHY

★

WORKS CITED OR CONSULTED

CHAPTER ONE

Audubon, John James. *Birds of America*. Edinburgh, 1840.

Bent, Arthur Cleveland. *Life Histories of North American Wood Warblers*. Washington D.C.: Smithsonian Institution Press, 1953.

Hamel, Paul B. "Cerulean Warbler (*Dendroica cerulea*)." In *The Birds of North America* Issue 511, edited by A. Poole. Ithaca: Cornell Lab of Ornithology, 2000.

Hamel, Paul B. "Cerulean Warbler, *Dendroica cerulea*." In *Mirgatory Nongame Birds of Management Concern in the Northeast*, edited by K. J. Schneider and D. M. Pence. Newton Corner, Massachusetts: US Department of the Interior, Fish and Wildlife Service, 1992.

Hamel, Paul B., Deanna K. Dawson, and Patrick D. Keyser. "How We Can Learn More about the Cerulean Warbler (*Dendroica cerulea*)." *The Auk* 121.1 (2004): 7-14.

Robbins, Chandler S., John W. Fitzpatrick, and Paul B. Hamel. "A Warbler in Trouble: *Dendroica cerulea*." In *Ecology and Conservation of Neotropical Migrant Landbirds*, edited by J. M. Hagan III and D. W. Johnston. Washington, D.C.: Smithsonian Institution Press, 1992.

Weidensaul, Scott. *Of a Feather: A Brief History of American Birding*. Orlando: Harcourt, 2007.

Wilson, Alexander. *American Ornithology*, Volume II. Philadelphia: Bradford and Inskeep, 1810.

CHAPTER THREE

Angel, Patrick, Vic Davis, Jim Burger, Don Graves, and Carl Zipper. "The Appalachian Regional Reforestation Initiative." *The ARRI Forest Reclamation Advisory* 1 (December 2005): 1-2.

"Endangered and Threatened Wildlife and Plants; 12-Month Finding on a Petition to List the Cerulean Warbler (*Dendroica cerulea*) as Threatened With Critical Habitat." *Federal Register* 71.234 (December 6, 2006): 70717-70733.

Jones, Jason, Paolo Ramoni Perazzi, Erin H. Carruthers, and Raleigh J. Robertson. "Sociality and Feeding Behavior of the Cerulean Warbler in Venezuelan Shade-Coffee Plantations." *The Condor* 102.4 (2000): 958-962.

Link, William A., and John R. Sauer. "A Hierarchical Analysis of Population Change with Application to Cerulean Warblers." *Ecology* 83.10 (2002): 2832-2840.

Moreno, Maria Isabel, Paul Salaman, and David Pashley. "The Current Status of the Cerulean Warbler on its Winter Range." United States Fish and Wildlife Service Assessment, September 28, 2006.

Office of Surface Mining Reclamation and Enforcement. United States Government. http://www.osmre.gov/.

Rosenberg, Ken. "Introduction to the biology, distribution, and demography of the Cerulean Warbler." Paper presented at the 3rd Annual Cerulean Warbler Summit, Bogotá, Colombia, October 20-26, 2008.

Southern Environmental Law Center. *Petition Under the Endangered Species Act to List the Cerulean Warbler, Dendroica cerulea, as a Threatened Species.* October 31, 2000.

Weakland, Cathy A., and Petra Bohall Wood. "Cerulean Warbler (*Dendroica cerulea*) Microhabitat and Landscape-Level Habitat Characteristics in Southern West Virginia." *The Auk* 122.2 (2005): 497-508.

Weakland, Cathy A., and Petra Bohall Wood. "Cerulean warbler (*Dendroica cerulea*) microhabitat and landscape-level habitat characteristics in southern West Virginia in relation to Mountaintop Mining/Valley Fills." Final Project Report. Submitted to USGS Biological Resources Division Species-At-Risk Program, December 2002.

Wood, Petra Bohall, Scott B. Bosworth, and Randy Dettmers. "Cerulean Warbler Abundance and Occurrence Relative to Large-Scale Edge and Habitat Characteristics." *The Condor* 108 (2006): 154-165.

Wood, Petra Bohall, Jeffrey P. Duguay, and Jeffrey V. Nichols. "Cerulean warbler use of regenerated clearcut and two-age harvests." *Wildlife Society Bulletin* 33.3 (2005): 851-858.

CHAPTER FIVE

Meyers, Robert Cornelius V. *Life and Adventures of Lewis Wetzel, The Renowned Virginia Ranger and Scout.* Philadelphia: J. E. Potter, 1883.

Perkins, Kelly. "Cerulean Warbler Selection of Forest Canopy Gaps." Master of Science thesis, West Virginia University, 2006.

CHAPTER SIX

Hamel, Paul B. "Cerulean Warbler (*Dendroica cerulea*)." In *The Birds of North America* Issue 511, edited by A. Poole. Ithaca: Cornell Lab of Ornithology, 2000.

Patuxent Wildlife Research Center Bird Banding Laboratory. United States Geological Survey. https://www.pwrc.usgs.gov/bbl/.

Perkins, Kelly. "Cerulean Warbler Selection of Forest Canopy Gaps." Master of Science thesis, West Virginia University, 2006.

Roth, Kirk L., and Kamal Islam. "Do Cerulean Warblers (*Dendroica cerulea*) Exhibit Clustered Territoriality?" *The American Midland Naturalist* 157.2 (2007): 345-355.

Weakland, Cathy A., and Petra Bohall Wood. "Cerulean Warbler (*Dendroica cerulea*) Microhabitat and Landscape-Level Habitat Characteristics in Southern West Virginia." *The Auk* 122.2 (2005): 497-508.

CHAPTER SEVEN

Barg, Jennifer J., Jason Jones, M. Katharine Girvan, and Raleigh J. Robertson. "Within-pair Interactions and Parental Behavior of Cerulean Warblers Breeding in Eastern Ontario." *The Wilson Journal of Ornithology* 118.3 (2006): 316-325.

Beachy, Tiffany Ahren. "Cerulean Warbler (*Dendroica cerulea*) Breeding Ecology and Habitat Selection, Initial Response to Forest Management, and Association with Anthropogenic Disturbances in the Cumberland Mountains of Tennessee." Master of Science thesis, University of Tennessee, Knoxville, 2008.

Jones, Jason, and Raleigh J. Robertson. "Territory and Nest-site Selection of Cerulean Warblers in Eastern Ontario." *The Auk* 118.3 (2001): 727-735.

Jones, Kelly C., Kirk L. Roth, Kamal Islam, Paul B. Hamel, and Carl G. Smith III. "Incidence of Nest Material Kleptoparasitism Involving Cerulean Warblers." *The Wilson Journal of Ornithology* 119.2 (2007): 271-275.

Hamel, Paul B. "Cerulean Warbler (*Dendroica cerulea*)." In *The Birds of North America* Issue 511, edited by A. Poole. Ithaca: Cornell Lab of Ornithology, 2000.

Rogers, Christopher M. "Nesting Success and Breeding Biology of Cerulean Warblers in Michigan." *The Wilson Journal of Ornithology* 118.2 (2006): 145-151.

CHAPTER EIGHT

Botero, Jorge E. "Cerulean Warblers in Coffee-producing Regions of Colombia." Paper presented at the 2nd Annual Cerulean Warbler Summit, Morgantown, WV, February 14, 2007.

Caro, David, Maria Isabel Moreno, Paul Salaman, and Alonso Quevedo. "Conservation Efforts for the Cerulean Warbler (*Dendroica cerulea*) in Colombia." Paper presented at the 2nd Annual Cerulean Warbler Summit, Morgantown, WV, February 14, 2007.

Fischersworring, Verena. "Certification of coffee, cacao, and forest products and

practices: How it works." Paper presented at the 3rd Annual Cerulean Warbler Summit, Bogotá, Colombia, October 20-26, 2008.

González, Carlos. "Remarks from the Director of Specialty Coffees, Federacion Nacional de Cafeteros de Colombia." Paper presented at the 3rd Annual Cerulean Warbler
Summit, Bogotá, Colombia, October 20-26, 2008.

Moreno, Maria Isabel, Paul Salaman, and David Pashley. "The Current Status of the Cerulean Warbler on its Winter Range." USFWS Assessment, September 28, 2006.

Wild, Antony. *Coffee: A Dark History.* New York: W. W. Norton, 2005.

CHAPTER NINE

Burns, Shirley Stewart. *Bringing Down the Mountains: The Impact of Mountaintop Removal on Southern West Virginia Communities.* Morgantown: West Virginia University Press, 2007.

Hendryx, Michael, and Melissa M. Ahren. "Relations Between Health Indicators and
Residential Proximity to Coal Mining in West Virginia." *American Journal of Public
Health* 98.4 (April 2008): 669-671.

Rosenberg, Kenneth, Sara E. Barker, and Ronald W. Rohrbaugh. *An Atlas of Cerulean
Warbler Populations: Final Report to USFWS: 1997-2000 Breeding Seasons.* Ithaca:
Cornell Lab of Ornithology, 2000.

CHAPTER TEN

Burns, Shirley Stewart. *Bringing Down the Mountains: The Impact of Mountaintop Removal on Southern West Virginia Communities.* Morgantown: West Virginia University Press, 2007.

West Virginia Coal Association. "West Virginia Coal Facts 2005." http://www.wvcoal.
com.

Wood, Petra Bohall, Scott B. Bosworth, and Randy Dettmers. "Cerulean Warbler Abundance and Occurrence Relative to Large-Scale Edge and Habitat Characteristics."
The Condor 108 (2006): 154-165.

CHAPTER ELEVEN

Buehler, David A., Melinda J. Welton, and Tiffany A. Beachy. "Predicting Cerulean Warbler Habitat Use in the Cumberland Mountains of Tennessee." *The Journal of Wildlife Management* 70.6 (2008): 1764.

Tennessee Valley Authority. "Pubic Meeting: Koppers Coal Reserve Management Plan
Environmental Impact Statement Scoping." Handout. Cove Lake State Park Recreation Building, June 3, 2003.

CHAPTER THIRTEEN

Marina, Marty, and the Tennessee Wildlife Federation. *Coal Mining in Tennessee*. Nashville: Tennessee Wildlife Federation, 2005.

Save Our Cumberland Mountains. http://www.socm.org.

National Mining Association. http://www.nma.org.

Tennessee Wildlife Resources Agency. http://www.state.tn.us/twra/.

CHAPTER FOURTEEN

Hamel, Paul B. "Cerulean Warbler (*Dendroica cerulea*)." In *The Birds of North America* Issue 511, edited by A. Poole. Ithaca: Cornell Lab of Ornithology, 2000.

Mehlman, David. "An examination of the migration routes and stopover ecology of the Cerulean Warbler (*Dendroica cerulea*)." Paper presented at the IV Congreso Norteamericano de Ornitología, Veracruz, Mexico, October 3-7, 2006.

Welton, Melinda, David Anderson, Gabriel Colorado, and Tiffany A. Beachy. "Research on Migratory Routes and Occurrence of Cerulean Warbler during Migration." Paper presented at the 3rd Annual Cerulean Warbler Summit, Bogotá, Colombia. October 20-26, 2008.

Welton, Melinda, David Anderson, Edgar Selvin Perez, Gabriel Colorado, and David Mehlman. "Cerulean Warbler: In Search of Critical Migratory Habitat." Paper presented at the 2nd Annual Cerulean Warbler Summit, Morgantown, WV, February 14, 2007.

CHAPTER FIFTEEN

Barón, Jose David. "Status of the cacao industry in Latin America and expectations for the future: Are certification programs an option?" Paper presented at the 3rd Annual Cerulean Warbler Summit, Bogotá, Colombia, October 20-26, 2008.

Cadena, Gabriel. "Coffee industry in Colombia as an example of Latin American countries: A balance between quality, production, and sustainability." Paper presented at the 3rd Annual Cerulean Warbler Summit, Bogotá, Colombia, October 20-26, 2008.

Colorado, Gabriel, Paul B. Hamel, David Mehlman, and Amanda Rodewald. "Distribution and Ecology of Cerulean Warblers in the Andes: New Insights." Paper presented at the 3rd Annual Cerulean Warbler Summit, Bogotá, Colombia, October 20-26, 2008.

González, Carlos. "Remarks from the Director of Specialty Coffees, Federacion Nacional de Cafeteros de Colombia." Paper presented at the 3rd Annual Cerulean Warbler Summit, Bogotá, Colombia, October 20-26, 2008.

Mara, Pete. "The ecology of the non-breeding period: Lessons from the American Redstart." Paper presented at the 3rd Annual Cerulean Warbler Summit, Bogotá, Colombia, October 20-26, 2008.

Simons, G. L. *Colombia: A Brutal History.* London: Saqi, 2004.

Stafford, Frank, and Marco Palacios. *Colombia: Fragmented Land, Divided Society.* New York: Oxford University Press, 2002.

CHAPTER SIXTEEN

Barrera, Luz Dary. "Education, Communications, and Publicity." Working group discussion at the 3rd Annual Cerulean Warbler Summit, Bogotá, Colombia, October 20-26, 2008.

Caycedo, Paula. "Opportunities from the draft Cerulean Warbler Nonbreeding Season Conservation Plan." Paper presented at the 3rd Annual Cerulean Warbler Summit, Bogotá, Colombia, October 20-26, 2008.

CHAPTER SEVENTEEN

Botero, Jorge E., Lina M. Sánchez-Clavijo, and Rocío Espinosa. "The Cerulean Warbler in Colombia's Coffee-Growing Regions." Paper presented at the 3rd Annual Cerulean Warbler Summit, Bogotá, Colombia, October 20-26, 2008.

Caycedo, Paula. "Opportunities from the draft Cerulean Warbler Nonbreeding Season Conservation Plan." Paper presented at the 3rd Annual Cerulean Warbler Summit, Bogotá, Colombia, October 20-26, 2008.

González, Carlos. "Remarks from the Director of Specialty Coffees, Federación Nacional de Cafeteros de Colombia." Paper presented at the 3rd Annual Cerulean Warbler Summit, Bogotá, Colombia, October 20-26, 2008.

Guhl, Andrés. "Coffee and landscape in Colombia 1970-2002: Linking agricultural intensification and land use and landcover change." Paper presented at the 3rd Annual Cerulean Warbler Summit, Bogotá, Colombia, October 20-26, 2008.

Rendón, Juan David. "Cerulean Warbler Conservation Coffee." Panel discussion at the 3rd Annual Cerulean Warbler Summit, Bogotá, Colombia, October 20-26, 2008.

Rodewald, Amanda, Marja Bakermans, and Carlos Rengifo. "Winter ecology and survival of Cerulean Warblers in coffee plantations in Venezuela." Paper presented at the 3rd Annual Cerulean Warbler Summit, Bogotá, Colombia, October 20-26, 2008.

ACKNOWLEDGEMENTS

*T*HIS BOOK WOULD NOT EXIST without the efforts of many kind, generous, dedicated people. I must first thank Jesse, for everything. In the weeks following the shootings at Virginia Tech all I wanted to do was curl up in a ball and weep; without Jesse's encouragement, I wouldn't have embarked on my first cerulean adventure in the spring of 2007. Jesse was a veterinary student during the time that I wrote and researched this book, and, without resentment, he took care of our house, pets, bills, and all other important things while I was off having bird adventures that he wished he could participate in. Thank you, Jesse, for being a compassionate, supportive partner and husband. You're a much better person than I am. I love you.

I owe a huge debt of gratitude to Petra Bohall Wood. In addition to allowing me to interview her, Petra patiently answered my follow-up questions weeks and months (and even years) later. She was my go-to expert on all things cerulean. I also first learned about the cerulean's plight through Petra's presentation at a local Audubon Society meeting; thanks, Petra, for introducing me to my new obsession!

Without Greg George, who at the time was completing a PhD under Petra's direction, this book would not have been possible. Greg and the rest of his field crew (especially Patrick McElhone) in the Lewis Wetzel Wildlife Management Area in West Virginia welcomed me into their world of mist-netting, spot-mapping, nest-searching, and cold pizza. Greg didn't just get me "up close and personal" with a cerulean—he allowed me to have intimate connections with several. A thousand thank-yous to my friend Greg.

Like Greg, Tiffany Beachy and her field crew graciously allowed me to invade their field site in eastern Tennessee. Not only did Tiffany sit for extensive interviews, she fed me, took me camping, and found a fledgling cerulean for me. She translated for me (and many others) in Colombia, and it was a pleasure to be her roommate in Bogotá and San Vicente de Chucurí. Tiffany is a truly beautiful soul, and I am grateful for her friendship. Thanks, too, to Tiffany's sister Letisha, my creative writing student, for introducing us.

Despite his humble denials, Randy Dettmers is an expert nest-finder. Finding a cerulean warbler nest in a forest is kind of like finding a needle in a haystack, except that the nest is made of the forest; perhaps it's more accurate to compare finding a cerulean nest in a forest to finding one particular piece of hay in a haystack! Randy also took the time to carefully read and comment on the drafts of several chapters, offering his invaluable suggestions and encouragement, for which I am very appreciative.

Paul B. Hamel is a cerulean warbler rock star, and at first he intimidated me; he is *the* cerulean expert, and I was worried he would view my book project as intrusion on his turf. The exact opposite turned out to be true. Not only did Paul patiently answer my cerulean questions, he also shared his knowledge of Colombian history as well as charming stories about his interest in birds as a child. He welcomed me into the cerulean warbler community, invited me to participate fully in the Colombian cerulean summit, and even called on me later to help edit documents about ceruleans. I feel extremely fortunate to have spent time with Paul, and his important contributions to this book—and to the growing body of knowledge about ceruleans—cannot be overstated.

In addition to explaining his studies about kleptoparasitism and clustered territoriality to me, Kamal Islam (along with David Buehler) helped me identify a myriad of birds—especially tanagers—in Colombia. Thanks also to David for allowing me access to his graduate students. Birding in the Cerulean Warbler Reserve was one of the most memorable experiences of my life, and I am glad to have shared it with such a fun group of people. Thank you, too, to Tatiana and César of the *Federación Nacional de Cafeteros de Colombia*, and to Misael, our intrepid ProAves guide, for leading us on the adventure.

Thank you to Melinda Welton for sharing her expertise on cerulean warbler migration with me, and for sharing her hotel room in Bogotá. I regret not being able to accompany Melinda to her field sites in Central America, and I wish her luck in determining the exact route that ceruleans take on their hemispherical journeys.

Thanks to Patrick Angel of the Office of Surface Mining and Reclamation's Appalachian Regional Reforestation Initiative. He's a passionate advocate for reforesting surface mines, and I hope to work with him to that end in the future. Special thanks also to Brian Smith of the American Bird Conservancy for sharing his knowledge about ceruleans. The ABC works hard to conserve birds throughout the Americas; I hope readers of this book will join me in supporting them. Thanks, too, to Deanna Dawson of the Pawtuxent Wildlife Research Center for reading chapter drafts, offering invaluable suggestions, and for being my early-morning taxi buddy.

Thank you to the many cerulean warbler experts who talked with me informally about their work, and thanks to those who gave presentations during the Third Annual Cerulean Warbler Summit in Colombia. Their research and our conversations were vitally important to this book. Many of these folks invited me on additional cerulean expeditions in the US, Colombia, and elsewhere; one day I hope to take advantage of their offers. These experts include Jorge Botero, Chris Eberly, Gabriel Colorado, Jeff Larkin, David Mehlman, Maria Isabel Moreno, Sara Barker Swarthout, Amanda Rodewald, Ben Wigely, David Wiedenfield, Rachel Vallender, Than Boves, Gabriel Cadena, Luz Dary Barrera, Carlos González, Pete Marra, and Paula Caycedo. Thanks, too, to Ken Rosenberg (I tried to somehow fit your story about "Pus Bob" into the text, but unfortunately he didn't make the cut.)

Thanks also to the cerulean experts whose research I relied on, but whom I did not have the pleasure to meet, especially Jason Jones, Pat Keyser, Chuck Nicholson, Kirk Roth, John Sauer, Cathy Weakland, Scott Bosworth, Chandler Robbins, Raleigh Robertson, Ronald Rohrbaugh, Kelly Perkins, Jennifer Barg, Kelly Jones, William Link, Katharine Garvin, David Caro, Diego Calderón, and Christopher Rogers. I humbly apologize for leaving anyone off this list, and I regret not being able to meet every cerulean expert in person.

Thank you to Cristian Agudelo for the hospitality and the birthday Aguila. Thanks to Camila Gomez for being an incredible host. Thank you to Emilce Suarez Pimiento and the entire town of San Vicente de Chucurí for the dancing, the parade, the music, the kindness, and the open arms. I will definitely return someday.

Thank you to Tom Will for his humor, kindness, and the gift of his poetry. (And for speaking much better Spanish than me.) Thanks to John Confer for hanging out with me in Bogotá—maybe golden-wings will be next.

Thanks to my bad news bear, Jeff Mann, for the support, for the luscious teas, for loving our mountains, and for inviting me to accompany him on a fly-over tour of southern West Virginia. Jeff is a generous colleague, a passionate advocate, and a cherished friend. (But if Jeff tells you that cerulean warblers are good eating, don't believe him.) Thanks, too, to the Ohio Valley Environmental Coalition, Keeper of the Mountains Larry Gibson, and South Wings. Thanks to the Virginia Tech Department of English and the Armstrong Foundation for funding my travel and research.

Thanks to my friend and fellow bird-writer David Gessner for the encouragement, inspiration, and humor. Thanks to Scott Weidensaul, too, for his kind words. David and Scott are two of my favorite writers, and their support means a lot to me.

Thank you to the Hot Shots—Steve O., The Haas, Stalker, and Wayne Train—for making me a better writer and person. Thank you to my friends and colleagues for their unending support, especially Natalie Seabolt Dobson, Kevin Oderman, Sara Pritchard, Julie Mengert Oakey, Steve Oakey, Aileen Murphy, Robin Allnutt, Richard Allnutt, Lisa Leslie, Shelly Maycock, Jessica Noon, Mark Brazaitis, Gail Galloway Adams, and Ed Weathers. Thank you, Lucinda Roy, for the wisdom and strength.

Thank you to Daniel Kohan and Elizabeth Cogan of Ruka Press—not only for publishing this book, but also for being brave enough to venture into independent publishing. The world needs Ruka Press.

Thank you to my incredible agent, Russell Galen, for friendship and for believing in this book and in me. Without Russ's guidance, encouragement, and direction this book would not exist.

Thank you to Mom, Dad, Joe, and Aunt Mary; and to Mom F., Dad F., Dennis, and Liz; and to the rest of my crazy family. Thank you Mr. Bones, Liza Jane, Asha, and Cassady for the sanity and all the unconditional stuff.

And, of course, thank you to my little blue friends. May your trees be old, your mountains high, and your coffee plantations shaded.

ABOUT THE AUTHOR

KATIE FALLON'S NONFICTION HAS APPEARED in a variety of magazines and journals, including *Isotope: A Journal of Literary Nature and Science Writing, Ecotone: Imagining Place, Appalachian Heritage,* and *River Teeth: A Journal of Nonfiction Narrative.* Her essay, "Lost," published in the journal *The Fourth River,* was nominated for a Pushcart Prize in 2008, and "Hill of the Sacred Eagles" was a 2011 finalist in *Terrain.org: A Journal of the Built and Natural Environments's* annual contest. She teaches creative writing at West Virginia University in Morgantown, W.V., and is the director of education for the West Virginia Raptor Rehabilitation Center. She lives in Morgantown with her husband, Jesse, a veterinarian.

INDEX

green press

INITIATIVE

Ruka Press is committed to preserving ancient forests and natural resources. We elected to print this title on 100% post consumer recycled paper, processed chlorine free. As a result, for this printing, we have saved:

31 Trees (40' tall and 6-8" diameter)
13 Million BTUs of Total Energy
3,196 Pounds of Greenhouse Gases
14,412 Gallons of Wastewater
914 Pounds of Solid Waste

Ruka Press made this paper choice because our printer, Thomson-Shore, Inc., is a member of Green Press Initiative, a nonprofit program dedicated to supporting authors, publishers, and suppliers in their efforts to reduce their use of fiber obtained from endangered forests.

For more information, visit www.greenpressinitiative.org

Environmental impact estimates were made using the Environmental Defense Paper Calculator. For more information visit: www.papercalculator.org.

MIX
Paper from
responsible sources
FSC® C013483